Slave Songs and the Birth of African American Poetry

Slave Songs and the Birth of African American Poetry

Lauri Ramey

First published in 2008 by PALGRAVE MACMILLAN™
175 Fifth Avenue, New York, N.Y. 10010 and
Houndmills, Basingstoke, Hampshire, England RG21 6XS.
Companies and representatives throughout the world.

Palgrave Macmillan is the global academic imprint of the Palgrave Macmillan division of St. Martin's Press, LLC and of Palgrave Macmillan Ltd.

Macmillan® is a registered trademark in the United States, United Kingdom and other countries. Palgrave® is a registered trademark in the European Union and other countries.

ISBN: 978-1-4039-7569-0

Library of Congress Cataloging-in-Publication Data

Ramey, Lauri.
Slave songs and the birth of African American poetry / Lauri Ramey.
   p. cm.
 Includes bibliographical references and index.
 ISBN 1-4039-7569-8
 1. American poetry—African American authors—History and criticism. 2. Slaves—United States—Songs and music—History and criticism. 3. African Americans—Songs and music—History and criticism. I. Title.

PS310.N4R36 2008
811.009'896073—dc22   2007026847

A catalogue record of the book is available from the British Library.

Design by Scribe Inc.

First PALGRAVE MACMILLAN paperback edition: April 2010

10 9 8 7 6 5 4 3 2 1

Printed in the United States of America.

Transferred to Digital Printing in 2010.

Contents

Acknowledgments   vii

Preface   xi

Introduction   1

1   Slave Songs and the Lyric Poetry Traditions   17

2   Theology and Lyric Poetry in Slave Songs   57

3   Slave Songs as American Poetry   97

4   Border Crossing in Slave Songs   123

Bibliography   151

Notes   167

Index   191

Acknowledgments

My abiding appreciation is extended to Bryant Alexander, R. Victoria Arana, Joseph A. Bailey II, M.D., Alice Ogden Bellis, Kamau Brathwaite, Joanne M. Braxton, Colin D. Bucell, John Cleman, Jasper Cross, Park R. Dougherty and The Spiritual Society Preservation Project, Rita Dove, Shelley Fisher Fishkin, Terry Flores, Sarah Frankland, Jeanne Gee, the late Calvin Hernton, Anthony Joseph, Aldon Lynn Nielsen, Elisabeth Schüsssler Fiorenza, Yolanda Galvan, the late Dieter Georgi, Theodore and Francine Herst, F. Abiola Irele, Portia Maultsby, Harryette Mullen, Nii Ayikwei Parkes, Marjorie Perloff, Nathan Ramey, Arnold Rampersad, Ishmael Reed, President James M. Rosser of California State University, Los Angeles, Ted Sammons, The Spirituals Project at the University of Denver, Carl M. Selkin and the staff of the Natural History Museum of Los Angeles County, Jim Simmons, the brilliant students in my Fall 2006 graduate seminar *The African American Poetic Tradition*, Corey Taylor, Mark Turner, Robert von Hallberg, Vincent Wimbush, Kwasi Wiredu, and Glenn Yocum. Some of these individuals have generously shared their scholarly knowledge and offered invaluable suggestions on this manuscript and the subject. Others have provided support in equally meaningful ways, especially in the form of the encouragement that means so much during a project of long duration. I am greatly indebted to all of them for their generosity and sustenance.

My research was aided immeasurably by the helpful and knowledge-able reference staff of The Huntington Library, Special Collections in The Fisk University Library, The University Archives and Harvey Library at Hampton University, The Moorland-Spingarn Research Center at Howard University, and The Women in Jazz Archive in Swansea, Wales.

My sincere thanks for financial support that permitted travel, course release, the acquisition of resource materials, and other practical dimensions of writing and research. I benefited greatly from an Andrew W. Mellon Foundation Huntington Library Research Fellowship, a British Council Fellowship, a Cardiff University Research Grant, a Joseph A. Bailey II, M.D. Fellowship in the African American Experience from the American Communities Program/National Endowment for the Humanities Grant from California State University, Los Angeles, and a Katherine Carter Fund Grant from the Department of English at California State University, Los Angeles.

My thanks to Mansfield College, University of Oxford, for inviting me to speak about slave songs and home, which helped develop the ideas in chapter 2. I was honored to deliver the 2005 Joseph A. Bailey II, M.D. Lecture at California State University, Los Angeles on "Bodies, Space and Place in the Spirituals," which was instrumental in forming the ideas in chapter 4. I am grateful for the opportunity to speak at numerous academic conferences—through the support of my university—and to my colleagues who offered constructive suggestions. The Paul Laurence Dunbar Centennial Conference at Stanford University provided funds that enabled me to share my work in progress on Dunbar and slave songs, which appears in chapter 3. The Interpretation of Scriptures as a Force of Social Change Symposium in Frankfurt provided support that allowed me to speak about slave songs in that context, a line of thinking that has impacted the direction of this book profoundly. That conference was organized by the late Dieter Georgi, with whom I began a spirited dialogue about slave songs in 1999 when I spoke on the subject at the Society of Biblical Literature International Congress in Cape Town. He and the late Calvin Hernton inspired, interrogated, and encouraged me until the times of their passing, and they are very much present in these pages. An earlier and substantially different version of chapter 2 appeared as "The Theology of the Lyric Tradition in African American Spirituals" in *Journal of the American Academy of Religion* 70, no. 2 (2002).

The anonymous reviewer of my book proposal and sample chapters made numerous insightful suggestions that were extraordinarily constructive in guiding the completion of the book. For the original edition, Farideh Koohi- Kamali, my former editor at Palgrave Macmillan, and her assistant Julia Cohen, offered support, patience, guidance, enthusiasm, and trust that were beyond parallel. I might never have finished this book without them at my back. I am equally indebted to my superb editor Brigitte Shull and editorial assistant extraordinaire Lee Norton for their continuing commitment to this book, and for their dedicated skill and effort in bringing this new edition to fruition. It is hard to imagine a finer copyeditor than Yvette Chin, who offered the perfect combination of patience, expertise, and mindreading, as each of those skills was needed. My thanks to Katie Fahey also, and all of those at Palgrave Macmillan whose knowledge and professionalism has been invaluable.

The original idea for this book came from Martin Ramey. In 1997, we were both teaching at Hampton University, and I was researching Hampton's collection of archival materials that were to become the foundation of the African American Poetry Archive, with the support of President William R. Harvey, which I also wish to acknowledge. Martin innocently asked, "Why aren't spirituals considered lyric poetry?" From that question, nearly a decade of thought and research, and a book, has transpired. Most academicians are reluctant to give away their ideas in spite of our ideals of "the scholarly conversation" in which we participate and to which we contribute. As a religious studies scholar, Martin not only gave me his idea but tirelessly offered knowledge of his field, and no doubt at some very inconvenient hours. I owe him my deepest gratitude (and ever my love) for asking the question—which had never occurred to me—that started the search for an answer. That answer, as I hope is evident from this book, is that slave songs should be considered lyric poetry, and readers are deprived by not seeing them in that light. I have tried to do justice to the poets of slave songs and regret my own errors and failings to do so. There is no mock humility in saying that these poets were *gli migliori fabbri*.

Preface

Often regarded as the most important body of folk songs created on American soil, African American slave songs as they have been passed down and inherited are likely to have had their roots in the mid- to late-eighteenth century. Some scholars, such as Miles Mark Fisher, believe that they were transported by the first Negroes who were brought as slaves to North America in 1619.[1] It is certain that they are older than the period when they first were formally transcribed and recorded in print, in the nineteenth century. But their precise time of origin, specific sources, and processes of composition remain mysterious and have been subjects for debate since these songs first were collected by figures such as Richard Allen, William Francis Allen, Charles P. Ware, Rev. Marshall W. Taylor, Lucy McKim Garrison, and Thomas Wentworth Higginson.

Consistently described by early observers using the terms "weird," "wild," "primitive," "quaint," "unforgettable," "other-worldly," "uncanny," "barbaric," "unearthly," "disjointed," "senseless," "pathetic," "naïve," "supernatural," "curious," "monotonous," "childlike," "repetitive," "strange" and "peculiar," paradoxically, slave songs also were criticized for being directly modeled in imagery, diction, and structure on white revival hymns. Any similarities to white Protestant, Methodist, and revival hymns were used by scholars such as George Pullen Jackson, Richard Wallascheck, Newman I. White, and Edmund S. Lorenz to demonstrate the fundamental lack of originality in slave songs in order to diminish their importance and prove that the slave poets were merely imitative—actually, that they were not poets at all. White hymns of the day undoubtedly influenced the slaves, who would have encountered them while being converted into Christianity, but it was evident to other early transcribers and auditors that this material had become something unmistakably different through the slave poets' imaginative transformations.

Numerous observers noted their distinctiveness from the language and performance of white church music in the use of some of the following features, many of which are African survivals:

- Dancing in a circle during the "ring shouts" that took place after formal church services or in secret
- Clapping of hands or the body referred to as "patting juba"
- Rhythmic arm movements
- Coordinated foot shuffling and tapping
- Bodily swaying
- Shouts of loud abandon
- Ecstatic displays of jubilation
- Uncanny imagery whose references to enslavement—even on the literal level—transcended conventional Christian imagery of being in the body
- Interchangeable segments of lyrics with the same lines, images, phrases, or stanzas reappearing in multiple songs
- Extensive use of repetition, which often took place in triads
- Lines and verses whose lengths vary
- Irregular rhyme and general lack of stress on rhyme
- Extensive lexical or phrasal repetition
- Frequent thematic discontinuities—or what might be thought of as intuitive poetic leaps—between verses and refrains
- Complex rhythmical patterns
- Continuous and overlapping use of the antiphonal structure referred to as call-and-response, where a leader (or leaders, who would rotate during long sessions)—whose knowledge of the "catalogue" of slave songs would generally be particularly extensive—would start singing a particular song, and the group would echo lines serving as refrains
- Satirical humor and ironic wit
- Ostensibly religious songs that do not appear to have conventional Christian themes and diction
- Extended development of biblical narratives
- Vernacular diction and unusual syntax
- Direct address of ancestors, biblical figures, heroic models and spirit guides

- Absence of the Western philosophical framework of Cartesian dualism, which allowed the mind to be described as traveling freely from the body
- Satan shown as a trickster figure
- Sense of time that viewed the future as a direct and immediate extension of the present, with past and present as dominant modes of consciousness
- Description of human relationships and connections as being maintained even in a state of absence, including after death
- Stress on the importance of community for every individual.

By the middle of the nineteenth century—or even earlier, as described with horror by John F. Watson[2]—slave songs appear to have been recognized as a distinctive cultural development within the slave community, but no one at the time seemed to be entirely sure of what they were, where they came from, and most of all, how to evaluate them. Some early responders found them mesmerizingly beautiful, alternately describing them either as heartbreakingly sad or upliftingly cheerful. Others, like Watson, were appalled by their barbarity and wildness. Some early auditors were merely puzzled by their oddity, and others experienced a combination of these reactions.

The poetical qualities of slave songs were noted by a number of early commentators, but that was as far as it went. Thomas Wentworth Higginson wrote that slave songs were "a flower of poetry."[3] William E. Barton's 1899 collection, *Old Plantation Hymns; a collection of hitherto unpublished melodies of the slave and the freeman, with historical and descriptive notes*, notably uses the technical diction applied to poetry in referring to "the variable character of the couplets which make up the stanzas."[4] W. E. B. Du Bois wrote in "The Sorrow Songs" in *The Souls of Black Folk* that the words of slave songs "conceal much of real poetry and meaning beneath conventional theology and unmeaning rhapsody."[5] Also employing literary diction, William Francis Allen wrote that slave songs "will dash heroically through a trochaic tune at the head of a column of iambs with wonderful skill."[6] Mark Twain called them "utterly beautiful" and wrote that, in slave songs, "America has produced the perfectest flower of the ages."[7] More recent commentators have continued to mention the poetic qualities of slave songs, but the terms "poetry" and the "poetic" have largely remained metaphorical, suggesting occasional imaginative inventiveness, memorable images or figures, or unexpected displays of verbal dexterity, rather than literary designations meaning part of a canonical body of American or even African American literature. In spite of these gestures that acknowledge their flights of "poeticism," the "folk" association has been perpetuated over recognition of slave songs as art.

Slave songs have been generally appreciated and studied for their musical significance, influence, and beauty, including serving as the foundation of gospel, jazz, and the blues. Their role in the formation and expression of African American Christianity explains the slaves' process of Christianization and demonstrates how the adoption of Western religious beliefs aided in their survival and sustenance. Historically and sociologically, slave songs created a system of coded communication in the slaves' efforts to build a functioning community, to elude detection by slaveholders when arranging shouts, meetings, escape routes and plans, giving warnings of "pattyrollers" (patrollers), and to offer one another the support and encouragement to carry on.

The roots of African American slave songs partially lay in African customs, community, and oral communication. They also directly reflect the immediate circumstances of slavery and plantation life in America. What F. Abiola Irele calls "The African Imagination" provided common ground and enabled the "black and unknown bards," as they are referred to by James Weldon Johnson in his poem by that name, to blend vestiges of their ancestral homelands with American influences to produce something utterly unique. Although they came from widely diverse geographical and linguistic backgrounds in Africa, the slaves would have shared music and dance as key elements in their ways of marking significant events and establishing a sense of individual and community identity.

While the issue of Africanisms has been a source of critical debate since slave songs first were preserved and written about, there is equal evidence that slave songs are a hybrid of African references, customs, and ontology juxtaposed with direct and immediate experiences of American slave culture. These influences include the adoption of Christianity, the religion of the slaveholders, which has been melded to African customs and suited to the slaves' psychological and emotional needs and worldview in slave songs; commentary on the daily routines and rhythms of particular kinds of enforced labor; reflections on current political events that traveled through word of mouth via slave songs; the development of fluency in English as a new language; and the construction of a community across barriers of language and culture with other slaves who might share no common links beyond their African roots, the experience of being snatched away from home, their present shared location, and current status in life as chattel. Logic as well as concrete evidence suggest that, when transplanted unwillingly to their new surroundings, the slaves would have carried with them aspects of their cultures of origin as a mechanism to retain a sense of personhood and forge a new sense of community when cut off from past connections.

John Lovell Jr. has accounted for more than 6,000 slave songs, making them in all likelihood the largest early canon of American verse. The most famous and popular include the following:

- "Ain't Gonna Study War No More"
- "Swing Low, Sweet Chariot"
- "You Got to Walk That Lonesome Valley"
- "Michael, Row the Boat Ashore"
- "Nobody Knows the Trouble I've Seen"
- "Sometimes I Feel Like a Motherless Child"
- "When the Saints Go Marching In"
- "Come By Heah, Lawd" ("Kumbaya")
- "Go Down Moses"
- "Go Tell It on the Mountain"
- "Joshua Fit De Battle of Jericho"
- "Do Lord, Do Lord, Do Remember Me"
- "Gimme That Old Time Religion"
- "I am a Poor Wayfaring Stranger"
- "Many Thousand Gone" ("No More Auction Block For Me")
- "Oh, Freedom!"
- "Let Us Break Bread Together On Our Knees"
- "Lord, I Want to Be a Christian in My Heart"
- "Rise, Shine, Give God the Glory"
- "Rock of Ages"
- "There's a Meeting Here Tonight"
- "This Little Light of Mine"

This brief listing of many that could have been selected of these classic songs—whose lyrics have been known, loved, translated into
countless languages, treasured internationally, endlessly given new
arrangements, recorded and sung in churches, opera recitals, choral,
rock, folk and gospel performances, and at political and labor rallies,
often by individuals who are unaware that they are slave songs—
reflects a remarkable achievement. But even more remarkable is the
consistent exclusion of slave songs (and information on their prove-
nance) from anthologies, classrooms, and general attention when seriously considering and appreciating the full, rich historical range of
American poetry.

Slave songs rarely are considered as lyric poetry and typically do not
appear in the major instructional anthologies of either African
American or American poetry or literature. When they are included, it
generally is in special categories such as "vernacular poetry," "folk
songs," "slave creations," "oral verse," "plantation songs," or simply "the
spirituals," and not in the category of "poetry." The absence of slave
songs from discussions of American lyric poetry is a serious oversight
that reflects more on the formation and the exclusivity of the American
poetry canon than on the literary qualities of slave songs themselves.

Their importance to the African American poetical tradition can be
traced through their influence on countless African American poets,
including James Weldon Johnson, Paul Laurence Dunbar, Melvin B.
Tolson, Calvin C. Hernton, Margaret Walker, Waring Cuney, Sterling
A. Brown, Robert Hayden, Sonia Sanchez, Lance Jeffers, Amiri Baraka,
Claude McKay, Langston Hughes, and Raymond Patterson, among
many others. Sterling A. Brown attributed a significant measure of
their importance to the fact that they were self-defining, rather than an
external description of the African American experience. Alain Locke
considered them not only to be a racial product but to possess universal meaning for all of American culture. Yet they remain excluded from
serious literary consideration. John Lovell Jr. summed up the situation
with hands-up frustration and impassioned bluntness:

> And so we still have 800 to 1,000 original songs, comprising an epic tradi-
> tion in the class of the Iliad, the Songs of Roland, or the Lays of the
> Nibelungs, with no clear analysis of the soil from which they sprung or the
> process of their growth. In other epic traditions, patient scholars have
> found seeds of racial and national culture. They look there first. And yet

for how many years have the dabblers in American "Negroitis" ignored or treated with disgraceful cavalierness the heart of the Negro spirituals![8]

The lyrics of these indigenous American creations have a compelling power, sophistication, and complexity consistent with traditional expectations for lyric poetry. "I am a Poor Wayfarin' Stranger"; "Don't be Weary, Traveler"; "Nobody Knows the Trouble I've Seen"; "Oh Mary, Don't You Weep"; "My Lord What a Mornin'"; "Go, Tell It on the Mountain"; "Roll, Jordan, Roll"; "Were You There When They Crucified My Lord?"; "Lay This Body Down"; "Wade in the Water"; "Go Down, Moses"; and "No More Auction Block For Me," among numerous other examples of classic slave songs, are an integral part of America's literary treasures. The humble and anonymous nature of their authors *should* have no bearing on a full appreciation of their inventive imagery, rhetorical sophistication, and emotional pathos. The lyrics of slave songs have been foundational in reflecting and establishing the special identity of the individual African Americans who created them, and they are a unique and irreplaceable body of American poetry.

The erasure of slave songs as lyric poetry—versus folk music, religious hymns, or historical vestiges of plantation culture—is a reflection on how we conceive of the American lyric poetry genre, and how (and why) the American and African American poetry canons have developed as they have. Some of our finest and earliest American poems—which even now remain invisible as part of the lyric poetry tradition—were produced by anonymous African American slaves. The scope and significance of this body of writing as a major touchstone of American culture—in conjunction with some possible explanations for the consistent pattern of slave songs' neglect as poetry—is the focus of this book.

The profusion of writings on slave songs attests to the interest that they have held throughout the world since the 1860s, but little is available in the way of in-depth and current literary scholarship. A limited range of sources is available that discuss them in the context of music or religion or aimed at a popular audience. As a result, while slave songs have been treated with respect, the existing resources have led to a situation where they are regarded primarily as folk songs, artifacts of oral or vernacular culture, historical documents, cultural relics of slavery, the roots of gospel or blues, or as part of the development of African American Christianity. While slave songs play an important role in all of these contexts, they are also central to the literary legacy of America and should be regarded as such.

This book discusses slave songs as lyric poetry, providing current critical and cultural analysis and bringing them into the present by discussing their continuing literary influence. Using the methodologies of fields including African American literature, American studies, poetry and poetics, postcolonial studies, cultural studies, religious studies, philosophy, and cognitive science, an interdisciplinary approach offers detailed analysis of slave songs' primary themes, stylistic devices, and imaginative metaphorical structures combining American experience with European inflections and African survivals resulting in highly original literary works. Literary criticism reframes slave songs to prove that they stand up to appreciative scrutiny as an authentic, significant and enduring body of lyric poetry with continuing influence. By showing the beauty and value of slave songs, I propose a reconsideration of both canons—American and African American—by calling for their consistent inclusion, which entails a reassessment of the contribution of African American poetry to early American poetry.

Considered as lyric poetry, slave songs are a record of the slave poets' ability to overcome adversity and illuminate the strength of slave society in achieving unprecedented cultural production under circumstances of dire repression. Viewing slave songs primarily as music or historical footnotes is a misrepresentation of their significance as living cultural artifacts, contemporaneous records of the daily experiences of these individuals and their society, a major body of poetry born of long suffering, and timeless expressions of the human ability to refuse to be destroyed by inhumanity. The finest examples stand up to anything produced in the American poetry tradition. Referred to by W. E. B. Du Bois as the sorrow songs, he justly claimed that they were "the most beautiful expression of human experience born this side of the seas."[9]

Introduction

Since the mid-nineteenth century, a wealth of writings on African American slave songs has been produced internationally by devoted amateurs and scholars in multiple disciplines, which serves as testimony to the virtually universal appeal of this inspirational, heart-rending, mystical, satirical, tragic, hopeful, pragmatic, and altogether multifaceted body of music and verse. Slave songs have been collected, recorded, performed, and studied as artifacts of slave culture, windows of insight into the sociopolitics of plantation life, a repository of African survivals for a diasporic population, the "true history" of plantation life for the slaves, the roots of African American musical forms including gospel and the blues, a treasured body of American and/or African American folklore, and one of the bedrocks of African American Christianity. But the relationship of slave songs to either "American" or "African American" poetry has been one of curious disregard.

The major purpose of this book is to address that omission, examine how it came about, and conclude that slave songs are entitled to a place at the foundation of the American and African American poetry canons. As a literary study, this book's primary focus is language and the critical questions associated with poetry and poetics. I set the stage in chapter 1 by reviewing the intersection of the oral and textual lyric poetry traditions. We see how slave songs connect those two artificially separated genres to create a quintessentially American product that echoes and binds the Western and African lyric poetry traditions.

There are invaluable resources available—aimed both at academic and popular audiences—that discuss slave songs, but they are almost exclusively relegated to music, religion, sociology, and history. From an intellectual and preservationist perspective, these studies and the respect that they have shown to slave songs—which otherwise might have disappeared from the cultural record at any number of moments in history—represent a monumental achievement. But the existing materials on slave songs have resulted in a situation where they are not considered part of the American or African American "high art" literary tradition when we conceive of the irreplaceable treasures of American lyric poetry; this tragic invisibility has diminished both canons. Hiding in plain sight is a magnificent body—perhaps even the first canonical body—of American poetry that has a compelling claim to be regarded as an indispensable part of the nation's literary roots.

Most of the primary sources consisting of collections of slave songs were published between the 1850s and the 1880s, with interest in finding new examples dramatically dwindling since that time because the major songs were believed to have been either found, lost, or forgotten. According to Irving Sablosky, many of these collectors knew by the 1860s that these cultural expressions were part of a life that was over and done: "When the historic volume of *Negro Slave Songs of the United States* [sic] (by Lucy McKim Garrison, William Francis Allen, and Charles P. Ware) was published in 1867, it uncovered for the world a music that was already of the past. . . . Spirituals endured because their beauty and the depth of religious feeling they embodied were imperishable."[1] By 1899, when William E. Barton published his *Old Plantation Hymns; a collection of hitherto unpublished melodies of the slave and the freeman, with historical and descriptive notes*, even though he purportedly was presenting both new "hymns" and new versions of those that were already known, Barton also wrote that the best of slave songs had been discovered and preserved, and it would be quite something if any new ones were to be found.[2]

The influential texts published during this explosion of interest in slave songs included Fredrika Bremer's *The Homes of the New World: Impressions of America, Volumes 1 and 2* (1853); Frances Anne Kemble's *Journal of a Residence on a Georgian Plantation in 1838–1839* (1863); William Francis Allen, Charles Pickard Ware, and Lucy McKim Garrison's *Slave Songs of the United States* (1867); *The Story of the Jubilee Singers; with their Songs* by J. B. T. Marsh (1875); *Jubilee Songs: As Sung by the Jubilee Singers of Fisk University*, edited by Theodore F.

Seward (1872); Thomas Wentworth Higginson's *Army Life in a Black Regiment and Other Writings* (which contained the important essay "Negro Spirituals") (1869); Rev. Gustavus D. Pike's *The Singing Campaign for Ten Thousand Pounds: Jubilee Singers in Great Britain* (1875); Rev. Marshall W. Taylor's *Plantation Melodies* (1882); and *Cabin and Plantation Songs as Sung by the Hampton Students* arranged by Thomas P. Fenner, Frederic G. Rathbun, and Miss Bessie Cleaveland (1874).

Two interconnected themes appear in a number of these early and important commentaries and collections that seem to denote almost antithetical, or at least paradoxical, responses to slave songs. There is an attitude of fascination in encountering something almost indescribably "weird"—a word used repeatedly, even in later collections by some African American critics—coupled with an urgency to preserve these strange phenomena. Many of these commentators and collectors who remarked on slave songs' "wild beauty" (where the erotic attraction, repulsion, and fear are unmistakable) were simultaneously entranced by their "strangeness" and repulsed by it. Comments of aesthetic appreciation—if, in fact, they were provided at all—almost invariably were counterbalanced by remarks reinforcing their otherness, difference, and even their naïve impropriety—that is, their ignorant, non-Western, noncivilized essence. This impression served to intensify images of the slaves' Africanness—their Orientalism, to form an analogical comparison with Edward Said's term—and primitivism, which was augmented by their lack of subject position due to slave songs' anonymity.

The result, in terms of literary appraisal and categorization (or noncategorization) has been to marginalize slave songs for nearly two centuries, based on the moment in time when slave songs solidified as we might recognize them today. Part of the distancing of the African American slaves and their songs resulted from their mode of worship, which was described by white observers as unlike anything they had ever experienced. Another part resulted from the slaves' state of exilic homelessness, embodied in the lyrics of slave songs such as "Motherless Child," which generated sentimental pity in white audiences long past Emancipation. These topics are addressed in chapter 2 in the context of theology and literature, which are conjoined themes throughout the history of the lyric poetry tradition. Chapter 3 looks at the "othering" of the slaves and their cultural products from the perspective of the classical tropes of *forma* and *figura*, authenticity and imitation, as they apply to concepts of Americanness and foreignness, and discusses how this constellation of images also may have contributed to slave songs' past and present invisibility as poetry.

Colonel Thomas Wentworth Higginson—thrilled to have found something "essentially poetic" (not quite the same thing as discovering "poetry") coming from such an unlikely source—seemed to have been quite dipped in Romantic nostalgia when he first encountered "live" performances of slave songs as sung by his black Army recruits. His initial attraction to slave songs as "quaint" and "plaintive" oddities came about because

> the present writer had been a faithful student of the Scottish ballads, and had always envied Sir Walter the delight of tracing them out amid their own heather, and of writing them down from the lips of aged crones. It was a strange enjoyment, therefore, to be suddenly brought into the midst of a kindred world of unwritten songs, as simple and indigenous as the Border Minstrelsy, more uniformly plaintive, almost always more quaint, and often as essentially poetic.[3]

As he transcribed them, Higginson compared the words of slave songs to "some captured bird or insect" and "after examination, put it by." He called the songs "strange plants," which were sung "harshly" as the "dusky figures" performed a "rhythmical barbaric dance." When he finished writing down the words of a slave song, he called it a "new specimen."[4] Equally odd is the comparison of the black soldiers to the aged Scottish crones, and he repeats the baffling comparison in his reading of the "detached and impersonal refrain" of one of the slave songs, "Cry Holy," which he claims "gives it strikingly the character of the Scotch and Scandinavian ballads." The refrain is:

> Cry holy, holy!
> Look at de people dat is born of God.[5]

Considering how little this example calls "strikingly" or otherwise to mind either Scottish or Scandinavian ballads, and without much explanation for the comparison offered by Higginson, one might speculate that Higginson's comparison—though there is no doubt that he found many of their lyrics beautiful and emotionally moving—was a way to code their "strangeness" or non-Americanness or "folkness." The comment also reflects Higginson's excitement at finding a "primitive" and unspoiled product of nature, one of the central motifs of chapter 1 in the context of the lyric tradition and chapter 3 in relation to the development of American and African American identities and canons.

Higginson was not alone in his raptures that combined admiration with unconscious misunderstanding and cultural superiority. On hearing the Fisk Jubilee Singers perform slave songs during their British tour in 1873, Scottish author George MacDonald commented on "the mingling of the pathetic with the unconscious comic in the rude hymns."[6] Theodore F. Seward, who compiled an early collection of the Fisk Jubilee Singers' songs "under the auspices of the American Missionary Association," referred to slave songs as "the simple, ecstatic utterances of wholly untutored minds."[7] Such responses are the subject of chapter 4 of this book where they are treated in relation to slave songs' variable interpretations and deliberately coded levels of meaning. In that chapter, I discuss the selective receptions of slave songs by differing audiences, and how such multiple understandings and interpretations were transmitted by means of creative metaphors and other sophisticated literary, linguistic, psychological, and philosophical processes.

It is a psychologically and socioculturally challenging notion that slavery has produced aesthetic beauty and that kidnapped and enslaved individuals could have been the progenitors of an esteemed American literary tradition. Some of the antipathy towards slave songs also came from some of the newly freed African Americans who experienced an initial period of understandable revulsion towards anything having to do with plantation culture during and after Reconstruction.[8] It was only in the twentieth century that slave songs began to regain some acceptance within the African American community. Part of this new respect—and even the fact of keeping slave songs alive to the present—can be credited to the role played by the Historically Black Colleges and Universities (HBCUs) in performing them publicly and framing them as a treasured legacy. Paradoxically, that gesture also was fed by white audiences who were nostalgic for plantation culture. One of the few things that many black and white individuals alike seemed to agree on after Emancipation were that slave songs should not be considered poetry. For many African Americans, it was because these songs were a vestige of the most terrible experience in their own or their ancestors' lives. For many white Americans, it was because it was unimaginable that African Americans—still widely discriminated against—had produced something as august as lyric poetry.

As a specific example of this recuperation and how the dual forces aligned, the Fisk Jubilee Singers' program originally consisted mainly of classical and popular standards with two or three slave songs sprinkled in.[9] Their first tour began in October 1871, but it was not until March 1872 that the program shifted to consist primarily of slave songs. At first it was a hard sell for George Leonard White, their director and guiding spirit, to persuade the Fisk Jubilee Singers to perform slave songs. But a lukewarm reception to their program at Oberlin College on November 16, 1871, was rescued by a desperate decision to sing "Steal Away" at the end, which produced what was reported to be a rapt assembly, a respectable collection plate of $139 and much-needed additional bookings.[10] Even the Fisk Jubilee Singers' first recording, made in 1909, did not exclusively consist of slave songs, in contrast with the later collections; it included "Old Black Joe" by Stephen Foster, and recitations of the poems "Banjo Song" and "When Malindy Sings" by Paul Laurence Dunbar. The situation of the Fisk Jubilee Singers holds similarities to that of Dunbar himself, whose vernacular poetry experienced a popularity that his formal verse never fully reached.

Reflecting the progressively deteriorating interest in African American cultural products—and especially, their recognition as being American—a letter written by Lucy McKim (later Garrison) was published in the November 8, 1862, issue of *Dwight's Journal of Music*. McKim was discussing her experience of hearing the slave song "Roll, Jordan, Roll": "That same hymn was sung by thousands of negroes on the 4th of July last, when they marched in procession under the Stars and Stripes, cheering them for the first time as the 'flag of *our* country.'"[11] McKim was elated to witness the evolution of enslaved Africans into African Americans who saw the American flag representing them as much as it did her. But fifty years later, John Wesley Work quoted a Mr. Damrosch who articulated his confusion—doubtless shared by many—between "race" and "nation" when it came to identifying African Americans and their aesthetic expressions as American:

> The Negro's music isn't ours, it is the Negro's. Nothing more charac-
> teristic of a race exists, but it is characteristic of the Negro, not the
> American race. Through it a primitive people poured out its emotions
> with wonderful expressiveness. It no more expresses our emotions than
> Indian music does.[12]

It is a sad but important symbol that by 1915—when Mr. Damrosch's comments appeared in John Wesley Work's *Folk Song of the American Negro*—Allen, Ware, and Garrison's *Slave Songs of the United States*, arguably the first and most important collection of slave songs, was out of print. I am persuaded of the sincerity of Higginson, Allen, Garrison, and others in their heroic efforts to transcribe and preserve slave songs. But the question lingers as to whether a coalescence of ambivalence towards race, slavery, and the products of slavery—such as the characterizations by Higginson and comments that I will note by James Weldon Johnson, John Wesley Work, and Roland Hayes—contributed to the history of reception of slave songs and their failure to be conceived of as poetry instead of as "essentially poetic."

This initial distancing away from slave songs was followed by an attitude of new appreciation and identification that was also fed by the New Negro Movement, and encouragement by Alain Locke and others to look with pride on these hallmarks of African American culture. In his essay on slave songs in *The New Negro* (1925), Alain Locke argued that slave songs were both uniquely black and uniquely American, a reminder of the uncertain relationship between what it meant to be American and what it meant to be black in America, which is addressed in chapter 3 of this book. Using slave songs as a symbol of race pride and the achievements of African Americans, Locke speculated that, in time, the Negro spirituals (a term used commonly to refer to slave songs, which I will discuss) could become America's folk songs. Optimistically, although with a small caveat ("if the spirituals are what we think them to be"), Locke affirmed his belief—while acknowledging that America was not ready for it yet—that the songs would stand the test of time and eventually fill that role:

> The spirituals are really the most characteristic product of the race genius as yet in America. But the very elements which make them uniquely expressive of the Negro make them at the same time deeply representative of the soil that produced them. Thus, as uniquely spiritual products of American life, they become nationally as well as racially characteristic. It may not be readily conceded now that the song of the Negro is America's folk song; but if the spirituals are what we think them to be, a classic folk expression, then this is their ultimate destiny.[13]

Frequently repeating the word "folk" throughout this essay, Locke was setting up readers for the relatively modest goal of accepting African American products as having been made by the "folk" of America. How much more shocking would it have been in 1925—the year that James Weldon Johnson and J. Rosamond Johnson published the first volume of *The Books of American Negro Spirituals*—to have intimated, as J. W. Johnson did, also very guardedly in his introduction to that first volume, that the spirituals could be poetry, or—to paraphrase Locke—"the poem of the Negro is America's poem"?

Mirroring the thirty-year period that served as the seminal era for transcribing and preserving slave songs, the 1970s were a bellwether era for scholarship on this subject. This decade was a remarkably compressed and dynamic time for research relating to slave songs, coinciding with a general interest in African American studies, issues of civil rights and related nationally focused topics reflecting a burst of American self-archiving. It is astounding to think that during this ten-year period such path-breaking and definitive works in their fields were published—still the key texts in terms of historical research for the study of slave songs—such as *Black Culture and Black Consciousness* by Lawrence W. Levine (1977), *Slave Religion* by Albert J. Raboteau (1978), *The Spirituals and the Blues* by James Cone (1972), *The Slave Community* by John W. Blassingame (1972), *Sinful Tunes and Spirituals: Black Folk Music to the Civil War* by Dena J. Epstein (1977), *Black Song: The Forge and the Flame: The Story of How the Afro-American Spiritual Was Hammered Out* by John Lovell Jr. (1972),[14] *Deep River and The Negro Spiritual Speaks of Life and Death* by Howard Thurman (1975), and *Roll, Jordan, Roll* by Eugene D. Genovese (1972).

Two very thorough studies providing historical and sociological perspectives closer to the period of the songs themselves are *Afro-American Folksongs: A Study in Racial and National Music* by Henry Edward Krehbiel (1913) and *Folk Song of the American Negro* by John Wesley Work (1915). *The Social Implications of Early Negro Music in the United States*, edited by Bernard Katz, contains reprints of some fascinating, seminal assessments of slave songs that appeared in nineteenth-century periodicals, and Eileen Southern's *Readings in Black American Music* (1983) is another invaluable compilation of historical documents. Research on slave songs has diminished since these major periods of examination: the early era of collection and commentary in the mid-nineteenth century; the early twentieth-century production of fewer but nonetheless important works; and the explosion in the 1970s of religious, theological, musical, sociological, political, and historical research.

Historically, literary attention to slave songs largely has been relegated to essays, introductory materials to collections (mostly published decades ago) and discussions of their lyrics in studies primarily based in other disciplines or whose purposes are not literary analysis. That is true of the majority of brilliant texts cited above, though Lovell was an exception as a literary scholar. This situation is being perpetuated in current research. Some excellent recent scholarship on slave songs includes the essay "Biblical Themes in the R. Nathaniel Dett Collection *Religious Folk-Songs of the Negro (1927)*" by James Abbington in *African Americans and the Bible*, edited by Vincent L. Wimbush, which is in religious studies; "Secular Folk Music" by Dena J. Epstein with contributions from Rosita M. Sands and "Religious Music" by Mellonee Burnim in *African American Music: An Introduction*, which is in music; *The Music of Black Americans: A History* by Eileen Southern, an indispensable work, also in music, though Professor Southern discusses the relationship between black music and poetry with insight and sensitivity; "The Sorrow Songs: Laments from Ancient Israel and the African American Diaspora" by Wilma Ann Bailey in *Yet with a Steady Beat: Contemporary U.S. Afrocentric Biblical Interpretation* edited by Randall C. Bailey, which is in religious studies; *Culture on the Margins: The Black Spiritual and the Rise of American Cultural Interpretation* by Jon Cruz, which is in sociology and African American studies; *Wade in the Water: The Wisdom of the Spirituals* by Arthur C. Jones, in psychology and religious studies; and *Dark Midnight When I Rise: The Story of the Fisk Jubilee Singers: How Black Music Changed America and the World* by Andrew Ward, in biography. In addition to these resources, "The Sorrow Songs," chapter XIV of *The Souls of Black Folk* (1903) by W. E. B. Du Bois, is a unique and foundational essay that should be read by anyone interested in the topic.

In this book, I have chosen mainly to use the phrase "slave songs" rather than the perhaps better known and more widely used term "spirituals." I have used the term "spirituals" when I am citing someone else who has used that specific term. In most of the technical literary analysis, especially in chapter 1, I generally used the term "poem" because that is the context in which I am addressing slave songs—as poetry. To refer to them as examples of this genre underscores the main assertions of this book and coheres with the methodology, concepts, and traditions of literary studies that I have applied to these texts. By primarily alternating between the terms, "poem" and "slave song," my goal is to demonstrate that they transcend categories that fail to recognize them as a diverse and multifaceted body of art. At the same time, it would be a betrayal of their identity not to equally acknowledge the circumstances of their production and authorship insofar as it is possible.

I hope that the following chapters offer ample defense for my insistence on using the term "lyric poetry" when defining and categorizing the genre of slave songs. But why have I chosen to call these poems "slave songs" rather than the more familiar "spirituals"? For a number of reasons. I object to the use of a term that presents a skewed or partial portrait of a population (even if it is, as in this case, meant to be "positive") if it effectively deprives them of the full range of human emotions, reactions, desires, personhood, uniqueness, self-determination, and agency. The use of the term "spirituals" became popularized because it served to artificially or fraudulently characterize enslaved Africans—whether motivated by abolitionism, evangelism, racism, naiveté, or ignorance—as a holy, pure, and sanitized group. At its worst, such a term could have pernicious implications: a group born for Christ-like suffering is fulfilling its divine fate through mistreatment. "Slave songs" is a more direct and honest description and clarification of the horrors in which these poems were created and the context in which they should be considered. The term "spirituals" echoed an often stated and distorted view that the slaves thought only of religion, sang strictly of salvation and the afterlife, and were an endlessly tolerant population that patiently waited without malice for their freedom whenever it arrived sometime in the future.

In order to portray the slaves in this light of partial humanity—though the gesture may have been well-meant—some editors, abolitionists, commentators and concerned others thought it necessary to divide the slaves' words into separate categories. Metaphorically speaking, they may as well have segmented the slave poets themselves, and the subject of metaphorical representations of ontological wholeness and partial wholeness is a major focus of chapter 4 in this book. The songs that were sung on all occasions—with varying words, speeds, rhythms and movements, depending on the settings and circumstances—became parsed into work songs, secular songs, ballads, corn ditties—which were not as widely collected or preserved. There is too much documentary evidence that no such neat distinctions were made by the slaves themselves in using their songs, and many were sung on all occasions, though sometimes with differing lyrics and speeds. Henry Edward Krehbiel argued, "The singular fact to be noted here is that the American negro's 'spirituals' were also his working songs, and the significance which this circumstance has with relation to their mood and mode."[15] Roland Hayes, the great opera singer who did so much to immortalize slave songs, wrote, "His religion, his song, became a working principle; the promise had to be all around him. In work and church and field, song and word became functional, integrated."[16]

But the term spirituals as a reference to "the religious folk-songs" has largely come to represent metonymically the virtual totality of this musical, literary, and social body. So I have avoided the word "spirituals" as code for all slave songs to make it clear that not all of the songs were spiritual and to avoid the delimiting action of applying functional categories to what I believe to be the essential expansiveness and diversity of lyric poetry. An additional justification for this decision is the evidence of variants of slave songs with an almost prismatic array of moods, themes, dictions, phrasings, points of view, imagery, and tones. This malleability that is at the very heart of slave songs is masked by slotting them into fixed categories represented by stable texts. As Lawrence Levine surmises, "It is possible that a greater number of religious than non-religious songs have survived because slaves were more willing to sing these ostensibly innocent songs to white collectors who in turn were more willing to record them since they fit easily with their positive and negative images of the Negro."[17]

I also have chosen to use the term "slave songs" to echo the generously descriptive historical designation used by Allen, Ware, and Garrison in their seminal collection *Slave Songs of the United States* before the term "spirituals" became code implying that all slave songs were religious in nature. The fact that religious and evangelical societies such as the American Missionary Association had abolitionist ties and sponsorship roles at some of the HBCUs (Fisk, for example) and organizations for the support of the slaves and newly emancipated slaves also helps explain this desire to portray the slaves as wholly pure and deserving of freedom. But the result was a caricature, as it would have been of any group of people, by denying them a complete human identity.[18] In an implicit acknowledgment that a selection of songs that is wholly religious cannot represent the totality of any population (and that not all slave songs were "spirituals"), James Weldon Johnson wrote, "The Spirituals together with the secular songs—the work songs and the sex songs—furnish a full expression of the life and thought of the otherwise inarticulate masses of the Negro race in the United States."[19] But Johnson's phrase "otherwise inarticulate masses" should be noted in relation to the ambivalence that I flagged previously, which is a topic discussed in chapter 1.

Finally, as is implicit, the term "slave songs" enables me to effectively address some of the stereotypes of the stoically suffering slaves, who were often depicted as child-like embodiments of desexualized sub- or non-humanity, or by some of the abolitionists and others mentioned, as examples of Christ-like transcendence of such things as negative human emotions. Numerous sources claim that the slaves expressed neither anger nor resentment in their songs, and were interested in nothing except prayer and salvation. In a March 1892 article in *New England Magazine* titled "Negro Camp Meeting Melodies," Henry Cleveland Wood wrote of the Negro, "He never wearies of attending church; it comprises not only his religious, but his social life. He cares little for pastime or entertainment, in general. He manages to extract both from his devotional exercises, and is satisfied."[20]

John Wesley Work wrote, "In all his song there is neither trace nor hint of hatred or revenge. It is most assuredly divine in human nature, that such a stupendous burden as human bondage, with all its inherent sorrows and heart breakings could fail to arouse in the heart of the slave sentiments of hatred and revenge against his master."[21] Work's comment is an example of the ambivalence mentioned previously. The following remark from Roland Hayes similarly seems to be in tension with his earlier cited comment: "You may search the entire collection of Aframerican religious folk songs extent—which number in the hundreds—and you will not find one word of hate or malice anywhere expressed in them."[22]

Slave songs are certainly beloved, but beloved as what? What is being perpetuated, and what might be lost, by failing to classify them as examples of the culturally esteemed genre of lyric poetry whose features they demonstrably share? I believe that slave songs have been marginalized due to historical developments and cultural practices that have determined what constitutes both American and African American poetry rather than slave songs' inherent features, operations, or especially, limitations. The American and African American poetry canons are rife with exclusions, including poetry that is formally innovative. The uniqueness of slave songs—their extraordinary originality, commented on by so many of the early collectors (while simultaneously decrying their derivative and unoriginal character as nothing more than ignorant imitations of the entire white world's existing song catalogue)—should make the finest of them a source of lasting pride as some of the most truly original and, ironically, most influential examples of American poetry, along with Whitman and Dickinson. I do not mean that statement hyperbolically, as I hope to demonstrate in chapter 1. But it may well be that the unprecedented, or *hapax legomenon*, nature of slave songs—much as the uniqueness of "the peculiar institution" itself—has served to marginalize them from both canons.

If we partly judge poetry by the influence it has had on other poets, it would be far more difficult to find examples of African American poets who have not been influenced by slave songs than those who have. Curiously, as suggested by my earlier listing of major scholarly resources dealing with slave songs, there are surprisingly few literary studies. Secondary materials on slave songs in the field of literature include Alain Locke's essay on the spirituals in *The New Negro* (1925). Sterling A. Brown introduces the section on folk literature in *The Negro Caravan* (1941) with a discussion of "The Spirituals" and "Slave Seculars" and has an important essay called "Negro Folk Poetry" in *Negro Poetry and Drama and the Negro in American Fiction* (1972). LeRoi Jones's *Blues People: The Negro Experience in White America and the Music that Developed From It* links early Afro-Christian music and worship to later forms of black music and creates a theoretical trajectory to show how they merged to construct black citizenship (1963). Ralph Ellison discusses slave songs in *Shadow & Act* (1953). Slave songs are subtextually present in James Baldwin's essay "Many Thousands Gone" from *Notes of a Native Son* (1955). Frederick Douglass discusses them in *Narrative of the Life of Frederick Douglass, An American Slave, Written by Himself* (1845), which I address in chapter 4.

In addition to these biographical or literary critical discussions of slave songs by important writers—and the list is indicative and not exhaustive—they have had significant influence on writers of all races and genres, including Mark Twain, Toni Morrison, William Styron (quite controversially, in his use of *The Confessions of Nat Turner*), and William Faulkner, among numerous others, in America and internationally. This influence on literary thinking and creation makes slave songs' absence from literary tradition all the more puzzling. If we examine slave songs with the same levels of technical, historical, and theoretical scrutiny that we would apply to any canonical poetry, they display all of the features and provide all of the pleasures associated with the finest lyric poetry in terms of form, complexity, theme, purpose, substance, effect, value, and operation.

The disparate and linked influences that contribute to the character of slave songs still do not "explain" them. Above all, they—like all genuine poetry—are original artifacts deriving from pre-existing forms and components and made into something new. The exercise of reducing them to a composite of sources deflects from an appreciation of their power and uniqueness. We can recognize that a stew is a complex amalgamation of flavors and ingredients but fail to enjoy the new creation by focusing on a systematic address of every herb and spice tossed into the pot. If this is how we treat slave songs, we have not progressed very far beyond the musicologists arguing in the nineteenth century over the influence on slave songs of Scottish barroom ballads and German school songs. Now let's look at this magnificent body of American and African American poetry.

CHAPTER 1

Slave Songs and the Lyric Poetry Traditions

Since the advent of Romanticism in the early nineteenth century, the fine line between "primitive" and "literary" poetry has become increasingly blurred. William Wordsworth's "1800 Preface to *Lyrical Ballads*" is probably the most frequently cited touchstone for modern conceptions of the lyric poem. In describing the goal of his revolutionary collection, Wordsworth felt it necessary to explain in the "Preface": "It was published as an experiment, which I hoped might be of some use to ascertain how far, by fitting to metrical arrangement a selection of the real language of men in a state of vivid sensation, that sort of pleasure and that quantity of pleasure may be imparted, which a poet may rationally endeavor to impart."[1] "The real language of men" is a phrase whose implications have been argued for more than two hundred years. At the very least, lyric poetry is now widely accepted as conveying the voices of particular individuals, speaking in their own dictions (or dramatizing those of characters), addressing their own communities, and selecting from a wide range of "acceptable" forms or prosodic features employed either conventionally or innovatively. Since the time of Wordsworth, readers have tended to expect poetry to preserve the vivid animation of speech-in-conversation versus elevated diction, Latinate and archaic phrases, and to represent a personal utterance rather than an expression of the state or praise to a patron or nation.

After the Romantic era—and following modernism's promotion of free verse—poets, readers, and critics became more receptive to exploring influences beyond the Western canon and its classical sources.

Experimentation with varied prosodic patterns flourished, as did the use of poetic diction that came from "the real language of men"—or, as William Carlos Williams put it, "from the mouths of Polish mothers." This opening up of the lyric also represented a return to the ancient roots of the genre and mirrored many of the values and practices of the African oral tradition, which I will discuss in detail as this chapter progresses, particularly focusing on F. Abiola Irele's touchstone work in conceptualizing oral discourse as authentic literature.[2] Irele's views of African oral literature wholly invalidate any possible argument against conceiving of slave songs as poetry—and in fact, establishes them as an ideal bridge in lyric poetry between oral and written traditions.[3]

In the late twentieth century, interest has continued to intensify in poetry's performative properties and oral traditions that foreground the sonic and auditory features of language that Ezra Pound called "melopoeia." In "primitive," vernacular, or oral poems, elements such as repetition, rhythm, expressions of spontaneous emotion, physical movement, sound divorced from semantic content, text as score versus text as art object, chanting, improvisation, and group dynamics are placed on an equivalent or even more prominent plane than operations perceived as literary. Some of these conventional text-based characteristics would include

- stress on figured language;
- a consistent pattern of rhyme and meter;
- employment of a constrained group of accepted conventional poetic forms associated with education or skill;
- minimal repetition, which is used primarily for emphasis or special semantic impact rather than sonic effect or a social purpose;
- literary or scholarly allusions;
- the development of elaborate intellectual conceits;
- brevity, recalling Edgar Allan Poe's dictum in "The Poetic Principle": "I hold that a long poem does not exist. I maintain that the phrase 'a long poem' is simply a flat contradiction in terms."[4]

Dell Hymes, Dennis Tedlock, and Jerome Rothenberg are regarded as the moving forces behind "ethnopoetics"—an area of poetic exploration, study, and collection that aims to recuperate and validate "primitive" and oral poetry produced by marginalized cultures as an essential part of the world's lyric treasures. Ethnopoetics was popularized through the anthologies *Technicians of the Sacred*, edited by Jerome Rothenberg (1968); *America a Prophecy*, edited by Jerome Rothenberg and George Quasha (1974); and *Alcheringa*, edited by Jerome Rothenberg and Dennis Tedlock, which was the first magazine devoted to ethnopoetics (published from 1970–76). To theoretically ground the movement, intensify the focus on the talk of "real men," and continue to shake the lyric poetry hierarchy based on the Greek–Latin–English lineage that excluded poetries produced by cultures that were described as "primitive" and "savage," Jerome Rothenberg and Diane Rothenberg co-edited a selection of essays called *Symposium of the Whole: A Range of Discourse Toward an Ethnopoetics* (1983). According to the book's "Pre-Face," the editors were calling for a "redefinition of poetry in terms of cultural specifics with an emphasis on those cultural traditions to which the West gave names like 'pagan,' 'gentile,' 'tribal,' 'oral,' and 'ethnic.'"[5]

Ethnopoetics was one of several movements launched in the 1970s and 1980s that paid serious attention to the oral, physical and non-Western dimensions of poetry. Such approaches served as a reminder that lyric poetry traditionally had a connection to orality and performance, primarily through music but also through dance, drama, and oratory. The Society for the Study of Native Arts and Sciences was a related venture of the same era whose goals were to "develop an ecological and crosscultural perspective linking various scientific, social and artistic fields; to nurture a holistic view of the arts, sciences, humanities and healing; and to publish literature on the relationship of mind, body and nature."[6]

Such poetries—either created or rediscovered in the late twentieth century—represented a return to lyric traditions that prevailed prior to the last two hundred years during which time poetry became more closely associated with a fixed, page-based text. These primitive poetries, ethnopoetries, ecopoetries, and performance poetries were both new and a recuperation of something ancient by hearkening back to models spanning from the classical Greek tradition to the ballad tradition. These bodies of song and verse include forms that aim for a "holistic" view of poetry as a spiritual or community-building "act," demonstrate an explicit interest in performance, audience engagement, cultural diversity, oral practices, spiritual exploration, and highlight correspondences between humanity and nature. Examples would include the populist approaches of the Beat poets, the Buddhism of Allen Ginsberg, and ecological orientations implying a certain economy of life of poets such as Wendell Berry and Gary Snyder.

Without articulating an explicitly theological position, such approaches to lyric poetry have shown an attitude of receptivity to

- nontangible experiences associated with spiritual and natural systems;
- unmediated and spontaneous emotional expression;
- nonerudite and nonallusive references;
- imagery whose reference points are natural cycles rather than intellectual or literary touchstones of Western culture;
- poetry as a cross-cultural vehicle that does not exclusively privilege the literary and societal values of Western civilization, or reflect a common educational and class background in its creators or audiences;
- the body as an integral dimension of poetry;
- combining the aesthetic and religious;
- actively exploring connections between humanity and nature.

Poets and scholars associated with these movements have made inroads in persuading audiences that "primitive," oral, "naïve," marginalized, choral, group, "spiritual," non-Western, or anonymous verse—or poetry reflecting these wide-ranging influences—could hold a place of consideration in the canon of lyric poetry. But in his "Pre-Face" to *Technicians of the Sacred*, Jerome Rothenberg addressed the difficulties involved in identifying certain cultures and their poetries as "primitive" or other such terms that potentially imply an absence of sophistication. Rothenberg opened the "Pre-Face" with the subheading "Primitive Means Complex," by which he meant that such poetry can be extended in length; combined with music, dance, and myth; open in form; and "collective" in its authorship and presentation. Rothenberg's chief concern was that, based on these differences from conventional Western conceptions of the lyric poetry genre, if the art seems strange to audiences, then so it would appear without a fair and open-minded judgment as to the poetry's purposes, means, and effects. Rothenberg summarized this circular problem of arrogant or dismissive preconceptions fulfilling themselves endlessly: "The work is foreign & in its complexity is often elusive, a question of gestalt or configuration, of the angle from which the work is seen. If you expect a primitive work to be simple or naïve, you will probably end up seeing a simple or naïve work. . . . The problem is fundamental for as long as we approach these works from the outside—& we're likely fated to be doing that forever."[7]

For that reason, Rothenberg openly discussed his concerns about the terminology that he grudgingly chose to use, explaining that "non-literate" and "non-technological" were considered as alternative terms to "primitive" but were rejected as being "too emphatic in pointing to supposed 'lacks.'"[8] It is to Rothenberg's credit that he flagged his discomfort with the rhetorics of presentation in publishing "primitive" poetry.

But the questions are begged: how *do* we nonqualitatively address such conditions as "pre-literate" versus "post-literate"[9]—terms that Rothenberg also used—or avoid juxtaposing the "primitive" with the "modern," "advanced," or "sophisticated"? How do we come from a traditional understanding of lyric poetry deriving from the Greeks to develop an appreciation of oral products from non-Western cultures, recognizing that different sets of critical, social, and expressive values may well be in operation? Conversely, how do we break through preconceptions that these poetries are so radically different and come to recognize how they fulfill many of the same functions and offer many of the same rewards? How do we end the cycle—which Rothenberg fears will last forever—of expecting the primitive when faced with what is "different" and, therefore, of seeing only naïveté when dealing with the aesthetic and communicative practices and values of diverse cultures? Those are some of the interrelated questions to which I will pose some possible answers in this chapter in discussing the intersections of the text-based and oral lyric poetry traditions and the potential hinge between them that slave songs might effectively represent.

Strangely—in spite of this opening of the lyric to oral, spiritual, and non-Western influences—even in Jerome Rothenberg and George Quasha's landmark anthology *America a Prophecy*, where the editors brilliantly reconstruct "a new reading of American poetry from pre-Columbian times to the present," anonymous chants and lyrics are included from numerous American Indian tribes (e.g., Nez Percé, Dakota, Sioux) as well as from the Shakers. But slave songs, which are

a wholly indigenous American product, are not included in this landmark collection that ostensibly gathered and preserved the roots of
American poetry. The selection of poems from America in the international anthology *Technicians of the Sacred* is comprised entirely of
anonymous poems from members of eleven different American
Indian tribes. The principle of selection according to the book's "Pre-
Face" is that the poems representing America were selected "as ana-
logues to the 'primitive work' selected from throughout the
world"[10]—yet there, too, are no slave songs.

  In addition to collections deliberately designed to concentrate on oral
poetry, slave songs have been marginalized from general teaching
anthologies of American poetry. Some anthologies of African American
literature and African American poetry contain slave songs, though this
is not universally true, and these collections typically do not categorize
them as lyric poetry. The major anthologies of American literature do
not include slave songs, except occasionally in brief mentions as musical
folk products and certainly not as lyric poetry. In spite of recent efforts at
multicultural representation in standard anthologies of American literature, slave songs remain peculiarly missing. Here is a brisk summary of
slave songs' history as inimitably produced by Lovell:

> James Weldon Johnson, R. C. Harrison, and Alain Locke have
> sketched the periods of the creation and appreciation of the spiritual.
> They tell us that the spirituals were probably started on their way
> about 100 years before slavery died; that the heyday of the spiritual was
> about 1830 to 1865; that from 1865 to 1880 aroused Americans were
> collecting them, like fine orchids or trampled old masters; that from
> 1880 to 1910, men like Harris, Page, and Smith were using them for
> local color; that since 1910, Negroes, notably Du Bois and Johnson,
> have rolled them through their subjective consciousnesses, with
> admirable results.[11]

  Usually, the period that is approximately contemporaneous with
slave songs is represented in poetry by anonymous American Indian
poems and conventional figures that have long been canonized: Edgar
Allan Poe, William Cullen Bryant, Ralph Waldo Emerson, Walt
Whitman, Emily Dickinson, and so forth. Sometimes early African
American poetry is represented by Phillis Wheatley, who emulated
neoclassical forms and traditions. Even though Wheatley might engage

in various strategies of subversion, her poetry is intended to be an example of received and recognized Anglo-American taste. Even *The Heath Anthology of American Literature*, edited by Paul Lauter, which has a strong multicultural outlook and does include some references to the "spirituals," explicitly refers to them as examples of American "song" as distinguished from poetry.

The Oxford University Press *Anthology of Modern American Poetry*, edited by Cary Nelson (a massive undertaking) opens with poems by Walt Whitman and Emily Dickinson from the early 1860s, the period when slave songs were known, transcribed, organized into collections, and made available. The Oxford anthology contains a section called "Angel Island: Poems by Chinese Immigrants, 1910–1940," introduced by an editorial note explaining that these poems were written anonymously on barrack walls during the racist and horrific detainment of Chinese immigrants to America who were "essentially imprisoned on the island" while awaiting their fates, which was either entry via San Francisco or deportation, while other groups of people were quickly processed for entrance. Nelson writes that "[t]hese poets were not only inscribing a record of their passage; they were also giving a cultural education to those that would follow them. Indeed, some of the poems comment on one another."[12] That situation would be remarkably parallel to that of the enslaved African Americans who anonymously created poetry commenting on their situation to sustain themselves, leave behind cultural information for others, and produce a body of highly self-referential and allusive poems commenting on other poems within the canon of slave songs.

Another section of the Oxford anthology is called "Japanese American Concentration Camp Haiku, 1942–1944," which contains haiku written by Japanese Americans when forced into internment camps following the bombing of Pearl Harbor. It is explained that the authors were "amateur poets" who had been members of haiku writing clubs before they were sent to the camps. Few details are known about these individuals, but brief biographical comments accompany their names in the introduction to the section and in the anthology's table of contents. However, at the end of the introduction, the editor writes, "In order to emphasize the narrative potential that is revealed when the poems are treated as a collective enterprise, we have removed the poets' names from the poems here."[13]

In light of these inclusions—and the exclusion that I am about to point out—note the editorial intention stated in the preface to the anthology: "The long American poetic dialogue about race that began with the nineteenth-century Abolitionist movement becomes a powerful feature of twentieth-century poetry. White poets, black poets, Asian poets, Chicano poets, and Native American poets take up race here, reflecting on our history, interrogating both whiteness and blackness, and producing searing statements of astonishing condensation to be found nowhere else in our culture."[14] Anthologies cannot do and include everything, and the Oxford collection is outstanding in many respects, not least of which are the two extremely interesting sections mentioned here. Yet it seems odd to mention the "American poetic dialogue about race that began with the nineteenth-century Abolitionist movement"—especially when slave songs awakened many white Americans to the humanity, suffering, and rich emotional and cultural lives of the slaves—not to include the very poems that are at the heart of that dialogue, according to such preeminent figures as William Edward Burghardt Du Bois, Booker T. Washington, and Frederick Douglass. In the Oxford anthology, we find poetry by "amateurs," representatives of American minority populations, and anonymous authors. Based on these grounds, one wonders what was the process of editorial selection that could justify the exclusion or oversight of slave songs, unless it is on the basis of merit—an issue that I hope to conclusively address and put to rest with focused attention to their lyrics, significance, and value.

The situation is not appreciably different in anthologies of African American poetry in terms of their generic designation, though they do appear in that context more often. *The Negro Caravan*, edited by Sterling A. Brown, Arthur P. Davis, and Ulysses Lee, contains a section called "Poetry" and a separate section called "Folk Literature." Slave songs appear in *The Negro Caravan* as "Folk Literature" under the subheadings "Spirituals" and "Slave Seculars." In *The Black Poets*, edited by Dudley Randall, slave songs, which are classified as "Spirituals," are placed in a separate section from what Randall terms "Literary Poetry." In Richard Barksdale and Keneth Kinnamon's *Black Writers of America*, they are placed under "Folk Literature" as "Songs," which is the way that Frederick Douglass refers to them in his autobiography. To W. E. B. Du Bois, in *The Souls of Black Folk*, they are famously called "The Sorrow Songs." In *Trouble the Water*, Jerry W. Ward Jr. categorizes them as "Oral

Poetry/Slave Creations." *Blackamerican Literature* by Ruth Miller places them under the heading "Folk Poetry." *The Norton Anthology of African American Literature*, edited by Henry Louis Gates Jr. and Nellie Y. McKay, slots them as "Spirituals" under the heading "The Vernacular Tradition." Patricia Liggins Hill, in *Call and Response*, classifies them as "Lyric*al* [my emphasis] Poetry" in the sense of African (versus African American) compositions whose lyrical qualities derive from their musicality as performed. Still, the inclusion of slave songs in these anthologies indicates that they have a large audience that sees them as part of African American cultural heritage, although their role as "poetry," and potentially even as "American poetry," continues to be under erasure.

Of equal significance, there are numerous anthologies of African American literature and poetry that do not contain slave songs at all. Instead they sketch a canon that begins—mirroring the representation of African American poetry in anthologies of American literature— with a formal (though with slightly more figures represented) poetic "literary" tradition, most typically Phillis Wheatley, George Moses Horton, Frances Ellen Watkins Harper, and Jupiter Hammon. There are no slave songs in *African American Poetry: An Anthology, 1773–1927*, edited by Joan R. Sherman, though the introductory note to the volume refers to spirituals as verse "that embraced 'low' black folk culture and music," a category that also contains "jazz, ballads and blues."[15] The editor attributes this interest in what she calls "low black culture" to the influence of "the race-proud writings of W. E. B. Du Bois," but this explanation still did not lead to the inclusion of slave songs in the collection. No slave songs are included in *American Negro Poetry*, edited by Arna Bontemps; *The Vintage Book of African American Poetry*, edited by Michael S. Harper and Anthony Walton; *Selected African American Writing from 1760 to 1910*, edited by Arthur P. Davis, J. Saunders Redding, and Joyce Ann Joyce; or *The Prentice Hall Anthology of African American Literature*, edited by Rochelle Smith and Sharon L. Jones.[16]

Henry Louis Gates Jr. has pointed out an apparently lone example of an anthologist who made a committed effort to respectfully showcase such African American cultural products as slave songs in an aesthetically rarefied context. *An Anthology of American Negro Literature* (1929), edited by V. F. Calverton (né George Goetz), was the first collection whose aim it was to form a black canon accounting for vernacular products. Calverton considered "Spirituals," "Blues," and "Labor Songs" each to comprise a genre of black literature and thought vernacular African American art was the only truly original art produced in this country. According to Calverton, the white American was still "seeking European approval of his artistic endeavors, [while] the Negro in his art forms has never sought the acclaim of any culture other than his own. This is particularly true of those forms of Negro art that come directly from the people."[17] But judging by the anthologies that followed, Calverton's efforts to show the literary quality of slave songs failed to result in widespread acceptance of their artistic worth among readers and scholars.

Why haven't slave songs become part of the American or African American poetry canons? Is it because they are anonymous or fundamentally religious expressions? Or is it because they mix the religious with the secular or build heavily on repetition and structural formulae? Or is it because multiple versions are available or because their origins are unknown? Consider the following passage:

> The best of [these] lyrics, both religious and secular, seem remarkably fresh despite the fact that in both theme and form they are extremely conventional—at times almost stylized. . . . For although all good poets bring something of their own observing to the tradition they are following, the writers of [these] lyrics are especially distinguished for their unself-consciousness and immediacy. Just as there was no consciousness on the part of [these] people of anachronism—historical differences in time or place—there seems to have been no self-consciousness about their attempts to express themselves in poetic terms: convention apparently liberated them, instead of oppressing them, in the way that it is often supposed to do. It is with perfect naturalness that the poet relives the scene, standing with the mother Mary beside the cross on which her son hangs; or the poet [who] visualizes the mystery of the conception of Jesus through the Holy Spirit in terms of the most natural of mysteries, the falling dew; or the poet . . . cheerfully regards Adam's sin and its dire consequences as a kind of childish naughtiness and punishment that had the tremendous effect of bringing Christ to earth. The very simplicity of the poet's attitude achieves the most striking artistic results.
>
> It is impossible to date the lyrics with any certainty. In general, we know only that the poems must be earlier than the manuscripts in which they appear, but because of the fact that an early lyric might

have been reworded by a later scribe in such a way as to make it appear late, we can rarely tell by how many years any given lyric preceded the manuscript that records it. The sources of the texts printed here are too diverse to be listed. Spelling has been normalized.[18]

This description, from the *Norton Anthology of English Literature*, refers to the anonymous and often religious Middle English lyric poems that are typically viewed as foundational to the British poetry canon. As it appears here, with the phrase "Middle English" deleted, this passage is quite an accurate description of the tone, structure, and intent of slave songs, as well as their style and mode of composition. Why then don't slave songs hold a similar position in the American literary canon to that of Middle English lyrics in the British canon?

The answer does not seem to lie in the fact of their content being primarily religious. In spite of Wordsworth's new stress in 1800 on the voice of the poet as a plain-spoken individual addressing daily events in a state of heightened emotion, M. H. Abrams reminds us that Wordsworth also wrote, "The grand store-house of enthusiastic and meditative Imagination . . . in these unfavourable times . . . is the prophetic and lyrical parts of the holy Scriptures."[19] Abrams believed that "[w]e pay inadequate heed to the extent and persistence with which the writings of Wordsworth and his English contemporaries reflect not only the language and rhythms but also the design, the imagery, and many of the central moral values of the Bible."[20] In his address to the Folk-Lore Society of Texas in 1912, W. H. Thomas emphasized the importance of Judeo-Christian religion in the English poetical tradition and explicitly correlated it with the same pattern of development found in slave songs: "If you consider these songs as the negro's literature, you will notice some striking parallels between its history and that of English literature. As all of you know, English literature for several centuries was little more than paraphrases of various parts of the Bible."[21] Roland Hayes wrote that "The salvation of man is always the greatest theme of master works in literature and art."[22] Hayes also explicitly connected religion with poetry in slave songs by identifying faith as the source of the slave poets' artistic inspiration and by using Milton's *Paradise Lost* as a framing device for the translation of their religious ecstasy into artistic expression:

I have had occasion already to refer to this as a quality of poetic incantation on the song sermons of my people. No less an authority than Saint Augustine is cited by Charles Burney (English critic of the eighteenth century) on that specific quality:

> When we are unable to find words worthy of the Divinity, we do well to address him with confused sounds of joy and thanksgiving.

And how true appears to me the following quotation from Milton's Paradise Lost in summing up the kind of ecstacy, the spring of inner singing that radiates forth from hosts of souls of my people:

> . . . All
> The multitude of Angels, with a shout
> Loud as from numbers without number, sweet
> As from bless'd voices, uttering joy, heav'n rung
> With jubilee, and loud Hosannas fill'd
> Th' eternal regions.

It is curious how in our times such religious poetic creations as the Hebrew chant, Palestrina; Lassus, Gregorian chant, the great masses of Bach, Beethoven, the monumental Biblical oratorios, the religious folk songs of my people, have become concert fare, and sometimes museum pieces, that we study with the rational abstract aloofness of the scholar and student. Yet it would seem to me that only in finding our way back to the simple truth to which these human documents testify can we find the key to the spirit inherent in them.[23]

Booker T. Washington's description of slave songs also combined the religious and the literary in attributing the impact of these poems to their conflation of the spontaneous overflow of powerful emotions with the lyrical inspiration that derives from faith: "The plantation songs known as the 'spirituals' are the spontaneous outbursts of intense religious fervor. There is in the plantation songs a pathos and a beauty that appeals to a wide range of tastes, and their harmony makes abiding impressions upon persons of the highest culture. The music of these songs goes to the heart because it comes from the heart."[24] In applying the critical evaluation of "beauty" and referring to an appreciation by "persons of the highest culture," Washington explicitly applied aesthetic criteria to slave songs as art objects. In his assessment, they were not diminished by their emotional expansiveness, humble origins or holy inspiration; rather, as with Hayes, Washington regarded those features as recommendations for placing slave songs alongside the world's greatest art and calling them pinnacles of Western culture.

The question of why history has so consistently disregarded slave songs as lyric poetry is more sociological than aesthetic. Speculation might well lead back to the heated nineteenth-century debates regarding their authorship and sources. There are assertions from critics and musicologists that slave songs were stolen from white European hymns because black slaves would not have been capable of this level of sophistication or originality, or, conversely, that there was no sophistication or originality at all, an issue that is discussed in chapter 3.

The largely illiterate slaves were orally taught Bible lessons and transformed this material into verse in their own language reflecting their own environment. This transcendently beautiful poetry was largely ignored, derided, or regarded as an indescribable curiosity. Yet even earlier than the Middle English lyrics previously cited, we have "Caedmon's Hymn" (ca. 658–680) generally considered the first poem extant in English, and scholars accept that it melds Christian themes and Germanic pagan verse without raising the slightest issue of "originality," "theft," or strangeness. In fact, Caedmon, who was a simple illiterate shepherd, was praised for taking the Bible lessons taught to him and turning them into sublimely inspiring poetry in his own language suited to his times and circumstances (the first word of the poem is "now"). Caedmon is described by Bede as "learning by listening," surpassing his own teachers by creating poems about such standard Biblical themes as "the exodus of Israel into the promised land" and "the sweetness of the heavenly kingdom."[25]

Through the poem's cultural blending, the Father-God becomes a holy protector and divine architect; its genius is to have converted earlier, non-Christian heroic verse into something fundamentally new with a Judeo-Christian focus reflecting the contemporaneous world. No one questioned the beauty, efficacy, and power of Caedmon in being able to turn common Bible stories into poetry in spite of his humble identity as an illiterate laborer. For the very reasons of his identity and limitations, Caedmon was extolled as being specially chosen as the creator of God's poetry—not man's poetry—by adapting existing sources with such sweetness that they resulted in poetry that could change people's lives.[26]

Why is there such a dramatic difference in audience regard and reception in two literary circumstances with such striking similarity? Without claiming that slave songs have been modeled on mainstream Anglo-American literary trends, many of the slaves could read, attended church, and were exposed to the diction, imagery, and intonations of the Bible. They inherited and maintained a rich cultural body of African traditions, which they blended with a new set of experiences in American slavery to create a hybridized poetry that reflected all of its influences to result in something new. They also moved their genre forward progressively, maintaining certain links with history but wanting to add their own stamp, as any poet does with the art of the past. So why then are slave songs not perceived as an enrichment to Anglophone lyric poetry using the same open-minded vision that welcomes "Caedmon's Hymn," Middle English lyrics, international ethnopoetics, American Indian chants, Chinese barrack poems, and Japanese concentration camp haiku?

In the lyric poetry tradition—apart from some of the more broad-minded and recuperative efforts to expand and reimagine the canon such as those mentioned—it is interesting to note that there is an entry for spirituals in *Princeton Encyclopedia of Poetry and Poetics*, but the entry is less than one-quarter column in length and nowhere does it use the word "poetry" to describe them. Instead, they are referred to as "religious folk songs of the American Negro," "folk art," and "Jubilee Songs" whose "lyrics have no set form."[27] These descriptions are especially intriguing since two frequent responses when I refer to slave songs as lyric poetry are: "But aren't they just church music?" and "But aren't they just folk songs?" The standard definition, even in a scholarly tome, underscores a frequent impression that they are formless and naïve cultural products generally used for purposes of Christian worship.

But it was not the melodies or their identity as "church music" or "song" that put fear in the hearts of the slaveholders who forbade the slaves to sing these songs on the plantation; rather it was because they recognized the subversive content of their lyrics. It was not solely the harmonies that kept suicide rates among slaves at a relatively low level, or that enabled the establishment of an authentic self-sustaining community, including the development of African American Christianity. It was not the music of slave songs that contributed to the successful operation of the Underground Railroad or that revived slave songs at other points of political trauma in twentieth-century America, such as during the Civil Rights Movement and the Vietnam War. Slave songs have been preserved and passed down in musical form, and the complex dimensions of their creation and performance are essential elements of their production, reception, beauty, function and identity. Music is also a critical component of African American expression as well as an integral part of the history of the lyric poetry tradition.[28] But much of the inspiration that has made slave songs a source of practical and emotional sustenance, inspiration, solace, truth, beauty, information, wisdom, guidance, knowledge, personal growth, fellowship, and transcendence—in short, everything that we have traditionally sought and found in lyric poetry—has come from their words.

With conflicting and shifting definitions of lyric poetry from the ancient Greeks to the present, perhaps the one continuous defining feature extending from the roots of the tradition to the present is lyric poetry's relationship—whether explicit or implicit—with music. That relationship might consist of notes and words that have been designed to correspond with each other in the original compositional process, in the musical use of individual or group voices in a song, in the setting of a poem's lyrics to music, or in using musical instruments to accompany the words. The music also might serve as a historical nod to poetry's ancient roots, with the poem expressing "musicality" rather than music per se. It can be a ghostly vestigial or metaphorical presence vibrating through the poem in such auditory and structuring devices as alliteration, rhythm, or rhyme; mellifluous phrasing, or melodic patterns conveyed through the syntactic structure or diction; line breaks to signify breath pauses; repetition or refrain (chorus and echo); the actual or implied call-and-response of direct audience (reader or listener) address by creating a conceptual space for a reply to the poet; and onomatopoeia and other sorts of sound symbolism. *Princeton Encyclopedia of Poetry and Poetics* suggests ways in which musical representationality is intrinsic to lyric poetry:

> in lyric poetry, the musical element is intrinsic to the work intellectually as well as aesthetically: it becomes the focal point for the poet's perceptions as they are given a verbalized form to convey emotional and rational values. . . . Although lyric poetry is not music, it is representational of music in its sound patterns, basing its meter and rhyme on the regular linear measure of the song; or more remotely, it employs cadence and consonance to approximate the tonal variation of a chant or intonation. Thus the lyric retains structural or substantive evidence

of its melodic origins, and it is this factor which serves as the categorical principle of poetic lyricism.[29]

Northrop Frye stresses the almost always analogical meaning of "musical" that maintains when applying it to poetry based on his idea that the two features that poetry actually shares with music are sound and rhythm, which Frye relates to Aristotle's original identification of "melos" (actual music) as one of the six defining traits of poetry.[30] In "Introduction: Lexis and Melos," Frye states that the critical objective of his essay is

> to establish an intelligible meaning for the term "musical" in literary criticism. By "musical" I mean a quality in literature denoting a substantial analogy to, and in many cases an actual influence from, the art of music. It is perhaps worth mentioning, at the risk of being obvious, that this is not what the word ordinarily means to the literary critic. To him it usually means "sounding nice." . . . The term musical as ordinarily used is a value term meaning that the poet has produced a pleasant variety of vowel sounds and has managed to avoid the more unpronounceable clusters of consonants that abound in English. If he does this, he is musical, whether or not he knows a whole note from a half rest.[31]

In commenting on the defining features of the lyric poetry genre, David Lindley states that a "significant number are written for music or out of a musical impulse"[32] and that "[t]he true affinity of poetic rhythm with that of music, therefore, lies not in metre or rhythm abstracted from words, but in the subtlety with which a poet deploys the resources of a language's rhythmic possibility in relation with meaning, syntax, rhyme and other patterns of sound."[33] Pierre Ronsard connects the musical dimension of poetry to instrumentation as well as the human voice or voices, which implies a social or community function: "Poetry without instruments or without the grace of one or more voices is in no way appealing."[34]

Although the lyric of the last two hundred years has been dominated by the voice of the solo poet expressing an individual consciousness, W. R. (Walter Ralph) Johnson, with Ronsard, links a dimension of musicality with the expression of identity—group and individual—by reminding us that "in ancient formulations of lyric, both solo and choral poetry were equally valid and equally important, each of them necessary to the total shaping of the human personality. . . . Human beings have, after all, not only private emotions and selves but also public emotions and selves."[35] Lindley explains that the lyric often combines music, emotional spontaneity, individuality, and the social function: "many speak of heightened feeling in a poetic present and are uttered by a voice in the first person,"[36] while at the same time "the public praise of heroes in Pindar [and] the love songs or drinking songs of Sappho or Anacreon [a]ll . . . had specific social functions."[37] These social functions, in addition to praise, love, and drinking, included exhortations to battle, elegies, epitaphs, fables, personal invectives, religious rituals, political satires, and expressions of the values of the community.

The diversity and evolution of lyric poetry, even in classical Greek manifestations and with the continuous undercurrent of musicality, underscore the point—implied by Rothenberg—that literary engagement benefits by accepting and accommodating change. Especially in relation to lyric poetry—which is perhaps the most flexible of all genres in spite of its reputation for structural rigidity and a fundamentally conservative canon—an inevitable conclusion emerges from an overview of its history that a strict definition of genre bears interrogation when the lyric has taken so many forms and enacted so many functions. Lindley cites Paul Hernadi's *Beyond Genre* to support this concept of the multi-headedness of the lyric, where Hernadi "represents the territory of the lyric diagrammatically, moving between 'meditative poetry' and 'quasi-dramatic monologue' on one axis, 'songlike poems' and 'objective correlative' on the other."[38]

In addition to music, musicality, and the varied social functions, from praise to drinking to love to war—as well as the brevity mentioned by Poe—another traditional part of the terrain of lyric poetry, as cited by Lindley and others, has been the exploration of subjectivity and personal identity. According to Lindley, lyric "is held to apply to poems employing a first-person speaker, and, by extension, to indicate a preoccupation with the expression of individual feeling or emotion. The distinction between a poet speaking in his own voice or speaking through a character was made by Plato, but a close connection of lyric with a first-person speaker was most firmly established by German writers of the Romantic period, and became standard in nineteenth-century England, when Ruskin defined lyric poetry as 'the expression by a poet of his own feelings.'"[39]

Princeton Encyclopedia of Poetry and Poetics pushes back even further the identification of the lyric with the voice of the individual and the expression of emotion. James William Johnson, who wrote the entry on lyric poetry, places this complex of associations in the Renaissance where "the lyric's preoccupation with the subjective dovetailed neatly with humanistic interest in the varied forms of human emotion" and extends the connection philosophically to Hegel's view of the lyric as "an intensely subjective personal expression."[40]

W. R. Johnson also focuses on the lyric as a vehicle for the exploration of identity by using the poetic "I" to connect the modern lyric with the ancient Greek tradition. But W. R. Johnson offers a modified view that combines Romantic and post-Romantic conceptions of the lyric as an outpouring of personal emotional expression with a classical (Greek to Roman copies of Greek) identification of the lyric as functional discourse. Based on classical examples such as Archilochus and Sappho, and then tracing their methods to the present, W. R. Johnson considers it to be the special nature of the lyric to be able to bind the speaker and the audience in a way that is both intimate and communal: "In shaping emotions, then, the lyric poet performs two very different, indeed, opposite functions simultaneously: he particularizes a universal emotion or cluster of emotions, such as all men share—that is to say, he dramatizes the universal, makes it vivid and plausible; and at the same time, he universalizes an experience that is or was peculiarly his own, thus rendering it clear and intelligible. It is this delicate yet powerful fusion of the individual and universal that characterizes good lyric poetry."[41]

So far, we have a composite of features that consistently and historically seems to characterize the lyric poetry genre as bearing a strain of music or something perceived as "musicality" (going back to its original identity as song accompanied by a lyre), conveying strong, authentic, and unmediated emotional reactions, expressing the voice of an individual, articulating the relationship between an individual and the community, or universalizing the individual's experience to represent the values or attitudes of the community or all of humanity.

W. R. Johnson sees the lyric as a "rhetorical triangle" formed by the speaker, the reader or listener, and the subject of the poem, with emphases shifting in different eras.[42] For example, he considers Romanticism to have placed particular stress on the speaker, as we have seen with Wordsworth's "Preface," while Modernism focused more on metapoetic concerns by foregrounding the discourse itself. Johnson explicitly traces this triangular structure to Aristotle's concept of oration. This correlation is both inventive—I share his perversity here—and extremely useful for our purposes in relation to slave songs. In the ancient Greek lyric, Johnson has identified a connection between the oral presentation of information and the expression of a speaker's personal identity to an audience in order to convey a specific lesson, example, or message about character, ideals, and values. As we will see shortly, Johnson's persuasive argument also beautifully mirrors F. Abiola Irele's contention that the African oral tradition is literary. Johnson explains his position:

> Although it may seem perverse to connect Aristotle's concept of oratory with lyric, I think it can be argued that Greek lyric shows a "situation of discourse" (speaker, discourse, hearer) similar to that which obtains in oratory. This similarity is most pronounced in "epideictic" or "display" oratory, in which the speaker, as against the legal or political orator, is not attempting to persuade his hearer to make a judgment on a practical matter (guilt or innocence in the courtroom, war or peace in the assembly) but is praising or blaming some quality or mode in human nature with a view to educating his hearer, to helping him see what sort of person he can or should become, what sort of person he should not be. In short, the epideictic orator, like the lyric poet, is concerned to offer paradigms of identity, patterns of schooled volition, and he does this by exalting or censuring certain traits in human character with vivid examples of what these traits are like, *may be* like, when we experience them in others and ourselves.[43]

Slave songs are filled with such "paradigms of identity"—the positive and negative moral lessons presented decoratively—that Johnson attaches to the role of the epideictic orator as lyric poet:

> Hypocrite and the concubine,
> Livin' among the swine,
> They run to God with the lips and tongue,
> And leave all the heart behind.[44]

~

> Watch out my sister
> How you walk on the cross,

Yo' foot might slip an' yo' soul get lost.[45]

~

Heav'n, heav'n,
Ev'rybody talkin' 'bout heav'n ain't goin' there,
heav'n, heav'n,
Goin' to shout all over God's heav'n.[46]

~

Mourn hard, mourn hard,
mourn hard, sinner, yo' none too late;
Something spoke unto my soul,
Come down, sinner, yo' none too late;
"Go in peace and sin no mo',"
Come down, sinner, yo' none too late.[47]

~

Religion's like a blooming rose,
Washed in the blood of the Lamb,
As none but those that feel it knows,
Washed in the blood of the Lamb.[48]

~

Your foes shall not before you stand,
Let my people go;
And you'll possess fair Canaan's land,
Let my people go.
We need not always weep and moan,
Let my people go;
And wear these slavery chains forlorn,
Let my people go.[49]

~

Keep a-inchin' along,
like a po' inch worm.[50]

~

You'd better min' how you talk (sing, shout),
you'd better min' what you talk about (sing about, shout about),
For you got to give account in Judgment,
You'd better min'.[51]

Johnson traces the lyric's triadic structure whose constituent elements
are the speaker, the listener, and the poem's subject from the time of
the Greek lyric to "the Latin lyric that continued and refined the
Greek tradition, and [of] the medieval and early modern European
lyric that inherited and further refined the Graeco-Roman lyric tradition."[52] That leaves us where *Princeton Encyclopedia of Poetry and
Poetics* dropped us off: with a subjective, emotional, and musical lyric
in the Renaissance.

Although the lyric of the last two hundred years has been dominated by the voice of the solo poet expressing an individual consciousness, Johnson reminds us that

> in ancient formulations of lyric, both solo and choral poetry were
> equally valid and equally important, each of them necessary to the
> total shaping of the human personality. This sense of the dual, interde-
> pendent nature of lyric has all but vanished from our modern ways of
> thinking about poetry, about literature. . . . Human beings have, after
> all, not only private emotions and selves but also public emotions and
> selves.[53]

I fully concur with Johnson that from the nineteenth century to the
present, the lyric has been thought of as ruminative rather than horta-
tory, individual rather than communal, and "micro" rather than "macro"
in its scale and scope. We particularly do not regard the lyric as a common source of educating or character-building. But if we step back in
time before the Romantics, we find models for the sort of combina-
tory lyric that Johnson sketches—poetry produced by individuals
who recognize themselves as members of a community and who take
on leadership roles based on the force of their subjective identities as
conveyed in the discourse of rhetorical techniques. From ancient
Greece to neoclassical England, we find plentiful examples of lyric
poetry designed to educate and express values, but the georgic is probably the form of lyric poetry most closely associated with the goal of
imparting useful information.

Virgil is credited by Joseph Addison in "An Essay on Virgil's
Georgics" (1697), the foundational critical document on the georgic,

with being the first to copy the Greek masters of this form and intro-duce it into Rome—beating out Hesiod in both quality and chronol-ogy. The georgic is defined as "a didactic poem primarily intended to give directions concerning some skill, art, or science,"[54] but Addison's description of the form, and Virgil's achievements in using it, are more interesting. According to Addison, the finest examples of the georgic, which he believes were produced by Virgil, operate by indirection. Addison criticizes Hesiod for having "much more of the husbandman than the poet in his temperament,"[55] whereas Addison believes that in this form, "the precepts of husbandry are not to be delivered with the simplicity of a ploughman, but with the simplicity of a poet."[56] While Addison defends the purpose of the form as "giving plain and direct instructions to the reader," he poses the equivalent challenge that the most poetically successful way to do so "addresses itself wholly to the imagination" while it "conceals the precept in a description."[57]

The georgic was the form of lyric poetry designed to teach something, and according to Addison these could be "moral duties," "philosophical speculations," "rules of practice," or "signs in nature which precede the changes of the weather." The georgic shows that its creator "is altogether conversant among the fields and woods." It "has the most delightful part of nature for its province" and "raises in our minds a pleasing variety of scenes and landscapes, whilst wholly conversant with nature."[58]

The English tradition inherits two strains of the georgic. One, exem-plified by Hesiod, is intended to convey practical knowledge directly and without adornment. The other, as modeled on Virgil, operates through indirection. Information is gained circuitously through mental action as the poet stimulates readers' ideas on how to undertake a task. Slave songs tend to be most closely related to the Virgilian georgic, which conveys its meaning through indirection. This form relies heav-ily on metaphor and other types of inferential, allusive, or hidden ref-erences, which was a pragmatically valuable as well as poetically effective quality of slave songs as discussed in chapter 2. Details in this type of georgic are chosen for what they conceal as much as for what they reveal because, as Addison puts it, "the mind, which is always delighted at its own discoveries, only takes the hint from the poet, but seems to work out the rest by strength of her own faculties." For that reason, Addison particularly admires Virgil's handling of the form because Virgil "loves to suggest a truth indirectly, and without giving us a full and open view of it, to let us see just so much as will naturally lead the imagination into all the parts that lie concealed . . . thus to receive a precept that enters as it were through a by-way, and to apprehend an idea that draws a whole train after it. For here the mind, which is always delighted with its own discoveries, only takes the hint from the poet, and seems to work out the rest by the strength of her own faculties."[59] Although the physical world is ultimately the subject of the georgic, our apprehension of the world is materially changed for having encountered it in a transformed state through the language of the poem. Through our own efforts to decode the poem's meaning, we have also had an experience that transcends the transmission of pure information, which is what categorizes the georgic as lyric poetry. The same condition will be shown to apply to slave songs.

That is our history of the classical roots of the lyric genre, and we will see through some examples why the breadth encompassed by these forms is sufficient basis to claim that slave songs are lyric poetry. If anything, the history of the lyric strengthens the case. But to return to the start of the chapter and the critical values applied to English poetry: What are the conceptions of lyric poetry that came before the Romantic era against which Wordsworth was reacting? How has this history of the genre impacted more recent conceptions of poetry? Can we find an answer here as to why slave songs have been denied membership in the club? These Romantic and post-Romantic transformations include heightened attention to individual psychology in relation to one's social context, increased concern with spontaneous strong emotions, and diction, references, and perspectives that reflect "the real language of men" to a greater extent than the lyrics of most white hymns, if one is still tempted to think of slave songs solely as black church music. These are some of the features that I have mentioned in relation to developments in the lyric tradition of the past two hundred years.

Robert Pinsky also identifies two similar functions as necessarily operating in the lyric—one personal and one communal—which he views as being in some ways paradoxical but equally necessary in order for lyric poetry to serve as a cultural preserver while moving a society forward. The first role that Pinsky sees is "to mediate between the dead and the unborn: we must feel ready to answer, as if asked by the dead if we have handed on what they gave us, or asked by the unborn what we have for them."[60] The second role is to produce what Carolyn

Forché has termed "a poetry of witness."[61] Pinsky interprets Forché to mean "we must use the art to behold the actual evidence before us. We must answer for what we see."[62] This modern view of the lyric was expressed earlier in American poetry by Walt Whitman, who called English "the powerful language of resistance"[63] and believed that the poem was a dynamic, dialogic, and participatory experience: "The poem's existence is made up of a series of such re-creations; in a very real sense, it has many lives."[64] Whitman saw the lyric in America to be best suited by an open cadential form that metaphorically represented a chorus (echoing the Greek concept) of voices and that each individual's voice, by expressing its full individuality, serves to represent all identities and experiences existing within a society. "A series of re-creations" is a significant phrase for our purposes, because it suggests a ritual reenactment highly consistent with African oral tradition.

I am not suggesting that that the enslaved African poets in America were self-consciously working within a literary tradition based on Theocritus and Homer, then developed and suited to fit Roman culture by Virgil, Hesiod, and Varro, and then exploded into fragmentary trajectories as it entered the English tradition in a range of manifestations, including training in religion, ethics, one's place in society, cultural duties, gardening, and landscaping.[65] But slave songs display many features that parallel the significant historical and contemporary formal, psychological, and cultural shifts in the lyric poetry genre as based on classical tradition. They also have inspired countless numbers of African American poets whose poems allude to slave songs in the same way that poems in the lyric tradition historically refer to a core body of "alludable" texts—that is, commonly known and recognizable to an elect body of readers. Notably, although references in modern and contemporary African American poetry to slave songs are ubiquitous, slave songs—as has been shown—are not part of the African American lyric poetry canon, which is what one would expect with texts that are frequent sources of allusion.

If we consider the georgic broadly to be a "poetics of information," which incorporates both Hesiod's and Virgil's approaches, the modern and contemporary lyric poetry tradition continues to include examples of this mode, in spite of perceptions following Wordsworth that the lyric is an expression of powerful personal emotions and a poor way to transmit "knowledge." Poets such as William Butler Yeats,

W. H. Auden, and Robert Frost at times adopted an expansive—even oratorically based—form of address within the Anglophone canon intending to represent themselves archetypically in speaking as embodiments of their eras or cultures. Charles Olson had a didactic aim to impart information as an explicit part of his poetry's mandate, a goal that would have seemed quite conventional in the eighteenth century and earlier, as perceptively noted by Robert von Hallberg in *Charles Olson: The Scholar's Art*.[66] Ezra Pound's goals were explicitly pedagogical too; he had very specific information in mind that he incorporated in his poetry in order to educate his readers, selecting and presenting with great deliberateness what he believed they needed to know so that he could accomplish a particular agenda. Charles Reznikoff included information from newspaper clippings as a means of directly building into his poetry the impact of a historical cataclysm.

Within the modern and contemporary African American poetry tradition, we have parallel examples of poets providing a "poetics of information" based on specific cultural and historical knowledge intended for the readers' education and edification, and often using slave songs and the allusive references within slave songs—notably the Bible and the conditions of slavery themselves—as that content. This poetry, as with the other examples previously cited, often situates itself as personal expressions that also speak for wider cultural or even universal experiences. Melvin B. Tolson, Robert Hayden, and Rita Dove—as just a few examples among many—often incorporate documents and cultural information from African American lives and history as a mechanism to convey useful knowledge for the guidance of future generations. Samuel Allen's poem "Harriet Tubman aka Moses" directly alludes to slave songs and other oral testimony in the same way that any canonical poem in the lyric tradition alludes to pre-existing canonical literature. Rita Dove's Pulitzer Prize-winning poetry collection *Thomas and Beulah* is based on the history of her grandparents' relationship, making the personal both iconic and historical. Melvin B. Tolson's anthemic and historically encompassing poem "Dark Symphony" constructs and instructs on the cultural history of a race of people and uses a group of slave songs as the central motif of section II, "Lento Grave": "One More River to Cross," "Steal Away to Jesus," "The Crucifixion," "Swing Low, Sweet Chariot," and "Go Down, Moses."

Margaret Walker is another example of a twentieth-century African American poet whose writing is often intended to inform by combining the personal, historical, social, emotional, musical, and informational in a manner representative of much of the post-Romantic lyric poetry tradition. Walker's poem "For My People" (1937) is a narrative bricolage cataloguing cultural treasures handed down like heirlooms. The first stanza of Walker's poem echoes many of the qualities of Whitman: the generously encompassing formal structure of Whitman's open cadential form, oratorical rhythms, and a direct address of music and musicality; a sense of an inchoate and transcendent divine force or controlling spirit; quasi-narrative development; I–you rhetorical bond; and a goal of cataloguing a lengthy compendium of meaningful intimate and shared details of a population:

> For my people everywhere singing their slave songs
> repeatedly: their dirges and their ditties and their blues
> and jubilees, praying their prayers nightly to an
> unknown god, bending their knees humbly to an
> unseen power.[67]

Walker's poem "Amos, 1963" applies the formal and thematic patterns of slave songs (as discussed in chapter 2) by applying direct biblical lessons to her contemporaneous vision of African Americans' experience of social persecution in the South. She builds on the model established in slave songs of using a biblical figure to map the frames of the Old and New Testaments over her present, and she uses the historical role of African American Christianity as a guide, sword, promise, protector, and reckoner. As in slave songs, Walker takes phrases directly from the Bible, incorporates them into her poem as lessons to be learned and extrapolates on them as they apply to the specific and immediate situation of the audience of listeners or readers:

> Amos is a Shepherd of suffering sheep;
> A pastor preaching in the depths of Alabama
> Preaching social justice to the Southland
> Preaching to the poor a new gospel of love
> With the words of a god and the dreams of a man
> Amos is our loving Shepherd of the sheep
> Crying out to the stricken land
> "You have sold the righteous for silver

And the poor for a pair of shoes.
My God is a mighty avenger
And He shall come with His Rod in His Hand."
Preaching to the persecuted and the disinherited millions
Preaching love and justice to the solid southern land
Amos is a Prophet with a vision of brotherly love
With a vision and a dream of the red hills of Georgia
"When Justice shall roll down like water
And Righteousness like a mighty stream."
Amos is our Shepherd standing in the Shadow of our God
Tending his flocks all over the hills of Albany
And the seething streets of Selma and of bitter Birmingham.[68]

The implication that slavery has continuous ramifications is suggested in "Amos, 1963" by the slave song structure, which becomes the hinge connecting four other states chronologically and analogically:[69] (1) Amos in the time frame of the Old Testament, where he prophesies God's vengeance, the return of the Messiah, and the establishment of justice for all people; (2) The Day of the Lord in the future where Amos's prophecies will be fulfilled; (3) an implicit reference to the time of the New Testament through St. Stephen's and St. James's references to Amos's prophecies in The Book of Acts; and (4) the American south in 1963 during the Civil Rights era when Walker's poem was written, but with the ghostly echo of the nineteenth-century South via the allusion to slave songs. "Amos, 1963" uses knowledge of nature and the land—as in the Virgilian georgic—to provide the central metaphor. One of the ancestors, in this case the prophet Amos as a shepherd—which was his original occupation—serves as inspiration for a present-day pastor or prophet to predict God's vengeance and preach justice through an African survival of belief in connections across time and space among people of the black diaspora and ancestors, including biblical figures.

In this poem, the present-day shepherd who is referred to as ministering to his metaphorical flock is inspired by the original pastoral shepherd-prophet, Amos, to call for justice, not sacrifice. We recall two unique aspects of Amos's prophecies. He changed the interpretation of the Exodus tradition, which has been a powerful inspiration and symbol in African American culture since slavery, by opening it up to apply to other nations, not just Israel. Amos saw the election of the Israelites as conditional, not unconditional, as the Israelites believed it was. Amos, therefore, offered an even stronger claim to the slaves that God would intervene on their behalf to enact their own Exodus from slavery.

Amos's second unique prophecy was to offer a new vision of the concept of "The Day of the Lord," which he predicted to be a day of judgment against the rich, which they instead might have understood as their day of celebration. "Amos, 1963" also suggests that African Americans viewed Amos as the prophet of the poor. He warned of the consequences for those who were unjust to the poor and still thought they could be part of the elect, a stance that echoed slave songs' frequent criticism of the hypocrisy of slave holders in their practice of Christianity. In this poem, Amos becomes part of the fabric of African American Christianity by the implicit references to him in the Book of Acts but also by the explicit reference to the pastor in a prophetic role as a new Amos.

Through the connection with Amos, two central themes of slave songs enter Walker's poem as allusions. First, all Christians are connected across boundaries of time and space. Second, as part of the cycle of historical return, God will intervene against wickedness and act on behalf of African Americans in all times in history. He will defend African Americans in their struggles for freedom—whether from nineteenth-century slavery or for twentieth-century civil rights—because he has done so in support of his chosen people in the biblical past. Amos asks that "justice roll down like waters," an image of nature that echoes "Roll, Jordan, Roll," to return to the tradition of the georgic and other slave songs. In a final expression of cohesion with the georgic in its specific references to working on the land, we note that there is an exceptionally high number of allusions in the Book of Amos to "natural objects and agricultural occupations, as might be expected from the early life of the author."[70]

At their most sophisticated, both georgics and slave songs express similar senses of poetic values in conveying a complex and multilayered body of indirect information so that a reader or listener must work to decipher it. There can be cognitive, pragmatic, or circumstantial reasons for an audience's need to be actively engaged in decoding the meaning of any poem, and those conditions would apply to slave songs, as discussed in chapter 4 in relation to metaphor and multiple layers of meaning.

Slave songs were described as "poetic" or having the qualities of poetry by numerous early observers, and many later critics also discuss the "poetry" in their lyrics and music. In August 1899 in *The Century Magazine* XXXVI, Marion Alexander Haskell described the coastal or low-country slave songs as "poetic and imaginative."[71] In the October 1939 issue of *Journal of Negro Education*, John Lovell Jr. wrote metonymically of slave songs' creators: "He was writing some of the stoutest poetry ever created."[72] Some of these comments were surely intended as compliments, but "poetic" also suggests having features that are like poetry—damning with faint praise to perpetuate the impression of slave songs as copies or shadows rather than authentic originals. Instead of conveying the literary critical judgment that slave songs are lyric poetry, "poetic" implies that they contain pleasurable sounds or catchy expressions or show emotions rather than an artist's deliberate and controlled use of techniques to create a sustained and self-aware aesthetic effect. Rather, the underlying surprise at discovering "poetry" or "the poetic" among slaves is conveyed in comments (with its awkward metaphor) such as the one made in 1869 by Thomas Wentworth Higginson: "I was startled when I first came on such a flower of poetry in that dark soil."[73]

In *My Songs: Aframerican Religious Folk Songs Arranged and Interpreted by Roland Hayes*, the great opera singer and famous interpreter of slave songs made repeated references to their composers as poets and to slave songs as poetry: "The texts of these Aframerican religious folk songs are a blend of versified religious paraphrases and amplifying remarks of the poets."[74] Several times, Hayes called the creators of slave songs "Aframerican poets"[75] and pronounced the song "He Never Said a Mumberlin' Word" "the creation of an African who came to these shores already an accomplished bard."[76] Sterling A. Brown quotes an unnamed collector who wrote that "[t]he words of the best White Spirituals cannot compare as poetry with the words of the best Negro spirituals."[77] James Weldon Johnson referred to slave songs' creators as "bards" who knew "the power and beauty of the minstrel's lyre" in an allusion to the lyric tradition.[78] James Weldon Johnson elaborated the point by stating that, when reading slave songs, "[o]ccasionally we are startled by a flash of poetry of pure beauty."[79] However, Johnson also qualified his assessment of slave songs in terms that marginalized them from a "high art" literary tradition by

describing them as having a "primitive dignity,"[80] consistently categorizing them as naïve and as folk art, and admitting his view that
"[m]any of the lines are less than trite, and irrelevant repetition often
becomes tiresome."[81]

In contrast, one of the earliest statements to recognize that slave
songs were performing authentic poetic operations came from William
Francis Allen in his use of the technical terminology of prosody in the
introduction to *Slave Songs of the United States*, writing that slave songs
"will dash heroically through a trochaic tune at the head of a column of
iambs with wonderful skill." Allen also expressed surprise that no systematic effort had been made to preserve them.[82]

Just a few years later, slave songs did come to some of the wider
public attention that Allen, Higginson, and others had hoped for
through the intervention of key figures at some of the newly founded
HBCUs (Historically Black Colleges and Universities). George
Leonard White organized a troupe of students known as the Fisk
Jubilee Singers who traveled nationally and internationally giving a
series of world-renowned concerts from 1871–1903. Their extraordi-
nary list of achievements included an 1873 appearance before Queen
Victoria who requested that they sing "Go Down, Moses" and was
reported to have listened to their rendition "with manifest pleasure."[83]
Pamphlets containing the lyrics of songs performed by the Fisk Jubilee
Singers were distributed at their concerts but were first published in
book form in 1872 in a collection by Theodore Seward titled *Jubilee
Songs: Complete as Sung by the Jubilee Singers of Fisk University*. Rev.
Gustavus D. Pike published *The Jubilee Singers and Their Campaign
for Twenty Thousand Dollars* in 1873, followed by a revised edition in
1875 called *The Singing Campaign for Ten Thousand Pounds: Jubilee
Singers in Great Britain, Rev. Gustavus D. Pike, with an appendix con-
taining slave songs, rev. ed.* Pike's text contains a letter written by Mark
Twain saying how moved he was by the authenticity of the Fisk
Jubilee Singers[84] and a review of their 1875 appearance at the Crystal
Palace that appeared in *The Temperance Record* that cites Henry
Wadsworth Longfellow's poem of admiration for the singing of the
enslaved "negro":

Then, notably, there was the concert of the Fisk Jubilee Singers. Did Longfellow know of their singing or their coming? Surely he did when he wrote the poem of the slave singing at midnight.

> Loud he sang the Psalm of David!
> He, a negro and enslaved,
> Sung of Israel's victory,
> Sang of Zion, bright and free.
>
> And the voice of his devotion
> Filled my soul with strange emotion;
> For its tones by turns were glad,
> Sweetly solemn, wildly sad.

Longfellow must have prophetically beheld the temperance fête of 1873. How his heart would leap up could he have heard the sable off-shoots of slavery, slaves no more, mingling their voices with the blue-eyed, fair-haired Saxons![85]

J. B. T. Marsh's *The Story of the Jubilee Singers; with their Songs* went into its fourth edition in 1874. Thomas P. Fenner, the original band director of the Hampton Student Singers, Frederic G. Rathbun, and Bessie Cleaveland published a collection of their arrangements called *Cabin and Plantation Songs as Sung by the Hampton Students* in 1874, which went into a third edition by 1901, followed by a "new and enlarged edition" in 1927 under the title *Religious Folk-Songs of the Negro as Sung at Hampton Institute*, edited by R. Nathaniel Dett.

Slave songs were categorized by some collectors, editors, and arrangers according to ostensible themes, forms, and purposes, such as "spirituals," "religious folk songs," "cabin and plantation songs," "work songs," "Negro ballads," and "folk seculars," though such divisions are of limited value since slave songs often depict a highly permeable boundary between the sacred and mundane. In fact, this division might ultimately have proven to be misleading, if not outright marginalizing. Abolitionists, collectors, and even some prominent figures in African American culture had a variety of motives to portray the slaves (and later the former slaves) as being entirely devoted to Christian values. For instance, J. B. T. Marsh wrote of the Fisk Jubilee Singers, "Every member of the company is a professing Christian. . . . None of the singers use tobacco, . . . and they are all teetotallers."[86]

These externally imposed categories for slave songs—whether by arrangers, educators, or anthologists—resulted in compilations high-lighting the piety of the slaves and the nonfigural functionality of their songs, which may be one of the reasons they have not been viewed as poetry, although we have already demonstrated that their forms, themes, and purposes were entirely consistent with a variety of lyric modes.

Imposing such categories also does not necessarily reflect the way the slaves themselves understood the songs or the nature of their own existence. For example, the categories used by John Wesley Work and the songs chosen to exemplify his categories, were

- Joy Songs ("Good News, The Chariot's Coming"; "Oh, Religion is a Fortune, I Really Do Believe"; "Shout All Over God's Heaven"; "Great Camp Meeting");
- Sorrow Songs ("I'm Troubled in Mind"; "Nobody Knows the Trouble I See");
- Sorrow Songs with Note of Joy ("Soon-A-Will Be Done with the Troubles of the World"; "Swing Low, Sweet Chariot");
- Songs of Faith ("You May Bury Me in the East");
- Songs of Hope ("In Bright Mansions Above");
- Songs of Love ("I Know the Lord's Laid His Hands On Me"; "Old Time Religion");
- Songs of Determination ("Keep-A-Inching Along");
- Songs of Adoration ("He is King of Kings");
- Songs of Patience ("By and By");
- Songs of Courage ("Stay in the Field"; "March On");
- Songs of Humility ("Reign, Oh Reign").

The optimistic and religious dimension of these headings is unmistak-able, leading to questions of what naturally must have been left out.

Notably, with all of the categorizations, typologies, and functions that we have identified in the history of the lyric poetry tradition going all the way back to its classical roots, when and where have we seen such cate-gories employed? These descriptions are in a sense critical neologisms intended to locate these cultural artifacts not within a literary context but in a circumstance of production or in a characterization of the songs' producers and their culture—which are all ways of separating them from literature, whether consciously or not. R. Nathaniel Dett similarly grouped all slave songs into "Hymns of" categories

- admonition
- aspiration
- biblical themes
- Christian life
- Christmas
- church
- consolation
- death
- death of Christ
- deliverance
- encouragement
- faith and fellowship
- future life
- invitation
- Jesus Christ
- judgment
- meditation
- occasions
- penitence
- pilgrimage
- praise
- religion
- religious experience
- resurrection
- second coming
- tribulation[87]

Roland Hayes divided slave songs in his collection into Events of the Old Testament, Abstractions from the Teachings of Both Old and New Testaments, and The Life of Christ, which he divides into Christ's Birth, Boyhood and Ministry and The Passion of Our Lord. Such structuring foregrounds the purity of their religious sentiment both in their selection and presentation, as well as their singular utility.

If these lyrics were being thought of by their collectors as poetry, it must be as a type of highly functional georgic, more Hesiod than Hesiod. John Mason Brown even wrote a letter about slave songs that was published in December 1868 in *Lippincott's Magazine* that does sound very much like a description of the georgic: "In the department of farm or plantation songs there is much of singular music and poetry to be found," wrote Brown.[88] A comment about the African foundations of slave songs made by Roland Hayes conveys the didactic or pedagogical dimension of the georgic, as well as the new stress on spontaneous emotion in the Romantic and post-Romantic lyric: "African songs give instruction—often by allegory—and improvised song deals with a topical episode or emotion."[89] But based on the organizational structures in the major collections, the "directions concerning some skill, art, or science"[90]—which is the most basic definition offered by *Princeton Encyclopedia of Poetry and Poetics*—would seem to be solely about religion, so slave songs presumably were, and perhaps still are, seen and presented as something akin to georgics for the soul or didactic lyrics for religious training. But this characterization contradicts what will be discussed in chapter 2 and elsewhere in this book: the threat presented to some early audiences by the emotional exuberance and physical "wildness" in the performance of slave songs, as well as the danger thought to be contained in the subversive and militant nature of their lyrics.

These contradictions partly lie in the mode of slave songs as oral transmission and as a means of communication that was able to circumvent the prohibitions against literacy for the slaves by white, pro-slavery culture. In moving from Greek choruses via Whitman and ethnopoetics to the complexities of the "oral" as opposed to the "textual" dimensions of the lyric, we are ready to confront one of the greatest barriers to the acceptance of products of an oral "primitive" tradition into a canon that historically has been associated with education, race, privilege, class, esteem, gender, authority, authorship, and ownership, and which has certainly influenced the failure to frame slave songs as lyric poetry. I will demonstrate that there is a productive intersection—actually a creative blend, which is explained in detail in chapter 2—between African and Western lyric traditions, and slave songs reside in that cognitive space.

F. Abiola Irele has identified three levels of African orality: the first level is that of daily factual communication, the second level consists of rhetorical uses of language that are formulaic such as aphorisms and proverbs, and the third is the literary level where language is used imaginatively. While Irele explains that there is a communicative continuum flowing among these levels, the third level is the center of his focus and ours, in which he posits that there are "specimens in the oral tradition that are endowed with the same character of literariness as written texts" in that they consist of structured enunciations, which form a pattern of discourse and heavily rely on metaphors, tropes, and other figures of speech that create a second order of language with constitutive elements—*words*—foregrounded, organized in highly stylized ways, and subjected to artifice so as to carry a special charge of meaning. In other words, a literary text, whether oral or written, is language *intensified*.[91] The power of Irele's theory of the literary text as it relates to the oral transmission of slave songs—and my contention that slave songs are lyric poetry—is that it "provides an occasion for challenging the conventional Western view of textuality and consequently of literature as linear and spatial, which is based on the exclusive model of writing."[92]

What the early auditors and collectors are likely to have experienced as especially "weird" about slave songs is what Irele calls the "organic mode of existence" in oral literature: "In production, realization and transmission, the text inheres in the physiology of the human frame and is *expressed* as voice, in gestures, and in immediate performance."[93] That exuberant integration of language and movement would go far in explaining reactions such as James Hungerford's 1859 description in *The Old Plantation and What I Gathered There in an Autumn Month*:

> [W]hen the horn sounded for the afternoon service, the "colored brethren" were singing "Play on the Golden Harp" so loudly, and shouting and jumping so excitedly, that they did not notice the call of the horn. The preachers were all gathered in the stand, and the white congregation seated before them; they waited for nothing but for the negro singing to cease. The blacks, however, were too much preoccupied to notice the state of things. After some consultation among the preachers, Mr. Brown arose, and, facing the rear of the stand, said, in his loud and strong nasal voice, "Our colored brethren will endeavor to control their feelings; the hour for the afternoon service has arrived."[94]

In a more detailed description of the complete engagement of the body as part of the performative social interaction in African American worship, Fredrika Bremer made these observations in 1850:

> They sang so that it was a pleasure to hear, with all their souls and with all their bodies in unison; for their bodies wagged, their heads nodded, their feet stamped, their knees shook, their elbows and hands beat time to the tune and the words which they sang with evident delight. One must see these people singing if one is rightly to understand their life.[95]

For Irele, "orality functions as the matrix of an African mode of discourse, and where literature is concerned, the griot[96] is its embodiment in every sense of the word. In other words, oral literature represents the basic intertext of the African imagination."[97] Irele defends the concept that "the African imagination" can be perpetuated in African American literature through African survivals and in the influences of a black diasporic culture, a perspective that supports the views of early scholars and observers who attributed many of the slaves' values and practices to African rituals and perspectives. Irele's comments are especially germane to the situation of slave songs:

> The current interest in the folk origins of African-American literature and the possible resources offered by an oral tradition in Black America is related, as we have seen, to the need to define the distinctive character of this literature. At the same time, it prompts the question as to whether there exists a link between the literature of the Black Diaspora and African literature in its indigenous inspiration, in the sense that I have been employing here. Certainly, a thematic connection exists, if only because of the reference to a common historical experience.[98]

Ultimately, that experience links back to an identification with "a Black literary tradition with roots in an oral tradition,"[99] and to Irele's crucial point that, based on the view of literature that he expresses, there is no philosophical, critical, theoretical, practical, cultural, or material basis for considering oral texts to be less exemplary of literariness than printed texts.

The African view of the oral text also entails improvisation, ingenuity, surprise, spontaneity, varied performance, and change with each instantiation, in contrast with predominant Western views of texts that have a "correct," unitary, and rigidified form on the page (apart from variations in readers' interpretations) that is meant to be read the same way each time it is encountered. We find a perfect example of the flexibility of the African tradition in the well-known survival in slave songs of their call-and-response structure. This antiphonal form is a well-documented inheritance of the African legacy displayed in slave songs that perfectly coincides with the social function inherent in the ancient classical roots of the lyric poetry tradition. It also chimes with the growth of interest in the twentieth-century discussed earlier in this chapter in diverse poetries connected to dance, prayer, and group cohesion. This structural dynamic can readily be seen as a manifestation of the intimate connection between individuals and the social group in slave songs. The call-and-response structure may have been an African inheritance, but it ideally suited the shared communal living and working environment of the slaves in their transplanted American culture and mirrored the thematic content of many slave songs (for example, songs involving group labor, such as hoeing, shucking corn, or rowing). This communalism that reflected African values was readily applied to the conditions of worship, domestic life, work, mourning, help, celebration, and other personal and social rites while slaves in America. Through its mirroring of the importance of both the individual and the group, the use of call-and-response enabled slave songs to serve as an important bridge between the slaves' views of themselves as disparate peoples from various African nations and as a cohesive new community that was something both African and American.

Call-and-response was, above all, an improvisatory structure with differing results each time a song would be performed. This structure must have had the marvelously freeing advantages of being self-determining but also requiring adaptability and concentration—a true break from the routine of work. The result was the fun of familiarity, variety, surprise, bonding, trance-like states, focus, excitement and energy. The leader had special gifts of verbal creativity or a large repertoire of lyrics and music memorized to cue those gathered on how to respond. There were multiple versions of melodies and lyrics on each plantation, and from one plantation to another, and new variants seem to have been a constant. The flexibility and spontaneity of slave songs were inherent in their structure and ever-changing presentations, as outlined in Irele's description of the African oral text. Those facts fly in the face of common perceptions of slave songs as having "correct versions" or being fixed texts with set lyrics, as would be the case with Western conventions, since it places slave songs in a context that makes them look more like church hymns than dynamic and self-regenerating oral poetry. The adaptability of slave songs was their hallmark, which ideally suited the slaves' current situation while preserving ties with their identities and histories. It enabled the slave poets to circumvent the laws against teaching slaves to read and write, and although we know such teachings took place, the penalties were dire. Kemble's comments offer wonderfully logical insights on the subject of teaching slaves to read and the penalties exacted:

> We have no laws forbidding us to teach our dogs and horses as much as they can comprehend; nobody is fined or imprisoned for reasoning upon knowledge, and liberty, to the beasts of the field, for they are incapable of such truths. But these themes are forbidden to slaves, not because they cannot, but because they can and would seize on them with avidity—receive them gladly, comprehend them quickly; and the masters' power over them would be annihilated at once and forever. But I have frequently heard, not that they were incapable of receiving instruction, but something much nearer the truth—that knowledge only makes them miserable: the moment they are in any degree enlightened, they become unhappy.[100]

Kemble later explains that "the penalties for teaching [the slaves to read] are very severe, heavy fines, increasing in amount for the second and third offence, and imprisonment for the third . . . and *death* has not been reckoned too heavy a penalty for those who venture to offer these unfortunate people the fruit of that forbidden tree of knowledge, their access to which has appeared to their owners the crowning danger of their own precarious existence among their terrible dependants."[101]

Here is a typical example of a slave song in call-and-response form from the J. B. T. Marsh collection *The Story of the Jubilee Singers; with their Songs*. The leader's call and the desired response that the leader elicits from the group are clearly telegraphed and would be simple to follow in an oral format, especially since the group would already be familiar with versions or constituent parts:

Where do you think I found my soul,
Listen to the angels shouting.
I found my soul at hell's dark door,
Listen to the angels shouting,
Before I lay in hell one day,
Listen to the angels shouting,
Run all the way, run all the way,
Run all the way my Lord,
Listen to the angels shouting.

Blow, Gabriel, blow,
Blow, Gabriel, blow,
Tell all the joyful news,
Listen to the angels shouting.
I don't know what sinner want to stay here for,
Listen to the angels shouting,
When he gets home he will sorrow no more,
Listen to the angels shouting,
Run all the way, run all the way,
Run all the way my Lord,
Brethren, will you come to the promised land,
Come all and sing with the heavenly band.[102]

By breaking through conventional Western notions of textuality and orality, which imply that there are two separate genres of lyric poetry, we can see how and why the fully embodied power and literary art of slave songs has remained underappreciated, since they have been considered largely in their later, secondary, and clipped-wing form as printed text. By viewing these poems in context—with their language reconnected to their theology, rhythm, voice, dance, and community—we can understand how effectively slave songs serve as a bridge and add to the totality of the lyric poetry traditions.

CHAPTER 2

Theology and Lyric
Poetry in Slave Songs

Lyric poetry historically has been used for theological purposes, beginning with the Homeric text in the ancient Greek world, which has served the dual role as "bible" for its own culture as well as perhaps the central Western canonical text for oral-to-written verse. In this sense, slave songs are part of an ancient tradition. As with a great deal of such sacred verse, slave songs embody both a permeable boundary between the sacred and secular and an intimate relationship between these two realms of experience. This duality is consistent with the canonical lyric poetic tradition—for instance, as embodied in the written work of William Langland, William Blake, John Donne, George Herbert, John Milton, Christopher Smart, and Gerard Manley Hopkins, as well as the oral cultures discussed in chapter 1—yet rarely has it been demonstrated with as much power and poignancy as in slave songs. Slave songs' value as lyric poetry is not negated by their theological value; rather, their literary, religious, and cultural significances are integrally related and mutually reinforcing.

The debate about origins and ownership that dominated the assessment of slave songs, at least through the nineteenth century, masks their significance as a new and important body of American poetry while they have been proven by scholars such as Eddie S. Glaude Jr., Jon Cruz, Dwight N. Hopkins, and Albert Raboteau to be an integral manifestation of the creation of an African American Christianity and culture. Hopkins lucidly argues that we find evidence in slave songs of an African American constitution of communal selfhood and a liberative theology. This identity was in part self-constituted as a social body and also contributed to by the oppression of the slave owners themselves, whose conduct and religious teachings offered a sounding board for the slaves to react against, and through which to define themselves. This vision of constructive reaction is foundational to the development of a black theology, which is exemplified for Hopkins in the emergence and increasing presence of the first person pronoun and what he terms "the power of naming one's own reality" through language, whose generative seeds he identifies in slave songs.[1] But the same features that have led to the construction of culture and individual identity also form an integral part of the value of slave songs as poetry.

A major aspect of what makes slave songs poetry rather than versi-fied Bible lessons is the free-floating imagery that moves across tem-poral and spatial barriers at will, joining conceptual spaces that cannot in reality be joined. Here we see a classical feature of the lyric tradition as well as an African ontological overlay and emergent feature of black theology. Slave songs link together sacred and secular imagery with an ease that bespeaks how closely these two worlds—if they even were separate spheres—were connected for their creators. By means of bib-lical imagery, these poets were able to forge an intimate connection with other times, places, and characters through the sheer vitality of their belief in such a way that all of time and space seem coextensive. Their inherited African perspective would have made them particu-larly comfortable with this worldview. Their circumstances as slaves in the American South might have made it a necessity. The Old and New Testaments offered them the content and context. We encounter in these poems an extraordinary expansion of mind and an unbounded vision of time, place, and identification brought "home" to the speaker, even if the speaker could not travel "home." This achievement seems particularly exceptional when we consider the limited physical and intellectual opportunities afforded these poets. Slave songs represent a combined act of refusal and self-constitution, accomplished by creative means and powered by religious belief.

In addition to adapting the slaveholders' Christianity to their needs and circumstances, the slave poets also drew on African tropes and sym-bology. Satan is often depicted as a trickster figure, as are unrepentant sinners, those who have not yet been born into Jesus, or those who claim to be Christians but are perceived as acting hypocritically (this behavior applies to both slaveholders and fellow slaves) in relation to the slaves' interpretation of the Bible. "View the Land" provides an example:

Ol' Satan's mad, and I am glad,
  View the land, view the land;
He missed the soul he thought he had.
  Oh, view the heav'nly land.
You say you're aiming for the skies,
  View the land, view the land;
Why don't you stop your telling lies?
  Oh, view the heav'nly land.
You say your Lord has set you free,
  View the land, view the land;
Why don't you let your neighbours be?
  Oh, view the heav'nly land.[2]

As another example, "Don't Yo' Hab Eberybody Fo' Yo' Fr'en" is a marvelously spirited and less well-known slave song transcribed in the Saint Helena Islands in 1924 by Nicholas George Julius Ballanta-(Taylor). Once again, we have a poem that demonstrates how much the slaves' lives—as shown in their art—were a composite of the "sacred" and "secular" with little distinction made between the holy and profane, or the religious and social. This intermingling reflects the values of African culture, which were then mapped over the slaves' understanding of a Christianity that was not restricted to church on Sunday. "Don't Yo' Hab Eberybody Fo' Yo' Fr'en" combines commentary on the nature of their view of true Christianity with a vivid sociological portrait of one dimension of slave culture:

Don't yo' hab eberybody fo' yo' fr'en
Don't yo' hab eberybody fo' yo' fr'en.

I tell yo' what yo' fr'en will do
Dey will sit and eat and drink wid yo'
  But when yo' trubble come
    Yo' fr'en begin to run.

Don't yo' hab eberybody fo' yo' fr'en
Don't yo' hab eberybody fo' yo' fr'en.

Meet yo' bruddah in de mornin'
  Ax him how he do
Yo' meet him again in de ebenin'
  He done tell a lie on yo.'

> Don't yo' hab eberybody fo' yo' fr'en
> Don't yo' hab eberybody fo' yo' fr'en.
> Don't yo' forsake yo' mother
> I tell yo' what yo' mus' do
> When yo' father forsake yo'
> Yo' mother will stand by you.
>
> Don't yo' hab eberybody fo' yo' fr'en
> Don't yo' hab eberybody fo' yo' fr'en.[3]

"Scandalize My Name" is another slave song with a similar direct and witty message, which also deals with the themes of betrayal, hypocrisy, and gossip from supposed Christians—even one's own family members—and appears in numerous collections of slave songs.[4]

As another wonderful example of a similar type of slave song combining social commentary on Christian practice and hypocrisy within the slave community—versus the Christian hypocrisy of slaveholders—the poem that I cite from Ballanta-(Taylor) is followed by another called "Jis Want Tell What a Liar Will Do," whose lyrics include the lines:

> He always come wid somet'ing new
> Steal yo' hawss wid false pretense
> and claim dat he is yo' bosom fr'en.'
>
> Ebery day when yo' look out,
> Yo' will see dat liar comin' to yo' house.
> Den dat liar will hab his way
> and tek a seat and stay all day.
>
> Jis about time yo' goin' change yo' mine
> Tell yo' a leetle truth and mek it shine.
>
> Jis about time he get his business fix
> He'll sweeten dat lie wid a leetle trick.
> If yo' Aunt Julia don't, yo' tell Aunt Jane,
> Do fo' Gawd's sake don't yo' call my name.
>
> Jis about time for har to leave
> He'll cause yo' heart and mine to grieve
> But he'll strictly tell you before he go
> Ef he ax yo' do yo' tell him I tell yo' so[5]

Among other African survivals in slave songs, as in African ontology, time is integrally connected to events and experiences, which are then linked to one another regardless of differences in chronology or space, as if metaphysics were suspended. The poets of slave songs show an uncanny conceptual ability to forge images and metaphors that allow them to virtually "fly" through the Old and New Testaments, levitating from their lives in enforced servitude and using models from the Bible to give them strength of mind, imagination on earth, and hope for a Christian reward in the future.

According to John Mbiti, the African perspective is to conceive of the future as a direct and almost immediate extension of the present moment, with past and present as the dominant states of consciousness, which would explain the slaves' view of heaven as a place very much like earth but with its most positive and idealized qualities accentuated. The image of heaven is typically a terrestrial mental construct, not materially different from the slaves' own perspective of what a perfect life on earth would consist of, and redolent with imagery of easy mobility, simple physical pleasures, respectful treatment, reconciliation with loved ones, and absence of overwork and abuse:

> Oh, when I git t'heaven gwine t'ease, ease,
> Me an' my God gwine t'do as we please,
> Sittin' down side o' de Holy Lamb,[6]

~

> O when I get to heav'n goin' to sing and shout,
> I'm goin' to lay down this heavy load,
> For there's no one there for to turn me out,[7]

~

> I'm gwine to sit down at the welcome table,
> I'm gwine to feast off milk and honey,
> I'm gwine to tell God how-a you sarved me,[8]

~

> Dere's no rain to wet you,
> O yes, I want to go home.
> Dere's no sun to burn you.
> Dere's no whips-a-crackin,[9]

~

I hope my mother (sister, brother) will be there,
In that beautiful world on high.[10]

There is a poignant preponderance of references to well-fitting and
comfortable clothing, the humble shoe, and walking freely, references
that are meant to be taken as literally as they are metaphorically:

I know my robe goin' to fit me well,[11]

~

O, walk 'em easy round de heaven,[12]

~

Do don't touch my garment, Good Lord, Good Lord,
Do don't touch my garment, Good Lord,
I'm gwine home.
Do don't touch my slippers, Good Lord, I'm gwine home,[13]

~

When I get to heab'n gwine put on my shoes,
Enter de chariot,
Travel along,
I'll walk all over heab'n an' spread de news,[14]

~

You can walk up in the air, Oh, my Lord?
These shoes I wear are gospel shoes, Oh, my Lord
and you can wear these if you choose,[15]

~

What kind of shoes is dem you wear?
Dat you may walk upon de air.[16]

The homely and poignant stress on walking in heaven unencumbered
and in comfortable shoes can be contextualized by reading the memoirs

from the Works Progress Administration Slave Narrative Collection compiled from 1936–1938. Mary Reynolds, age "100+" at the time of her interview, described the clothing that she wore on her plantation during slavery:

> Shoes was the worstest trouble. We weared rough gussets when it got cold, and it seemed powerful strange that they'd never get them to fit. Once when I was a young gal they got me a new pair and all brass studs in the toes. They was too little for me, but I had to wear them. The brass trimmin's cut into my ankles and them places got miserable bad. I rubs tallow in them sore places and wraps rags round them, and my sores got worser and worser. The scars are there to this day. [17]

That was the situation for a young girl in her apparel, treatment, and physical condition, which was better than the circumstances of many adult males. According to Eileen Southern and Josephine Wright in *Iconography of Music in African-American Culture (1770s–1920s)*, "field hands do not wear shoes." [18]

From the perspective of audience reception, there was certainly a fascination with the slaves' lack of a permanent home and the impact that it had on their songs and characters. Sources as early as William E. Barton in 1899 suggested that this state of rootlessness during slavery explained the African Americans' "fondness for eschatology, and the joy with which they anticipate the day of judgment and dwell upon its terrific and sublime features." [19] In a positive review of the November 1873 performances of the Fisk Jubilee Singers in Scotland, music professor Colin Brown of Andersonian University in Glasgow identified homelessness as a defining feature of African American cultural history whose presence in slave songs was the essence of their "naturalness." Brown defended the theme of homelessness as an expression of the artistic authenticity that generated an overwhelming emotional impact in the audience and compared its use, in an inverted way, to references to the importance of home as a parallel trope by the singers of Scottish ballads and Swedish folk songs:

> Surely their singing was not the less worthy of notice because they laid aside all professionalism and sang with the most perfect naturalness the songs of their homes. So with the Jubilee Singers, their songs are the songs of their people, for they had no homes. The melodies, in all their simplicity, are touching, effective, and characteristic. Why is it that at one time they stir up their audience to enthusiasm and melt them into tears? [20]

When slave songs were sung by free African Americans, the impact on audiences was heightened by this tendency to contemporaneously imagine and sentimentalize the black singers' (or their ancestors') formerly homeless condition and its psychological ramifications. This attitude also limited the ability of post-Emancipation audiences to accept the African Americans as authentic artists by perpetuating, in the last decades of the nineteenth century, a piteous view of them that kept them locked in the past in a state of deprivation. Their homelessness augmented the emotional impact of their former circumstances on audiences by triggering the Aristotelian "pity and catharsis" that comes from imagining how homelessness would have felt while experiencing the utterly alien nature of the singers and their ancestral condition.

Theodore Ledyard Cuyler, founding pastor of the Lafayette Avenue Presbyterian Church in Brooklyn and a friend of Henry Ward Beecher, invited the Fisk Jubilee Singers to perform at his church during their December 1871–January 1872 tour of New York. Dr. Cuyler wrote a letter to the *New York Tribune*, which was cited by J. B. T. Marsh in his 1875 edition of *The Story of the Jubilee Singers; with their Songs* that was evidently meant to be a glowing advertisement. Yet even after Emancipation, Dr. Cuyler—who had been an abolitionist—continued to view the Fisk Jubilee Singers metaphorically in terms of the Exodus tradition and as representatives of plantation culture. As Andrew Ward wrote in his magnificently detailed biographical account of the Fisk Jubilee Singers, "Cuyler's endorsement was riddled with unconscious racism."[21] We see this combination of sympathy and distancing, which remains firmly lodged in the framework of a romanticized past, in Dr. Cuyler's comments:

I never saw a cultivated Brooklyn assemblage so moved and melted under the magnetism of music before. The wild melodies of these emancipated slaves touched the fount of tears, and grey-haired men wept like little children. Their wonderful skill was put to the severest test when they attempted "Home, Sweet Home," before auditors who had heard the same household words from the lips of Jenny Lind and Parepa. Yet these emancipated bond-women—now that they know what the word home signifies—rendered that dear old song with a power and pathos never surpassed. Allow me to bespeak a universal welcome throughout the North for these living representatives of the only true native school of American music. We have long had enough

of its coarse caricatures in corked faces; our people can now listen to
the genuine soul-music of the slave cabins, before the Lord led His
children "out of the land of Egypt, out of bondage"![22]

Colin Brown's point of view is some distance away from that of Dr.
Cuyler. Brown formed no subtextual contrast between the audience as
a "cultivated . . . assemblage" and the singers as "emancipated slaves"
who produced "wild melodies" in contrast with "our people."
However, in spite of their differences, Brown and Cuyler both reflect
a common attitude in focusing on the implications of home for emancipated slaves and citing it as a major source of pathos in the performance of slave songs. Another dimension of the state of homelessness
during slavery was its practical perpetuation when the African Americans
were freed. The extent to which "home" genuinely was an abstract concept was reinforced by the absence of preparation for the freed slaves to
care for themselves and establish homes, a subject that is discussed by
numerous historians in detail and well documented in interviews and
autobiographies.[23]

Slave songs retain conventional Christian associations of a heavenly
home as the eternal reward of the true believer, conflating heaven,
home, the Promised Land, and the Jordan River as references that had
the capability of being substituted or serving as metaphors or codes
for one another, though with different shadings depending on their
poetic contexts. For example, the symbol of home could carry additional weight of a more literal nature for those who had little in the
way of a home on earth, if we are basing our definition of home on its
customary meaning: that is, as a place of stability, free movement, self-
determination, ownership, and safety. We see these visions of an
earthly home that is truly "heavenly"—with all of the ambivalence
implied by that correlation—embodied in the poetry of Paul
Laurence Dunbar, the son of a slave who was raised listening to slave
songs. His poem "Bein' Back Home" begins with the pleasures of
returning to a settled place of one's own in the opening line "Home
again, an' home to stay—." Yet it concludes with what might be
described as fatalistic comfort or eschatological homesteading with
these four faintly ominous and qualified ("Kind o'") lines:

> Kind o' nice to set aroun'
> On the old familiar groun',

> Knowin' that when Death does come,
> That he'll find you right at home.[24]

The influence of slave songs on Dunbar is unmistakable. Home is ultimately just a place where death will find you at the end of a painful life. But those moments of peace at home with family still provide the closest proximity to the rewards beyond mortality. With their ambivalently manufactured imagery of "lowly life" and the importance of "the hearthside," Dunbar's poetry and the accompanying illustrations highlight the compromised and constructed meaning of home as a legacy of slavery. A home on earth would be heaven in its fullest metaphorical sense to a population largely born into slavery, owned instead of owning, separated from family members and from the geographical and ancestral roots so crucial to most African cultures, and with such powerful ramifications for a diasporic people.

In slave songs, "home" rarely has a single and determinate meaning. It is a concept characterized by multiplicity, with a range of meanings that can be literal, but is more often metaphorical, theological, historical, futuristic, and even hypothetical, existing largely in the realm of the imagination and most often expressed in poetry and music. Associations of home radiate backwards and forwards in time to a past in Africa that such references aim to recapture. This act is not experiential—that is, for most of the slaves, knowledge of Africa was not firsthand but was inherited or mythical and needed to be reconstructed or "retro-recalled."

An effective way to conceive of the cultural role of Africa as well as the Bible for the slaves is by what Egyptologist Jan Assmann has termed "mnemohistory":[25] "Unlike history proper, mnemohistory is not concerned with the past as such, but only with the past as it is remembered. It surveys the story-lines of tradition, the webs of intertextuality, the diachronic continuities and discontinuities of reading the past."[26] Ronald Hendel explains that "[t]he data for mnemohistory are texts, artifacts and other evidence of cultural discourse about the remembered past, and its object is to discern how such cultural discourses are constituted and how they influence the cultural present."[27] Assmann's concept, according to Hendel, is to discern "the ways a culture 'shap[es] an identity by reconstructing its past.' The habits of cultural life and the multifarious interests of the present exert selective pressures on collective memories of the past, creating a version of the past with present relevance. How the past becomes a meaningful frame for the present is the particular burden of mnemohistory."[28]

Africa as the ancestral home would have presented just such "versions" of a remembered past, and especially a past that most of the slaves would not have known personally but knew through stories or other cultural vestiges. In many ways, the roles of Africa and the Old and New Testaments operated in a parallel fashion as material for the slaves to usefully adapt these worlds to suit constructively to build their present culture. Though Africa could not have been remembered as physical memory, it would have been one of the mnemohistorical associations of home, along with a rich array of other associations that created a meaningful present for the slaves. As mentioned, "home" was interpreted as heaven, that is, the final resting place projected in the future.

"Home" would have suggested an emotional respite with friends and family, having a place in one's ancestral or current community, a release from bondage, and freedom of spirit even if the body was in chains. Few literary symbols in any culture or era have operated with such resonant sophistication on such a prismatic wealth of conceptual planes (all proposed with equivalent authorial commitment) as slave songs' imagery of home and what will take place there. For the slave, heaven is not only communal but also deeply personal in the sense that, chiasmatically, it is finally a true home, and it truly is a final home. We see how simple yet complex home and heaven are as concepts, combining reconnection to family and friends, union with God, and states of peace, belonging, and freedom:

> Me and my Jesus gwineter meet and talk,
> I thank God I'm free at las'[29]

~

> Po' mourner's got a home at las'[30]
> No mo prayin and no mo dyin,
> when I get home,[31]

~

Oh, freedom! Oh, freedom!
Oh, freedom over me!
An' befo' I'd be a slave,
I'll be buried in my grave,
An' go home to my Lord an' be free,[32]

~

Steal away, steal away, steal away to Jesus;
Steal away, steal away home,
I ain't got long to stay here,[33]

~

Swing low, sweet chariot, comin' for to carry me home,
I looked over Jordan and what did I see,
Comin' for to carry me home,
a band of angels comin' after me,
Comin' for to carry me home,[34]

~

Deep river, my home is over Jordan,[35]

~

See dat forked lightnin'
Flash from tree to tree,
Callin' home God's chil'en;
Get home bimeby.

Keep prayin,' I do believe
We'll get home to heaven bimeby,[36]

~

I heard of a city called heaven
I'm striving to make it my home,[37]

~

Don't be weary, traveller,
come along home to Jesus.[38]

Home in slave songs usually refers to an abstract or metaphorical place, where speakers desire to travel either in the imagination or in the future. It does not necessarily entail an expectation of imminent bodily motion or even that travel to home will be taking place in their bodies or lifetimes. If any symbol was dominant and redolent in slave songs, it is the one of home, also associated with salvation and freedom: "Sometimes I feel like I got no home," "a long way from home," "ol' ark's a moverin', / and I'm goin' home," "I'm on my journey home," "Lord, I'm gwine home," "I want to go home in de mawnin,'" "My home is over Jordan," "Until I reach ma home / I nevuh intend to give de journey ovuh". Slave songs often connect home to an "elsewhere" that is not necessarily conceived of in material terms. Home was generally described as a place where the speakers were journeying, somewhere they had never been, an imagined or hypothetical place, or as an absence or aspiration.

When one longs to go home, typically there is a literal referent that is a specific place of familiarity, origin, or current domicile, with a speaker metaphorically wishing to return to that state of safety or comfort. In contrast, references to "home" in slave songs tend to be devoid of particular details, or references to a plausible return to a familiar or particular state or place. "Home" was most often the object of an expression of future or potential wishes or dreams characterized by references to absence, deprivation, and hope. It was usually connected to travel, motion, and somatic experiences of dislocated identity related to displacement. What we encounter in slave songs is more than a state of double voicing or what Homi Bhabha in the context of post-colonial studies has called liminality—that is, a twofold consciousness that expresses its own experience while also identifying with the colonizer. These poems convey an extraordinary expansion of mind, a mentally unfettered experience of time, place, and identity brought "home" to the speaker. This accomplishment is exceptional, especially when considering the extreme limits of the physical and intellectual opportunities afforded these poets.

To offer two frequent examples of how slave songs are authentically metaphorical, the history of interpretation enables us to understand that crossing the "River Jordan" (which is a related metaphor with some varying implications to "going home") metaphorically refers to crossing the Ohio River (perhaps specifically using the Underground Railroad), traveling to Canada or the North, dying, or passing into the eternal rewards of heaven. Going home—which is one of the most commonly used phrases in slave songs—is a tremendously multivalent symbol. Its metaphorical suggestions include being united or reunited with family (living or deceased); being at peace or feeling in a state of harmony with the universe; being surrounded in fellowship with other Christian believers; feeling connected to Jesus or God; or achieving a state of freedom, either by means of escape on earth—perhaps through the Underground Railroad or some prearranged friendly passage—or relief from life's tribulations through death. Both phrases—"over Jordan" and "going home"—have special significance to Christian slaves in their integral references to crossing over to an eternal home in heaven by means of faith, which is an almost omnipresent level of metaphorical resonance operating in the typically religious poems where these phrases do appear.

In terms of the Christianity expressed in slave songs, this conceptual orientation of African culture where "people set their minds not on future things, but chiefly in what has taken place" would influence notions of a future reward as well as the omnipresence of past occurrences (whether real or mythical, or a personal or ancestral inheritance).[39] Regarding the extension of the past into the present, another African cultural legacy in slave songs is that intimate and personal bonds are maintained among individuals even after death, which is reflected in slave songs in what seems to be an ability to reach into the sky, or heavens, or heaven (or across the Ohio River, or to Africa, or to another plantation) to touch ancestors and biblical figures alike.

The speakers in slave songs often depict themselves interacting with vivid immediacy in biblical stories and with biblical characters. At times, it appears that the Bible figures have been imported to the slaves' present circumstances in the nineteenth-century American South. At other times, it seems as if the speakers have been transported to the past frames of the Old and New Testaments' biblical narratives or to a future after the Second Coming to become firsthand witnesses to the scenes being described. In both sets of situations—including many slave songs where it cannot be precisely determined where the speakers and biblical figures are located—the figures from the Old and New Testaments are related to with the same sense of familiarity and intimacy as family members. Their situations are frequently described as mirroring those of the slaves by describing details of physically suffering, manually laboring, and having simple needs, such as wishing to sit, talk, and treat one another kindly according to the dictates of Christian principles.

Moses, Jacob, Noah, Peter, Jesus, Joshua, Mary, John, David, Gabriel, Daniel, and others are portrayed as being part of the living fabric of the slave poets' lives, and even in direct dialogue with them:

'Raslin' Jacob, let me go,
I will not let you go,[40]

~

I heard King Jesus say,
"Come here, I am de way,"
An' a little talk wid Jesus,
makes it right,[41]

~

O Mary, what you goin' to name that pretty little baby?,[42]

~

Go Mary, an' toll de bell;
Come, John, an' call de roll,[43]

~

Little David play on yo' harp,[44]

~

Daniel saw the stone
Cut out the mountain without hands.
Never saw such a man before,
Cut out the mountain without hands,[45]

~

Gabriel, blow your trumpet!,[46]

~

See fo' an' twenty elders on de'r knees,
See Gideon's army bowin' on de'r knees,
See Daniel 'mong de lions on de'r knees,[47]

~

We am climin' Jacob's ladder,
Ev'ry roun' goes higher, higher,
Soldiers of de cross,[48]

~

Oh, yonder comes my Jesus, Hallelujah,
I know him by-a his shinin', Hallelujah,[49]

~

Look-a how dey done my Lord,
He never said a mumblin' word,
He had to wear a thorny crown,

Saw him when he rise and fall,
Blood it come a twinklin' down,
Thomas say I won't believe,
won't believe, won't believe,
He said Thomas see my han',
He bow'd his head an' died.[50]

At other times, two or more temporal or spatial locations seem to be
activated simultaneously:

De angel roll de stone away;
De angel roll de stone away;
'Twas on a bright an' shiny morn,
When de trumpet begin to soun';

Sister Mary came a runnin'
at de break o' day,
Brought de news f'om heaben,
De stone done roll away.

De angel roll de stone away;
De angel roll de stone away;
'Twas on a bright an' shiny morn,
When de trumpet begin to soun';

I'm a lookin' for my Saviour,
tell me where he lay,
High up on de mountain,
De stone done roll away.

De angel roll de stone away;
De angel roll de stone away;
'Twas on a bright an' shiny morn,
When de trumpet begin to soun';

De soljahs dere a plenty,
standin' by de do',
But dey could not hinder,
De stone done roll away.

De angel roll de stone away;
De angel roll de stone away;
'Twas on a bright an' shiny morn,
When de trumpet begin to soun';

Pilate and his wise men,
didn't know what to say,
De miracle was on dem,
De stone done roll away.

De angel roll de stone away;
De angel roll de stone away;
'Twas on a bright an' shiny morn,
When de trumpet begin to soun.'[51]

The combination of settings is complex, activating heaven and earth, the American Southern culture of the speaker, and the New Testament time frame of Mary Magdalene, the angels, the Roman soldiers, Pontius Pilate, and Jesus at the time of his death and resurrection. The poem also brings together characters from disparate frames by joining biblical figures with a poetic persona who is presumed to be an African American slave. At least four time frames are activated in this poem, not all of which are accommodated by Cartesian physics:

- the past time frame of Jesus at the time of the resurrection, in the reference to the stone rolled away from the tomb in the refrain;
- the future time frame of the apocalypse, in the reference to the trumpet sounding, which is also juxtaposed in the refrain;
- the present time frame of the poetic persona, again imagined to be an African American slave in the nineteenth century;
- the mysterious time frame or frames when the speaker encounters the angel, who is described as performing actions in both the past and the future: this projection might involve imagining the speaker in the future at the time of the Second Coming when the trumpets are sounding, or in the past when the angel is rolling away the stone from Jesus's tomb (especially since the speaker is looking for Jesus, and also sees the soldiers and Pilate);
- finally, there is the equally mysterious time frame or frames in which the speaker encounters Mary Magdalene, who has come running at the break of day after returning from heaven to share the news that the stone has been rolled away from Jesus's tomb and he has been resurrected.

Metaphorically, we can read the text as suggesting that Mary Magdalene felt as if she were in a heavenly place when she discovered that Jesus had risen. As an alternative reading, she actually might have gone to heaven, either in the body, "out of the body," or in a dream state, based on two biblical examples that we can use as models. As we will see later in this chapter and throughout this book, these diverse means of travel would be entirely consistent with African models. The first biblical example is the story of Jacob's ladder from the Book of

Genesis. Jacob, in a dream state, climbs a ladder to heaven and is told by God that he and his descendents will be given the land that they occupy and will multiply plentifully. This biblical story was much beloved by the slaves in its prophetic power—similar to their attachment to the Exodus myth—and was a frequent theme in slave songs. Miles Mark Fisher identifies references to climbing Jacob's ladder in slave songs as early as 1824, and he connects the story to several of their recurring themes, notably imagery of progress for African Americans and the colonization of Liberia.[52] Although references to Jacob's ladder appear in slave songs most often, Jacob makes other frequent appearances, especially in the biblical story of his wrestling with an angel. In *Army Life in a Black Regiment*, Thomas Wentworth Higginson provides an early citation of the lyrics to "Wrestling Jacob," a popular slave song that appears in various forms in several later collections. Higginson also includes a more unusual set of lyrics that he calls "The Baby Gone Home," which connects Jacob's ladder to the frequent imagery of home as paradise in slave songs and whose first stanza is "De little baby gone home, / De little baby gone home, / De little baby gone home, / For to climb up Jacob's ladder."[53] To recuperate the reference to Mary Magdalene traveling to heaven and returning to the body on earth, we also have the model of 2 Corinthians 12, where Paul discusses a man—possibly himself—who goes to heaven, "whether in the body or out of the body, I do not know," receives revelations, and then returns to the earth in the flesh.

In all three of these ways of interpreting stanza 2 in the context of this poem, Mary Magdalene's experience of heaven and her communication to the poem's speaker that Jesus has been resurrected leads to a cohesive interpretation: it is a constant source of joy and discovery to be shared with others that Jesus is the savior to those who believe in him; such news is not restricted to any time in history, and conventional physical frames are not binding to a Christian. There is one metaphysical question remaining: Did Mary Magdalene travel to the nineteenth century after her journey to heaven to speak to the African American slave after the death of Jesus (in which case, time has radically compressed or expanded—either way, physics no longer applies), or was the slave transported to the time of the New Testament when Mary originally experienced Jesus's death and resurrection? The answer is shown not to matter. Both equally plausible readings of this beautifully mosaic-like poem—which has interwoven history, theology, and literature in a seamless totality—is that a Christian feels always present at the moment of salvation, and all believers are connected across barriers of time and space.

The slave poets sometimes cast themselves into the future, as if already in the afterlife or a postapocalyptic state, as in this rare example that originally appeared in an article by Henry Cleveland Wood in *New England Magazine* in March 1892:

> De sun run down in a purple stream,
> An' de moon hit bled ter death,
> An' my soul awoke from hits wicked dream,
> When hit felt my Saviour's breath.[54]

This remarkable poem or poetic fragment—echoing the comparison made between slave songs and "Sappho's of old" in 1873, by Professor Colin Brown[55]—opens with the vivid surrealism of its apocalyptic imagery in the first two lines and continues with the uncanny depiction of the ethereal separation of body and soul depicted in lines three and four. It is not the body but the soul of the speaker that is awakened in this magnificently condensed Christian rendering of waking from the dream of life to life everlasting. The poet here performs the astonishing achievement of capturing the moment of passing from the "wicked dream" of life to death, and then to eternal life through the Lord's sacrifice and blessing. It is an especially interesting feature of this poem that the soul is awakened not by the trumpet, as in conventional apocalyptic imagery, but by the savior's breath in an allusion to the Gospel of John. Before Jesus ascends, he breathes on his disciples and says to them, "Receive the Holy Spirit." It is an early act of forgiveness that takes place before the Second Coming, suggesting that the speaker in this slave song believes that the African American slaves, like the Hebrew slaves, are a chosen people who are marked for special blessing.

In 1872, twenty years before Wood's essay was published, the following lyrics appeared as the second verse of "Didn't My Lord Deliver Daniel?" in *Jubilee Songs: As Sung by the Jubilee Singers of Fisk University*:

> The moon run down in a purple stream,
> The sun forebear to shine,

And every star disappear,
King Jesus shall be mine.[56]

This version is far less successful as poetry than the one cited by Wood. With the substitution of "moon" for "sun" in line one, the imagery in lines one and two becomes more literal and predictable. The second line is too short and rhythmically awkward, with more prosaic diction, an inconsistent rhyme scheme, and less interesting choice of end rhyme words. But the similarities in the first couplet suggest that the beautiful fragment quoted by Wood might have appeared in some of the variants of "Didn't My Lord Deliver Daniel?" and as one of the "mosaic" parts of other slave songs. Certainly the diction and imagery of both stanzas is apocryphal and alludes to Revelation, echoing numerous references in slave songs to Judgment Day.

Another similar poem is "Moon went into de poplar tree, / An' star went into blood; / In dat mornin'."[57] The frequency of appearance ascertains that this mosaic of multiply appearing and interchangeable images was extremely compelling to the poets. A 1910 interview with a former slave contains the reminiscence: "It's like the plantation song, I said,

O the stars in the elements are falling,
And the moon drips away in the blood."[58]

Finally, the imagery strongly echoes the description by Nat Turner of the mystical vision that persuaded Turner that he was ordained for a divine purpose.[59] Lawrence W. Levine explains that "the sign that Turner sought proved to be the solar eclipse of February 1831," and "in the slaves' sacred world . . . magic and Christianity were integral ingredients."[60]

Sometimes the biblical figures and the slaves themselves appeared to be depicted ahistorically, that is, in two places simultaneously or in an indeterminate place created by slave songs, where barriers of time and space do not exist. "Mighty Day" exemplifies this locative flux or bi- or multi-location:

As I went down into Egypt,
I camped upon the ground.
At the sound of the trumpet,
the Holy Ghost came down.

And when the seal was opened,
The voice said, "Come and see,"
I went and stood a-lookin'
To see the mystery.

The red horse came a-gallopin',
And the black horse he came, too,
And the pale horse he came down the road,
And stole my father away.[61]

In the first stanza, the speaker is located in the past—from the perspective of a speaker who is presumed to be a nineteenth-century
slave—of the Old Testament at the time of the Exodus. In the second
stanza, the speaker shoots into the future—both from the perspective
of a slave in the nineteenth century and from the Old Testament—to
Judgment Day. The third stanza is explicitly apocalyptic in its narrative, which is taken from Revelation.

In another slave song, the lines "I never shall forget dat day / When
Jesus wash my sins away,"[62] do not explain where the speaker is in time
and space or who is being addressed. On the literal level, it appears that
a nineteenth-century African American slave is describing a direct personal memory of an event that took place in the past time frame of the
New Testament. We could read these lines as a conventional metaphorical interpretation of Christian theology, addressed to believers in different times and places, but that explanation does not adequately
account for the uncanny sense of *presentness*, authority, witness, and continuous, immediate access to this memory, which especially hinges on
the first-person pronoun. If we are to arrive at a fuller understanding of
this slave song, additional conceptual work is demanded.

In order to illuminate the complex cognitive operations of slave
songs and their implications, I am going to draw on the theoretical
construction referred to by Mark Turner and others as creative
metaphorical blends, cognitive blends, or blended spaces.[63] A blended
space results from a conceptual process produced by a disjunction
rather than from a similarity between two realms being metaphorically compared. It is this jarring contrast by which the mental work
takes place and the meaning of this dynamically unexpected
metaphorical relation is communicated. This operation, which occurs
in non-aesthetic as well as aesthetic uses of language, involves two
"'input' mental spaces . . . blended selectively into a separate mental

space called 'the blended space.'"[64] There is typically an asymmetry, rupture, or disanalogy of some type between the two domains being metaphorically related. Crucially, this juxtaposition results in emergent features in the blended space, features which are not contained in either of the input spaces. It is often the contrast or surface dissonance between the two situations rather than their harmonious correspondence, as with conventional metaphor, by which the meaning takes place. Blends create connections between the input spaces by establishing novel relationships of "identity, analogy and disanalogy, similarity, causality, change, time, intentionality, space, role, part-whole, or representation."[65]

It is also a central feature of blends that they result in "a human-scale" compression of thought, which brings greater manageability to complex and abstract information and ideas.[66] Blends make the inconceivable commensurate, allowing some powerful imaginative conjunctions to be constructed and fresh meanings to be conveyed. Creative blends tend to appear in literature where conventional metaphorical structures cannot represent a "new idea" that an author is seeking to express. This circumstance would apply to the poets of slave songs, who must be seen as working to create something new from the deliberately constrained materials allowed to them in terms of identity, culture, language, religion, and education. Their deprivations and limitations included the enforced Christian interpretations of the slave masters, deliberate renting of their family and cultural ties, and a panoply of physical, mental, and social controls. The poets of slave songs had a horrific paucity of resources available to them and were deprived of literacy and literature as well as anything like a literary tradition that expressed their experience. They had little but the Bible to work with and had to adapt it to their own experiences and perceptions. They were deprived of normal opportunities for communication, family relationships, native languages, individuation, self-fulfillment, self-determination, and personal and group agency and authority. But the desire to circumvent those limitations persevered against almost inconceivable odds.

As I will discuss in chapter 3, one of the major early arguments about slave songs was the question of their originality. A number of scholars have shown that slave songs did contain elements of borrowings from a plethora of existing hymns as well as other foundational sources. But given the limitations of access, openness, and freedom, how could they possibly be "copies" or "nothing new," as some early critics claimed? It is obvious that certain influences must have entered into the slaves' sphere, including ancestral vestiges, which is discussed in chapter 4 in relation to African philosophy. These influences had been transformed by the slave poets into works of art that were uniquely American and African American, with a recognizable identity in addition to shared references to Christian theology, and inventively adapted into new forms. The slaves needed substantial ingenuity to make this material their own, including starting to develop what is now seen as the emergence of a black theology from the cultural margins.[67] Creative blends were some of their most significant means of achieving these highly distinctive and original results that have produced lyric poetry of unique effect and lasting value.

By applying the concept of creative blends to slave songs, how can we view the series of questions in one of the most haunting and moving of these poems?

> Were you there when they crucified my Lord?
> Were you there when they nailed him to the tree?
> Were you there when they pierced him in the side?
> Were you there when the sun refused to shine?
> Were you there when they laid him in the tomb?

This series of questions is followed by an uncanny refrain that creates one of the poem's cognitive blends: "Oh, Sometimes it causes me to tremble, tremble, / Were you there when they crucified my Lord?"[68]

"Sometimes" implies an echoic series of repetitive responses taking place over an extended period of time, which is in contrast to the series of questions that each describe unique and isolated incidents. The brilliant addition of "sometimes" to the line reinforces the recurring shock that returns at intervals as a reminder to the speaker (and audience) of precisely what has been done to Jesus. Assuming that the persona who speaks the line "Sometimes it causes me to tremble" is a slave, this line could refer to a series of responses—the trembling—that take place over an extended period of time in the slaves' present, but that time and place cannot be reconciled logically with the rhetorical stance of the questions. Their phrasing suggests that the speaker has viewed these events firsthand, which would locate him in the chronological frame of the New Testament. In the compressed simplicity of the blended space, there is an uncanny resonance between

Jesus's crucifixion and death and their impact as continuous theological occurrences that exist outside of history. The blend also expresses the combination of the intimate and expansive by cross-referencing the enormity of Jesus's physical suffering with the slave and observer's human-scale response of trembling.

In one space in "Were You There When They Crucified My Lord?" we have a speaker in the nineteenth-century American South asking listeners if they observed an event that took place in the time and place of the New Testament. In order to make sense of these questions, we must step outside the usual confines of time-space physics and human biology. Based on pragmatics, we would infer that the speaker is located in the same time and place as those being addressed. But we know that this situation, if taken literally, is physically impossible given either of the two most logical interpretations. If the speaker were asking these questions of his or her contemporaries in the nineteenth-century American South, on biological grounds the answer cannot be "yes." Similarly, if the listeners were in the time and place of the New Testament, it would be pragmatically impossible to ask the question at all, though the answer might have been "yes." We can make sense of this slave song only by selectively activating information that allows for two equally impossible explanations. Either the addressees are located in the time and place of the New Testament—that is, the listeners are in a different place and era from the speaker and could have witnessed the crucifixion of Jesus—or the speaker is asking other listeners who are in the same time and place, that is, the nineteenth-century American South, if they personally observed an event that took place in the time and place of the New Testament.

Logically, the only person who would be in a historical position to answer "yes" to this series of questions being asked by a speaker in the nineteenth-century American South would have to be located in the time and place of the events recounted in the New Testament. In order to read any meaning into this slave song from this perspective, we must selectively activate our own ability to accept the idea that the slave poets believed they were addressing listeners across space and time. This is one metaphorical reading, but there is yet another metaphorical reading of this slave song. If the speaker in the nineteenth-century American South were addressing others in his or her own time and place, the speaker must be understood to be asking if the listeners have had a non-physical experience—if they have engaged with a type of gnostic immediacy with Jesus. This leap is more than imaginative; it is also mystical. In both readings, a blended space contains features found in neither of the input spaces. The two input spaces have been mapped over one another to generate a third metaphorical meaning: that is, true believers are able to connect with one another across time and space, as the restrictions of the mortal body do not apply. We can also apply Mark Turner's theory very effectively to our reading of "De Angel Roll De Stone Away."

There cannot be a literal or metaphorical reading of these lines that is earthly and not transcendent. If listeners were being addressed in the time and place of the New Testament, they were being asked if they had observed the death of Jesus and knew about the beginnings of Christianity. If listeners were being addressed in the time and place of the nineteenth-century American South, they were being asked if they were empathetically and spiritually affected by the historical knowledge of the crucifixion—that is, if they were Christians. Only through the construction of the blended space do we have access to the message that through the event of Jesus's crucifixion, all Christians are joined to one another across time and space. People who might otherwise have been seen as dissimilar (witnesses to the persecution and death of Jesus in the time and place of the New Testament, and African American slaves in the nineteenth-century American South) instead emerge in the blended space as analogous in their identity. Both groups were Christians who had witnessed persecution by oppressors and were therefore joined in a non-space–time state that Christianity promises as salvation through resurrection. Through the operations of the blend, we see the literal belief of the slaves in Christian immortality: in the blend, those who were in both input spaces (recall the use of the first person) were *alive*.

The operation of blends explains how the speakers in slave songs were able to have frequent conversations with biblical figures, though rarely with God. Here is where we see the advantages of metaphorical blends in their ability to create human-scale conceptions. Slave songs tend to address anthropomorphic figures, with whom the slaves could identify, which explains their greater focus on Jesus than on God. References to God tend to be in the form of expressions, such as "My Lord, what a morning!" rather than direct addresses to God with the intimacy reserved for the other biblical figures. These instantiations are so common that R. Nathaniel Dett includes a section in *Religious*

Folk Songs of the Negro that he calls "Hymns of Religious Experience," which contains slave songs that describe these direct encounters, including examples such as "Oh Peter, go ring dem bells, / I heard from heaven today."[69] We find an abundance of dialogues and monologues between the slaves and biblical figures dating back to the earliest collections. Some examples follow:

> Weep no more, Marta,
> Weep no more, Mary,
> Jesus rise from the dead,
> Happy morning,[70]

~

> Do, fader Mosey, gader your army,
> Sister Mary, stan' up for Jesus,[71]

~

> Jesus when he said to me, I am de voice,
> Like Jesus when he said to me,
> Ev'ry day.
> Like Jesus when he said to me,
> Come out de wilderness,
> Like Jesus when he said to me prepare de way,[72]

~

> Little David, play on your harp, Hallelu! hallelu!
> Little David, play on your harp, Hallelu! hallelu!
>
> 1. Little David was a shepherd boy,
> Killed Goliath and shouted for joy.
>
> 2. Joshua was the son of Nun,
> He never would quit till the work was done.
>
> 3. Done told you once, done told you twice,
> There're sinners in hell for shooting dice.[73]

John W. Work's version of this last set of lyrics from *American Negro Songs: 230 Folk Songs and Spirituals, Religious and Secular* indicates some of the intriguing variations that appear in published slave songs because of the method described by Eileen Southern as "wandering choruses" or "mosaics" by William E. Barton as early as 1899. I discuss this compositional process in chapter 3 and point out variants throughout this book to show the dynamic play of freedom and form in the performance of slave songs.

In the lyrics that Work provides for this almost ever-present slave song, the biblical references are restricted to the Old Testament (which is the same pattern found in James Weldon Johnson and J. Rosamond Johnson's first volume of *The Book of American Negro Spirituals*). They refer to Joshua as the son of Nun, bearing in mind the importance of family relationships and ancestry for the slaves who were deprived of both. David is depicted in three roles; he is a musician, a shepherd, and a fighter who battles with Goliath. These roles would provide models of active agency for the slaves—including the self-referential dimension of being conveyed in a song—whose lyrics often used metaphors of battle, resistance, and work and who celebrated music and lyrics as central to life, community, and communication.

This poem charmingly and significantly underscores the limitations—"misrepresentations" is not too strong a word—of designating all slave songs as "spirituals." The second verse is "Joshua was the son of Nun, / He never would quit till the work was done." The third and final stanza is "Done told you once, done told you twice, / There're sinners in hell for shooting dice." In combining biblical references with comments on both work and play, we can better understand the title of Work's collection and how it telegraphs his editorial goal to present a more complete picture of how these topics integrate in *American Negro Songs*. In "Little David," we find clear evidence that songs of manual labor and adult play, abiding faith and recognition of sin, pious Christian devotion and witty social satire, were not neatly divided into separate categories for the slave poets. We also see that the poets were not simple partially developed childlike beings lacking fundamental multidimensionality. Work's version of "Little David" supports a view that although the slaves were devout Christians, the "spirituals" were used by some white and black Americans to sanitize their public image and progressively represent them as being solely religious beings to promote several ideological and political agendas. When examined as a body, slave songs present resounding evidence that they are the literary expressions of creatively and intellectually gifted, fully embodied human beings.

By contrast, Work's version of these lyrics, "Little David, Play on Your Harp" in R. Nathaniel Dett's *Religious Folk-Songs of the Negro* (whose title conveys the alternative editorial perspective being conveyed by Dett of the slaves and their songs) combines Old and New Testament references in a blended space.[74] This version invokes Moses and the Exodus in the first stanza:

> God told Moses, O Lord!
> Go down into Egypt, O Lord!
> Tell ole Pharoah, O Lord! Loose my people, O Lord!

The second and third stanzas juxtapose both an allusion to the valley of the shadow of death from Psalm 23 in the Old Testament in stanza 2 with a combination of Old and New Testament references in stanza 3: the angels come down to earth "writing salvation." The model for this allusion could be both Revelation in the New Testament and Moses writing down the Ten Commandments in the Old Testament, which was the marker of God's relationship with the Hebrew slaves as a special people and made the Exodus possible, and the parallel event that enabled the African American slaves to believe that God would enable their own future freedom.

In addition to biblical figures, or sometimes in conjunction with them, friends and ancestors were also imported into the slaves' present and implied immediate future through slave songs:

> If you get there before I do,
> Coming for to carry me home,
> Tell all my friends I'm coming too;
> Coming for to carry me home,[75]

~

> Gwine to see my mother
> some o' dese mornin's,[76]

~

> Oh, my brother (Oh, my sister), did you come for to help me?
> Pray give me your right hand,[77]

~

> Oh get you ready, children,
> Don't you get weary,
> Dere's a great camp-meetin' in de Promised Land,[78]

~

> My mother's (father's, sister's, brother's) gone to glory,
> I wan' t' go there too, Lord,[79]

~

> Who dat a-comin' ovah yondah,
> look-a like my sister (brother),[80]

~

> O I hold my bruddder (sister)
> wid a tremblin' hand.[81]

We infer that these friends and relatives are a combination of the living and the dead, those who have slipped from reach or were about to; but in all cases, the connections were maintained through slave songs regardless of apparent disanalogies or barriers of time and space, just as they were with biblical figures and situations.

Understanding how blends operate aids us in recognizing some of the underlying beliefs and assumptions of slave songs' creators. Time, space, and matter are highly fluid and permeable, with conventional operations of physics suspended or only partially applying. The speakers appear to go back and forth in time, virtually at will, and often use imagery of paths to spiritual knowledge or salvation to do so:

> Oh, look up yonder, Lord, a-what I see,
> Den-a Hallelujah to-a de Lamb,
> My Jesus walkin' down de hebbenly road,
>
> Oh, look up yonder, Lord, a-what I see,
> Den-a Hallelujah to-a de Lamb,
> Dere's a long tall angel a-comin' a'ter me,
> . . .
> Wid a palms o' vicatry in-a my hand,

. . .
Wid a golden crown a-placed on my head,[82]

~

I wonder where my mother is gone
I heard f'om heaven today,

O, I'se been on de road into heaven, my Lord!
I can't stay behind!,

Before I'll be a slave
I'll be buried in my grave,
And go home to my Lord,
and be free.

Often, states are depicted that seem not to be wholly in the body or in the spirit—recalling the words used by Paul as a possible model for "De Angel Roll De Stone Away"—as if the speaker felt on the verge of dissolution, escape, or metamorphosis. The speaker is simply "elsewhere" in a mind that had the capability to be separated or freed from the physical body:

Sometimes I feel like I'm almos' gone,
Sometimes I feel like a feather in the air,[83]

~

I got a home in-a dat Rock,
Don't you see?
Between de earth an' sky,
Thought I heard my Saviour cry,
You got a home in-a dat Rock,
Don't you see?[84]

~

Where do you think I found my soul,
Listen to the angels shouting,
I found my soul at hell's dark door,
Listen to the angels shouting,[85]

~

> Gwinter meet my Jesus in de middle of de air,
> Oh your soul! oh my soul! I'm going to the churchyard
> To lay this body down.[86]

The information was sometimes ineffable or predictive, with a perspective that looked back from the future on the present, and from the present toward the future at the same time, as if time were a container with two open ends and certain knowledge is already at hand: "The ol' ark's a moverin' an' I'm goin' home,"[87] "I've heard of a city called heaven, / and I've started to make it my home," "My Lord, I'm mos' done toilin," "I feel like my time here ain't long," "I ain't got long to stay here," "One of dese mornings, it won't be long, / you'll look fo' me an' I'll be gone."

I will focus on one set of lyrics in particular to demonstrate even more emphatically the benefits of recognizing the major role played by creative blends in slave songs' "uncanny" effects or "unusual" impact, commented on by so many early auditors. I have selected "Oh Mary, Don't You Weep, Don't You Moan," a very common slave song, because it is in many ways typical. It follows many of the conventional patterns discussed in this chapter, and any number of other slave songs can be used to demonstrate the same analytical process. What follows is a composite version, which contains the verses that appear most commonly in the major collections.

> Oh Mary, don't you weep, don't you moan,
> Oh Mary, don't you weep, don't you moan,
> Pharoah's army got drownded,
> Oh Mary, don't you weep.
>
> One of dese mornings, bright and fair,
> Take my wings and cleave de air,
> Pharoah's army got drownded,
> Oh Mary, don't you weep.
>
> I thinks every day an I wish I could,
> Stan on de rock whar Moses stood,
> Pharoah's army got drownded,
> Oh Mary don't you weep.

One of dese mornings, round 5 o'clock.
Dis ol world gonna reel and rock,
    Pharoah's army got drownded,
    Oh Mary, don't you weep.

Don't know what my mother wants to stay here fuh,
Dis ole world ain't been no friend to huh,
    Pharoah's army got drownded,
    Oh Mary, don't you weep.

In the five stanzas reproduced here, we have disanalogies everywhere, most notably in the refrain: "Oh Mary don't you weep, don't you moan / Pharoah's army got drownded," where the two situations—one from the Old Testament and one from the New Testament—are not apparently similar. The disanalogies appear in every verse, as three states are invoked in these five verses, all inextricably connected: there is the political and legal state of being free on earth; heaven, as the site of release from earthly bondage—a doubly resonant symbol for slaves who are Christians; and by means of references to the Exodus tradition, the state of anticipation of release from bondage to freedom on earth through a projected identification with Moses and the Israelites.

In addition to these abstract spaces, four concrete places and circumstances are evoked: the time and place of the Exodus in the Old Testament; Mary at the time of Jesus's death as depicted in the New Testament; the nineteenth-century world of the slaves in the American South; and the future imagined by the slaves when God intervenes on their behalf—or, from the secular perspective, when they or forces working on their behalf prevail and they are made free (part of the function of slave songs, as an extension of the African griot tradition, was to share news of military and political developments, of which many slaves seemed to be aware).

Slave songs express a view that is explicitly Christian in depicting heaven as the final home of the true believer and belief in Jesus as the means of arriving there. As slaves, the theological implications of death are embraced with a particular passion as a sometimes potentially desirable alternative to the lives they are leading. Release to the freedom of the afterlife is consistently linked with imagery of release from bondage on earth. Slave songs also contain strong messages of political insurgency based on biblical principles of ethical conduct, including comments on the hypocrisy of Christian teachings and beliefs of slavery advocates. It seems likely that the slaves adopted an ironic distance from what they perceived as the Christianity of the slave-holders, which might help to explain their attachment to the Old Testament as their primary lens for interpreting the New Testament in their reversal of the Christianity of the masters and overseers. As Frederick Douglass wrote in his autobiography, "my master found religious sanction for his cruelty."[88]

Overwhelmingly, it is the Exodus tradition that maintains their faith and that appears to form a direct parallel to their immediate situation of being another chosen people in a state of enslavement. The Promised Land is a polyvalent symbol within the body of resonant poetic imagery in slave songs, operating similarly to the multiple meanings of heaven, home, freedom, and the Jordan River, among other important recurring terms. The Promised Land, within the context of the Exodus tradition, is the reward for their abiding faith. It represents freedom on earth, whether a return to Africa (or specifically Liberia), or the abstract condition of freedom as a state and conceptual construction. It is often used (see Douglass, Higginson, and others) to refer to the North, a place of escape and deliverance that specifically represents the land of freedom within the social and historical context of the African American slave poets; and it is heaven, the afterlife, or eternal rest in Christian terms. It is also the Exodus tradition that allowed the slave poets to apply Old Testament themes as literary tropes to their literal and immediate political circumstances, convinced that they would be freed on earth by God through their unwavering belief. The consistent presence of all of these realms and polysemous meanings for repeated terms such as "the Promised Land" shows that we are in a literary space that is replete with creative metaphors once we recognize them.

The first stanza of "Oh Mary, Don't You Weep, Don't You Moan" speaks from the persona's chronological present to one time frame in the past, while simultaneously referring to another time frame in the even more distant past. The speaker directly addresses Mary (and Martha, in some versions), who is located in the frame of the New Testament, and consoles her by telling her to remember another past, that of the Old Testament—which is the past in relation to Mary as well as the poet, but a past that is implied to be alive for them both. So we have three literary locations—including the frame of the poem itself—and three chronological periods invoked and in dialogue with one another in the first stanza. The first stanza also displays one of several conventional forms that is characteristic of slave songs: line one appears to be the first verse, serving to introduce the narrative, and then repeats as the last line of the first stanza to form an initial framing device. It then reverts in all subsequent stanzas into the refrain, so while it opens the poem as both the call and the response, it continues throughout the poem solely as the response to the leader's call.

The second stanza is one of the two prophetic "one of dese mornings" verses. It projects forward to an imagined future in the persona's lifetime, so that it may be read as taking place both in the persona's future and in an imaginative state. This projection is enacted by means of conventionalized imagery of metaphorical flight and rising into the air. This type of imagery often appears in slave songs in the form of birds, feathers, leaves, or travel across water, and may be read both as referring to flight to heaven after death, flight to freedom on the Underground Railroad, or flight to an imagined state of freedom on earth. These are the same sets of associations that have been discussed as being attached to other repeated redolent symbols in slave songs.[89]

Many versions of "Motherless Child" contain the line "Sometimes I feel like a feather in the air." Imagery of flying appears far too often to need to cite examples; if readers open any collection of slave songs, they will find poem after poem referring to flying, flying through the air, flying over water, and flying through the skies. Imagery of people as having wings or imagining themselves flying like birds also appears with great frequency. An especially beautiful poem using this wing imagery is found in the work of Roland Hayes, the opera singer who was such an inspired interpreter of slave songs. His interpretation of the flying imagery was, "It is a priceless heritage in my people's fantasy to set free serious concern—life, death, union with God—through the ability to laugh, to smile, to follow gaily in the steps of *poetic* [my emphasis] suggestion." The exquisite poem "Two Wings" cited by Hayes is

> Lord, I want two wings to veil my face,
>   I want two wings to fly away;
> Lord, I want two wings to veil my face,
>   And I want two wings for to fly away;
> Lord, I want two wings to veil my face,

> Lord, I want two wings to fly away.
> I want two wings to veil my face,
> And I want two wings for to fly away.
> O, meet me, Jesus, meet me,
> meet me in-a the air;
> And if these two wings fail me,
> Jus' give me another pair.
> O, I want two wings to veil my face, Lord,
> I want two wings to fly away, Lord,
> I want two wings to veil my face,
> And I want two wings for to fly away.
> I want two wings to veil my face, Lord,
> I want two wings to fly away, Lord,
> I want two wings to veil my face,
> And I want two wings for to fly away.[90]

Sometimes references to birds and wings—with heaven or escape—are combined in a composite image of wish fulfillment: "If I had only had wings like Noah's dove, / Oh, shepherd, feed-a my sheep. / I'd fly away to de heavens above."[91]

The third stanza of "Oh Mary, Don't You Weep, Don't You Moan," though not strictly prophetic, still builds on a prophetic tradition in its combination of wishful projection and a belief in the possibility of deliverance based on the Old Testament model. This stanza provides the poem's most explicit statement of identification of the persona with Moses and the Hebrew slaves, and it envisions a desired future by means of the example of the past. The fourth stanza, which is explicitly prophetic, echoes Revelation in the New Testament in its prediction of a future upheaval that the whole world will experience. The second stanza may be read this way as well, as the more horizontal view of the Old Testament is mapped over the more vertical view of the New Testament.

The final stanza addresses the immediate present by referring to the personal frame of the persona's mother. This stanza also forms an apparent ironic contradiction to the refrain or response, casting a seed of doubt on the persona's emphatic statement of belief. It is the persona who encourages Mary to keep faith but then appears to question her mother's own wish to remain alive due to the pain experienced by living in the world. This questioning implies a rejection of the physical and natural world entirely and invokes the imagery of the New Testament's promise of heaven as the reward and release from all human cares. But the closure is a strong statement that faltering faith will be restored, as the poem ends in the expected pattern that the reader now anticipates based on the form that has been established: "Don't you weep." This message is one of the most dominant of all themes in slave songs, which is both a message to others and a message of self-encouragement to keep going. The object of address has become universalized by this time to refer to an encompassing audience consisting of Mary, the African American slaves, the persona's mother, all Christian true believers and the readers of this poem.

The refrain—which we see has become the response to the call starting with the second stanza[92]—is "Oh Mary don't you weep, don't you moan, / Pharoah's army got drownded." But how does this apply to Mary? What kind of liberation does she need? The slaves wished to be freed to enter the Promised Land—potentially referring to the state of freedom, to heaven, or to Africa (the Promised Land from which they originated and were removed, in a reversal of the Exodus where the Hebrew slaves were delivered to a new homeland). Conversely, Mary is not a slave and does not anticipate being freed, as did the people of Israel under Pharoah's control in the metaphorical invocation of the Exodus tradition, or as did the African American slaves, to whom the reference to Pharoah did metaphorically apply. Therefore, we as readers activate certain features of the metaphorical domains but not others, just as the poets of slave songs used certain teachings from the Old and New Testaments for their purposes but chose to ignore others. Therefore, we must read this message to Mary as an exhortation to take comfort in God's ability to intervene on earth, regardless of anyone's station or situation. God had the ability to drown Pharoah and free the slaves during the time of the Exodus, could do the same in the nineteenth-century American South, and could bring comfort to Mary in her state of mourning at the time of Jesus's death. That act of compassion can be achieved by God's having sent Jesus to earth, letting Him rise from the dead, strengthening Mary's faith when losing her son, reuniting Mary with Jesus in heaven when freed from the mortal coil, and all of these possible actions and interpretations.

We find omnipresent examples of basic conventional metaphors in slave songs: life is a journey, life is a battle, life is a trial, life is being present here, staying alive is a contest, life is bondage, and life is a burden— and the correlates death is rest, death is going to a final destination, death is deliverance, and death is departure. Many of these basic metaphors are identified in one of the most helpful texts on the subject: *More Than Cool Reason: A Field Guide to Poetic Metaphor* by Mark Turner and George Lakoff. Slave songs are filled with these basic metaphors, which are human ways of organizing and conveying thought processes. These frequent uses of metaphor are clearly poetic and not literalized interpretations of the Bible, which add strength to the argument that slave songs are, in fact, poems—they are structured acts of reconstructing the Bible, values, knowledge, and experiences as art objects. We can already see how many of these basic metaphors appear repeatedly in slave songs by looking over the citations that appear in this chapter and throughout this book. In addition to the basic metaphors for life and death, there is frequent use of other metaphors: states are locations, the world is a wilderness, "time is a changer,"[93] and God is a guide on the journey of life. By understanding these metaphors, we understand the way slave songs operate as poems.

In addition to these conventional metaphors, we also find a high frequency of creative metaphorical blends, which are a special case of metaphor, as in "Oh Mary, Don't You Weep, Don't You Moan." Because there is a disanalogy between the metaphorical domains—Mary's situation is not one of slavery—certain features of the metaphorical realms are activated while others are not in order to make sense of this poem. In the context of this creative blend, "Pharoah's army got drownded" becomes a metaphor for the comfort offered by God, which the slaves believed was available to everyone who asked for it. Why shouldn't Mary moan? Why should the speaker's mother wish to remain on earth? Why does the Exodus story remain powerful? Not literally because God drowned Pharoah's army but because of the power of God. This poem also exemplifies a customary pattern, which is that most slave songs are not hymns of praise to God, unlike many of their contemporaneous counterparts in white Protestant hymns. Instead, they tend to celebrate the *actions* of God and the prophets of the Old Testament. When Jesus is represented, the characterization is typically modeled on Moses—echoing Matthew's Gospel, where Jesus is depicted as the new Moses in the Sermon on the Mount because he provides the new law—or on other Old Testament prophets or warriors, or an iconic representation of the poor sufferer.

In this poem, the action of drowning Pharoah's army becomes a highly expansive metaphor: it resulted in the freeing of the children of

Israel, which applies to the poetic persona here, but it means more than that because of the inclusion of Mary. What we have is an asymmetrical mapping of disanalogous realms being brought into relation to create a new meaning not contained in either frame of reference. As readers, we follow the poet's lead by having to activate certain features of the domains being compared in order to make literal and metaphorical sense of this poem. This making sense takes place through the operation of creative cognitive blends.

We see a similar blending of chronological and conceptual realms in an abundant number of slave songs, including "City Called Heaven" ("I've heard of a city called heaven / And I've started to make it my home"), "Motherless Child" ("Sometimes I feel like I'm almost gone"), "Nobody Knows Da Trouble I See" ("I never shall forget dat day / When Jesus wash my sins away"), "He Never Said A Mumbalin' Word" ("He bowed His head an' died, / An' He never said a mumblin' word"), "I Know Moonrise" ("I lie in de grave an' stretch out my arms, / I lay dis body down"), "Witness" ("My soul is a witness for my Lord"), "I Got a Home in Dat Rock" ("I got a home in dat rock, / Between de earth an' sky"), "Give me Jesus" ("Dark midnight was my cry"), "Were You There?" ("Were you there when they crucified my Lord?"), and "I Thank God I'm Free At Las'" ("Gwinter meet my Jesus in de middle of de air").

These metaphorical blends, which integrate realms that cannot be joined in the physical world, form a figural representation of the ability of the slave poets to transcend physical constraints through creative and imaginative means. The Christianity taught, which was designed to persuade the chattel to accept their state of enslavement as divinely ordained, resulted in a system of belief that restored control, sustenance, communal strength, and individual perseverance in the slaves. Created in conditions that were special, yet representative of the hardships that humanity has overcome, slave songs are clearly sacred lyric poems that are sufficiently literary to be categorized as such and sufficiently unique to be considered an essential component of the American poetry canon, as well as an embodiment of the fusion of the aesthetic and the devotional in African American art and culture.

CHAPTER 3

Slave Songs as American Poetry

The major nineteenth-century debate on slave songs, continuing in some quarters into the twentieth century, focused on the issue of originality. "The big guns of the white spiritual theory," as they are referred to by John Lovell Jr., are the "gentlemen-professors"—Newman I. White, Guy B. Johnson, and George Pullen Jackson—who leveled a series of charges against slave songs as not being "authentic" slave products. Some of their arguments were that there was no tradition of African song for them to have been built on; they were derived from the same revival songs sung by black and white worshippers alike, except they claimed that the white spirituals came first; and slave songs had similar themes and figures of speech mentioned in white European-based Protestant and Methodist hymns, for example, the Promised Land, Egyptian bondage, and freedom.[1] Coincidentally, they did mention only the white songs as the slaves' stolen source materials and failed to speculate on the Bible, church services, sermons and other oral teachings, or the experience of Christianization in Africa as potential influences.

James H. Cone's *The Spirituals and the Blues* cites the work of German musicologist Richard Wallaschek who in 1893 condemned, in a crescendo of charges, the ostensible scavenging by "the negroes" who "ignorantly borrowed" from "the national songs of all nations."[2] The quality of this type of negative scholarship is further exemplified by Professor Louise Pound, who claimed in 1918, as her sole evidence for black slaves copying white hymns, that her mother had learned the song "Weeping Mary"—identified by Henry Edward Krehbiel as a slave song—"in a period long antecedent to its recovery from the

Negroes."[3] All of these assertions of unoriginality led to the conclusion that slave songs had no unique cultural or artistic significance, because they contained no special reference to the circumstances of the African American slaves and were simply primitive, derivative versions of white European Protestant hymns.[4] These conclusions also contributed to the preexisting characterizations of the enslaved people as being imitative chattel rather than human subjects with the capacity for independent thought, action, and self-determination.

Slave songs bore inevitable similarities to revival hymns and white spirituals in the same way that slaves drew upon Bible stories to create a bonding master narrative of shared ancestry, memory, experiences, values, and religious guidance. There are numerous accounts—in such major scholarly works as Albert J. Raboteau's *Slave Religion*, Dena J. Epstein's *Sinful Tunes and Spirituals*, Lawrence W. Levine's *Black Culture and Black Consciousness*, and John W. Blassingame's *The Slave Community*—of the slaves' various modes of evangelization and worship that would have exposed them to white preachers, churches, and styles of services. But there are notable points of difference in the black songs, including facts first noted by John W. Work: two-thirds of slave songs are in the structure of call-and-response while there are no examples of white spirituals using this form, and their musical scales are different.[5] Miles Mark Fisher notes that the first white hymn to use the concept of "home" did not appear until nine years after a slave song on that theme.[6] In contrast with the attention paid by white hymns and spirituals to the Old and New Testaments—which tend to view the Old Testament through the perspective of the New Testament—slave songs also tend to draw more heavily on Old Testament themes to derive a sense of power, purpose, and identity in the present. There is more intimate personal identification with biblical figures, and there are more mystical slippages of bodies, times, and places. Some of these issues are discussed as instrumental features of slave songs as a means of crossing conceptual boundaries in chapter 4.

There were also significant rhetorical, theological, and ethical differences expressed in slave songs' phrasing, diction, and imagery, including what Zora Neale Hurston referred to as the "picture" words that are central to African American speech.[7] Listing other common themes in slave songs that differ from those in white spirituals provides insight into how the enslaved people understood the nature of their own existence, starting with the highly permeable boundary between the sacred and secular, which is an important African survival. Other unique themes include

- referring to particular types of physical labor (such as shucking corn, rowing ferry boats, stirring cooking pots, laboring in the fields in unison, or working on the railroad);
- depicting ancestors as being in direct contact with the slaves and carrying on conversations with them;
- characterizing personae in the poems who are able to move freely in time and space;
- metaphorically multi-layering imagery of home;
- providing satirical commentary, gossip, and news updates based on the African griot's traditional role;
- using vernacular diction;
- depicting religious hypocrisy of slaveholding culture by the selective interpretation of key aspects of Scripture;
- burlesquing or ironizing members of the community, including slaves, visitors, or members of the slave owner's household;
- "signifyin'" and double voicing;
- presenting unusually detailed imagery of transportation and localization (crossing water, flying, train travel) to be taken as instructions on meeting places, ring-shouts, slave worship services, and escape routes.

James Weldon Johnson noted the absence of "birth of Jesus" slave songs as opposed to the canon of white spirituals and hymns. Johnson observed that he was not aware of any "Christmas spirituals" apart from those written "quite some time after Emancipation" when views of Christmas as well as Christ had shifted. Johnson offered two intriguing potential explanations for this omission: "It may be that the old-time plantation preacher, nonplussed by the Immaculate Conception, touched upon the birth of Christ only lightly or not at all, and therefore, that part of the story of his life was not deeply impressed upon the bards. Or it may be that the Negro preferred to think of Jesus as God, as almighty, all-powerful to help; and that this idea could not be easily reconciled with his being born of a woman."[8] If we look toward the recurring themes of slave songs, we see that their essential nature is predicated upon the sufferings of the adult Jesus and the offered redemption—indeed, imagery of the power to overcome tribulation on earth. This identification would explain why the helpless innocence of the infant Jesus would not serve the psychological needs of the community. Jesus as a fellow sufferer did not have power commensurate with that of God in the theology of the slaves, as Charles H. Long has pointed out.[9]

The focus on the Old Testament in slave songs may also be attributed to the overwhelming importance of the Exodus tradition (and God's power, versus imagery of Jesus as a fellow sufferer and victim) to the African American slaves, which has been explored at length in many sources.[10] Raboteau uses the Exodus motif as a key symbol of differentiation between the slave-owning population's Christianity and that of the slaves.[11] For the slave-owning culture—that is, descendants of the culture of "the New Adam" where settlers explored and claimed their "Promised Land of Israel" in the form of America—a religious pact was fulfilled on the shores of their new home. However, for the slaves America was not Israel but Egypt, the place of bondage and alienation that separated them from their destiny. The poets of slave songs were buoyed by a historical precedent that gave them hope in the present and for the future: their banner was the model of the Old Testament slaves and their belief that God would act in the world once again to free them as well. God's ability to intervene in the present would have been a perspective shared by nineteenth-century black and white populations alike, but the slaves assuredly would have been seeking a very different form of direct action.[12] In many slave songs, we know that the North also represented the Promised Land, demonstrating the slave poets' ability to activate selectively varying features of the belief systems at hand to suit their needed meaning at the present moment. Slave songs were their own original creations, but the issues of copying, theft, lack of ownership, and status as a national product prevailed.

At the same time that they were being criticized for not being different, slave songs were being recognized by others as exemplifying a distinctive form of slave worship, and the songs were vilified for their impropriety. John F. Watson in *Methodist Error* (1819)—probably the first to refer on record to these songs, according to Eileen Southern and Dena J. Epstein—implicitly compared African American expression to that of the Jews in a number of respects: both populations' singing focused on the Old Testament, employed "*hyperboles* of

speech," was "naturally vehement, passionate and giddy," used language that "abound[ed] in extravagant metaphors," and was "extremely
figurative, sometimes to obscurity; and abound[ed] with familiar
objects of sense, for its comparisons and illustrations." When performing these songs, the worshippers were "so lively in their sensa-
tions, as to shout, and *leap*, and *dance*, and clap their hands, if joyful,"
and to howl if sorrowful. Watson makes the telling statement—with
implications that we shall later explore—that these individuals were
not expressing religion: rather, they were expressing "the natural temperament of the people." He formed this conclusion because "expressions" were sometimes heard and seen on occasions that were *not*
religious.

Some of the objections lodged by Watson are based on form and
structure, which significantly entails viewing these songs as aesthetic
objects. He commented that rather than being performed in constrained, modulated, and designated times and spaces, the "transports"
would suddenly stop and start again, "with a greater shrillness and loud-
ness than one could well imagine." Their performers were an "illiterate
people" whose expressions were "addressed to the external senses." The
language contained "highly wrought metaphors . . . and are accounted
for by their being all composed as poetry. 'Poetic license,' has now
become proverbial, and all admit that much *imagery* is essential to good
poetry." But the "illiterate Black slaves" were accused of singing disjointed phrases taken from multiple sources for hours on end and joining in long repeated choruses that were sometimes accompanied by the
rhythms of dance. They also were compared to the Welsh (as well as "the
people of the East," the French and the Greeks for various gross behav-
iors) who also produced "poor, bald, flat, disjointed hymns . . . singing
the same verse over and over again with all their might 30 or 40 times."
Moreover, in terms of proper religious authorship, this roster of advice
ends with the counsel of a Dr. Clarke who admonishes, " . . . never to
sing hymns of your own composing in public . . . unless you be a first
rate poet, such as only can occur in every ten or twenty *millions* of men;
for it argues incurable vanity."[13] In short, the slaves were not Christians,
not Americans, not white, not poets, not humble, not individuals, not
educated, and certainly not proper.

As late as 1913, Henry Edward Krehbiel wrote, "The oldest of
them are the most beautiful, and many of the most striking have never
yet been collected, partly because they contain elements, melodic as

well as rhythmical, which baffle the ingenuity of the early collectors."[14] Virtually all of the early collectors expressed concern that they were not "getting it right" and conveyed their worries about the differences between what they were able to record in contrast with the indescribable spectacles that they were hearing and witnessing. Slave songs simply appeared to be stunningly strange and difficult to capture by conventional means of music and poetry transcription due to their unique and African-inflected structural and presentational features based on oral rather than textual literary traditions.

Numerous observers commented (sometimes with horror) on slave songs' distinctiveness from white church music because of the involvement of the body with the spirit. For example, William E. Barton relates this story: "An old woman was trying to teach a younger woman a spiritual and she was having difficulty with the 'tune and time.' When the woman got her 'swaying and humming, patting her foot the while,' she started to catch on. The woman said, 'You'll nebbah larn 'em in de wuld till you sings dem in de sperrit.'"[15] In addition to dancing and physical motion, other African survivals included shouting, exuberant emotional expressions, and improvisation, as well as the compositional feature that Eileen Southern has termed "wandering" choruses.[16] Southern used this evocative term in relation to Richard Allen's 1801 hymnal, the first anthology compiled by a black preacher to be used by a black congregation. The original hymnal, which combined white hymns by Isaac Watts and others with slave songs, was titled *A Collection of Spiritual Songs and Hymns Selected by Various Authors by Richard Allen, African Minister*. A second edition followed. Southern identified Allen's hymnal as the first to include what she refers to as "wandering" choruses—that is, "choruses that are freely added to any hymn rather than affixed permanently to specific hymns,"[17] which is the characteristic pattern of virtually all slave songs. Southern elaborates on this crucial compositional process— which clearly echoes the patterns of oral literature as proposed by F. Abiola Irele in *The African Imagination*—in *The Music of Black Americans: A History*:[18]

> There are some words, some phrases, some lines that reappear so consistently from song to song that they can be regarded as "'wandering'" phrases and verses. Obviously at one time these wandering bits of text

were associated with specific songs, but it is now impossible to trace them back to the original settings. There are, for example, the places to which the slaves refer to in their songs—the wilderness, the valley, Jerusalem, Jericho, and the promised land. . . . Then there are the ubiquitous allusions to water, or to ships—particularly the ship of Zion.[19]

Southern also cites the repetition of common themes and ideas such as battle imagery, tiredness, biblical heroes, and Satan as the anti-hero,[20] values such as faith, optimism, and patience, and "religious concepts . . . interpreted in the light of the slave's everyday experiences."[21] Southern perceptively observes that these "wandering" choruses, which would require a high level of participation, attention, improvisation, and spontaneity, would heighten the communal component of slave songs' performance.[22]

William Barton made the impeccable choice to select the word and image "mosaics" to refer to the related process that Southern was inspired to call "wandering" choruses, but each of these metaphors has slightly different implications. In Barton's formulation,

> While the fitting together of couplets and refrains almost at random leads to some odd and incongruous combinations, upon the whole one is surprised to find with what good taste the mosaic is made, especially when the singing is led by an old-time leader with a wide range of couplets to choose from. Some of these men when confronted by an inquirer with notebook and pencil can hardly recall half a dozen of these stanzas; but by a sort of instinct rather than taste or judgment fit together words from different sources without a second's reflection or hesitation. It comes to pass sometimes that the words of a given hymn attach themselves to a given refrain so that one rarely hears them separately.[23]

To demonstrate how these mosaics or "wandering" choruses operate, here is a poem that serves as an example, which starts off with one motif and shifts direction as it progresses using the "wandering" chorus principle. The new borrowings seem to fit the poem especially well as Barton suggests in his concept of mosaics—and also to take the original concept of the first poem in some new thematic directions—until the poem eventually rigidifies into two separate poems once it becomes relatively fixed in published format.

The earliest version of "Pilgrim's Song" appears in 1901:

I'm a poor, wayfarin' stranger,
While journeyin' thro' this world of woe,
Yet there's no sickness, toil, and danger,
In that bright world to which I go,
I'm goin' there to see my father,
I'm goin' there no more to roam,
I'm just a goin' over Jordan,
I'm just a goin' over home.

I know dark clouds will gather round me,
I know my way is rough and steep,
Yet bright fields lie just before me,
Where God's redeemed their vigils keep,
I'm goin' there to see my mother,
She said she'd meet me when I come,
I'm just a goin' over Jordan,
I'm just a goin' over home.

I'll soon be free from ev'ry trial,
My body will sleep in the ole churchyard,
I'll drop the cross of self-denial,
And enter on my great reward,
I'm goin' there to see my Saviour,
To sing His praise in heaven's dome,
I'm just goin' over Jordan,
I'm just a goin' over home.[24]

The text appears unchanged in Dett's 1927 revised edition of the book titled *Religious Folk-Songs of the Negro as Sung at Hampton Institute*, but we find it curiously split into a second slave song that appears to be a double to the first, titled "Poor Pilgrim," and identified as having been collected by Dett himself:[25]

I am a poor wayfaring stranger
I sometimes know not where to roam
I heard of a city called heaven
I'm striving to make it my home.

Sometimes I'm both tossed and driven,
I sometimes know not where to roam,
I heard of a city called heaven,
I'm striving to make it my home.

My friends and relations forsake me,
And troubles roll round me so high,
I thought of the kind voice of Jesus
Saying "Poor pilgrim, I'm always nigh."

The title of the song seems to have become rigidified as "City Called
Heaven" at some point in time following the publication of the Dett
collection. It appears under that title in 1930 in Marc Connelly's
Broadway drama, *The Green Pastures: A Fable*, in which slave songs play
a major role.[26] It appears as "City Called Heaven" on the CDs *Toil and
Triumph* by Anthony Brown (2002) and *The Spirituals Project Choir*
(2001), which contain versions of the songs that appeared in a performance of *The Green Pastures*. The song also appears as "A City Called
Heaven" (with approximately the same lyrics as in all of the cited versions titled "City Called Heaven") in Moses Hogan's 2002 *Oxford Book
of Spirituals* in an arrangement by Leonard de Paur (b. 1915):

I am a po' pilgrim of sorrow,
I'm tossed in dis wide worl' alone.
No hope have I for tomorrow,
I've started to make Heav'n my home.

Sometimes I am "toss-ded" an' driven, Lord,
Sometimes I don't know where to roam,
I heard of a city called heaven.
I've started to make heaven my home.

My mother has reached that pure glory,
My father still walkin' in sin.
My brothers an' sisters won't own me,
because I am try'n' to get in.

Sometimes I am "toss-ded" an' driven, Lord,
sometimes I don't know where to roam,
I heard of a city called heaven,
I've started to make it my home.[27]

We begin in the earliest recorded version with imagery that is biblical
and diasporic, personal and representative of the state of all Christians
and all slaves. The speaker is a stranger because earth is not the natural
state for Christians who long to be reunited with Jesus by means of

"crossing over Jordan"—which is characteristic metaphorical imagery in slave songs suggesting travel to heaven or freedom. The speaker is also corporeally a stranger as someone who has been forcibly removed from his or her native culture, with the exilic and diasporic imagery operating with particularly strong symbolic resonance for Christians who are in exile from their homeland of Africa. The poem reflects New Testament imagery in the suggestion of God's redemption, the beautiful and unique metaphor of dropping the cross of self-denial in the Christ identification, and in the characteristic Old Testament imagery that is cross-mapped by referring to a state of exilic wandering in the wilderness, which is the metaphorical "world of woe." African survivals are reflected in connections to ancestors, predictive natural imagery, and a profusion of complex double-voiced and blended metaphors. The future, which is just beyond reach, is an immediate extension of the present and mirrors earthly life. But I want to be very clear in reinforcing the point that textual representations of slave songs are just versions, palimpsests, singular echoes, ghostly twins—they are not written documents in the Western poetic sense. This is the version where we see the highest incidences of "wandering" choruses or important constituent parts from a number of synchronically existing slave songs. The mosaic takes place in their construction, which has been sufficient to identify this poem—along with a melody (or a small body of melodies) to which it became identified—as distinct from other similar versions that were "generic." As not all poems are memorable, so not all slave songs are memorable.

Next we have the version coming from Dett called "Poor Pilgrim"—which, once again, I view as coexisting with the other version, not as having "replaced it" but as a new poem that it has generated in precisely the fashion described by Southern, Barton, and many of our other scholars, commentators, auditors and collectors. The poem has become drastically condensed and while the biblical and cognitive metaphorical Western and African substructures are still very much present (wandering in an unfriendly world, being a stranger on earth, home is heaven, home is a place in the future, life as a journey, pilgrimage, or state of exile, Jesus or heaven as salvation, all humans have now abandoned the pilgrim with Jesus as the only remaining friend) there is a remarkable new poetic element introduced in the couplet "I heard of a city called heaven, / I'm striving to make it my home," which has brilliantly cut through every other tribulation as the total answer. It implies the intrusion of the future into the present but no more so than in conventional metaphors—still, it is very beautiful and became a second independent authentic poem with a life as full and rich as the first with the new now historically living side by side in collections of slave songs.

But something especially exciting happens in the third version where a cognitive blend enters the poem, pushing the implied future of the second version into an authentic apocalyptic collision of time frames in the version that now seems to appear most often. We continue to see the "wandering" choruses—that is, the sad wandering pilgrim whose human connections from version one (stripped in version two) have been restored, and reconnected with the abiding presence of the love and future deliverance of Jesus. A new idea is introduced (which would be considered a "wandering" chorus, since it appears in many other slave songs as a value and a phrase that even if others aren't on the track of Christianity, the speaker will not be deterred).

Now "striving"—very notably—has become "started," so instead of trying to make heaven his or her home, in a sense the speaker is already living there in the final version. The metaphorical reading is that slavery is a state of mind that can be transcended through faith.

As a final comment on the metaphors used by Barton and Southern and their critical values, both the terms "mosaic" and "wandering" would have strong metaphorical resonance for a diasporic population, suggesting both migration and synthesis. Just so, Barton's term focuses not on the process as does Southern's, which beautifully implies a diasporic or migratory process of movement of the constituent linguistic units in slave songs. Rather, Barton's term concentrates on the result of that process as a changeable hybridized puzzle or work of cubist bricolage. The two terms together could not provide a more beautiful composite image for slave songs and their creators.

Since they first were transcribed and studied, there has been persistent fascination about who created African American slave songs. But this curiosity has been coupled with an implicit belief that an important part of their significance is as an expression of a homogeneous population rather than as the creation of individual authorship. Reading the literature on slave songs—reviews of public performances following Emancipation, critical accounts by musicologists, sociologists and other critics, and early transcriptions—most commentators have highlighted their anonymity and communal composition as central to their meaning. I believe that this is one of the reasons they have been consistently excluded from the canons of American and African American poetry, where individuality, originality, agency, self-determination, and ownership are viewed as premiums in literary production and cultural esteem. Here and there we have references to potential authors—"Maum Rizpah," Aunt Dinah, Sister Bemaugh, "the blind slave," "the rower," "old Ned"—who claim to have written specific songs—even Nat Turner ("Steal Away") and Harriet Tubman ("Go Down, Moses") have been credited with authoring some slave songs.

In other early writings on slave songs, we find their authorship shrouded in the mist of an almost insistent anonymity, with various explanations and motivations offered for that authorial "unknowability." A small number of commentators have expressed interest in discovering whether any slave songs had an actual author or originator, but they are in the minority, and most were contented with sketchy and inconclusive replies. For every Thomas Wentworth Higginson who is elated that he might have come upon "the true poet" who birthed a specific slave song, there are far more early collectors and commentators who expressed distrust of those claims or who understood that the cumulative construction of slave songs made the question of the "originator" a specious one, or at least very complicated. Other questions arise from this: The originator of what? A call? A response? A call and response that became fixed in relation to one another? A verse? An image? A melody? A refrain? A series of biblical allusions that became rigidified in their connection to a specific veiled commentary on an aspect of life on the plantation? A line that became a popular favorite to call for a secret meeting or to accompany a particular activity? We already know from documentary evidence, including the theory and research of Barton, Southern, Irele, and others that ideas of a fixed slave song are in contradiction to their lineage and new identity.

Other early commentators believed that one or a small number of gifted individuals were behind the genesis of each song, or at least core elements of it, which seems almost certainly true to anyone who has experienced the operations of improvisation and collaboration. But still the majority were committed to imaginaries of either non-originality or mystery as an inherent part of the detective story (a tale of fraudulence or mystical visitation, depending on one's perspective of the slaves—either revealing racist or abolitionist sympathies) behind slave songs. The focus on anonymity arises in a number of forms, from a number of sources, and with a number of motives, but the end result is acceptance—I would say almost an embrace—of the lyrics' lack of historically verifiable authorship.

Most claims of direct authority were dealt with as specious or tricksterism: in 1892, Henry Wood Cleveland wrote, "While gathering some of the most characteristic songs, I was informed by a dusky singer that I had been 'miscorrected' in regard to the words of one of them, and that to have him, for a small consideration, line it out to me while I wrote it down, would be the 'supernatural' way to get at the matter."[28] In 1925, Howard W. Odum and Guy B. Johnson wrote that "Negroes, in order to verify a boast that they know a certain song to exist, have been known to compose on the moment just such a song, mixing all sorts of songs together with the ideas that arise. Others who have been offered an attractive price for songs have composed them without scruples of conscience, and, when asked to sing them, have done so with perfect ease."[29] This focus on slave songs' misty and inaccessible origins has produced a dearth of serious literary appreciation and resulted variously in nostalgia, objectification, depreciation, exoticization, and sentimentalization. Most writings on slave songs reflect James Weldon Johnson's famous view that they were created by "black and unknown bards."

There are varied explanations and motivations for this focus on slave songs' anonymity and communal creation. It is a common perspective that it would have been dangerous to claim authorship because of the lyrics' subversive and coded messages. In chapter 4, I discuss the way many plantation owners and overseers took great pains to suppress the singing of slave songs because they realized that they had insurgent metaphorical meanings, such as reputedly playing a critical role in the Nat Turner Rebellion and in many slave escapes, including facilitating the work of Harriet Tubman and the operations of the Underground Railroad. In the "Negro Spirituals" chapter in *Army Life in a Black Regiment*, Thomas Wentworth Higginson writes that because of their political power, "[s]ome of the songs had played an historic part during the war." He cites the example of "We'll Soon Be Free," which he transcribes in his chapter, and says that Negroes had been jailed in Georgetown, South Carolina for singing that song because its refrain "was too dangerous an assertion." Later, the song "had been sung in secret to avoid detection."[30] The poem opens in the version transcribed by Higginson:

> We'll soon be free,
> We'll soon be free,
> We'll soon be free,
> When de Lord will call us home.

According to Higginson, a drummer-boy told him "Dey tink de Lord mean for say De Yankees."[31]

Another frequent critical reading of slave songs is to romanticize the deprivation of the slaves and former slaves as a class, which serves as a veil that maintains their anonymity as individuals and reinforces their face-lessness as members of a pitiful group—to paraphrase Paul Laurence Dunbar, "they wore the mask." In *The Singing Campaign for Ten Thousand Pounds: Jubilee Singers in Great Britain* by Rev. Gustavus D. Pike (1875), one of the laudatory prefatory endorsements is a colonial response to the Fisk Jubilee Singers' 1873 British tour. Titled "English Interest in Africa—A Reason for the Success of the Jubilee Singers," it states that "[t]he English are very fond of explorations and discoveries. Living on a narrow island, they stretch their aims and arms over the broad earth, any part of the globe not entirely discovered or explored is to them a golden opportunity to add to the extent of their domains and the glory of their achievements. Africa has been a land of unknown possibilities to them."[32] In this review, the singers of slave songs are not only unknown and implicitly uncharted (non-anthro-pomorphic) territory ("not entirely discovered or explored"), but they are not even African Americans.

Professor Colin Brown also anonymizes and alienates the Fisk Jubilee Singers in writing about his reaction to their performance: "their songs are the songs of their people," he writes, as if they can speak only in a unitary voice, and then he goes on to discuss "the singing of these strangers."[33] *The Daily Albion*'s review of the Fisk Jubilee Singers' performance spoke of "that strange sympathetic power, which is not the possession of an individual, but the dower of a race."[34] In the "Preface to the Music" written by Theodore F. Seward in this volume, Seward wrote: "the childlike, receptive minds of these unfortunates were wrought upon with a true inspiration, and that this gift was bestowed on them by an ever-watching Father, to quicken the pulses of life, and to keep them from that state of hopeless apathy into which they were in danger of falling."[35] Even Seward presents them as a group—an evangelized group, versus the racialized group that they are described as by Brown—and refers to them as something like a neo-Aristotelian Greek chorus-as-hero hit with a divine lightning bolt of Romantic inspiration just at the moment they were about to fall off the cliff of despair, saved in part, perhaps, by the Christianization brought to them by the American Missionary Association.

Slave songs were often categorized as utilitarian rather than aesthetic, though they were differentiated from work songs, since the "spirituals" typically reflected the views that the slaves held no malice and were mainly interested in religion, as discussed in chapter 1. In 1840, Edwin F. Hatfield compiled a volume of poems called *Freedom's Lyre: or, Psalms, Hymns and Sacred Songs, for the Slave and his Friends*, which he divided into such useful sections as "Cries of the Slave to God," "Cries of the Slave to Man," "The Slave Comforted," "The Slave Exhorted to Patience and Hope," and "The Rights of the Slave." Again, we see the slaves depicted deliberately and sentimentally as a group with practical needs and concerns and as a non-differentiated mass with whom Hatfield may dramatically empathize and to whom he has offered this volume of inspirational poetry to which they would presumably have had no legal means of access in 1840. In 1892, Henry Cleveland Wood generalized a population in such a way that it also dehumanized and de-individuated the former slaves: "The Negro never wearies of attending church; it comprises not only his religious, but his social life. He cares little for pastime or entertainment, in general. He manages to extract both from his devotional exercises, and is satisfied."[36] This sense of pure and pious functionalism attached to African American culture has continued to set slave songs apart from any poetry that was considered part of a high art tradition.

This vision of slave songs as having been produced by a group or class—an issue complicated by the African oral tradition and value placed on community, as discussed in chapter 1—and not reflecting the ingenuity of individual artists also was perpetuated by African American commentators, though with different perspectives and motivations. In "The Sorrow Songs" chapter of *The Souls of Black Folk*, W. E. B. Du Bois referred to slave songs as "the soul of the black slave" and "the voices of my brothers and sisters." For Du Bois, there was a heroic ancestral communalism that he recognized as his own and could partake of in what he called "The articulate message of the slave to the world." In 1882, the African American Rev. Marshall W. Taylor similarly framed slave songs as the work of a people rather than of individuals, writing "If you would know the colored people, learn their songs."[37]

Looming over critical accounts of slave songs' value were questions both of their Americanness and their originality. Their identification with Africanness was used to undermine their status as an American product, though at least it proved their originality by rescuing them from the charge (lodged most loudly by Wallaschek) of being derivative of white European hymns. Also, by being associated with Africa's primitivism and savagery, slave songs were further removed from being categorized as an American product, since "the big guns of the white spiritual theory," as they were so fondly called by Lovell, most assuredly would have eschewed Africa's barbarism and lack of sophistication as *American* traits. In addition to deciding whether or not slave songs were "original" or merely copies of existing white-authored lyrics, the debate splinters into two additional, related issues: who created these songs, and are they authentically "American"?

The subtextual concern with authorial anonymity and collaborative production is perpetuated in the debate over whether slave songs could be considered part of American culture. Lucy McKim wrote in 1862: "They are valuable as an expression of the character and life of the race which is playing such a conspicuous part in our history."[38] "Our" makes it unclear whether "they" are merely playing a part or are part of "us." Henry Edward Krehbiel reveals that issues of authorship and race were intertwined with American identity and culture when discussing slave songs. The controversy extended into the twentieth century and "most of it has revolved around the questions of whether or not the songs were original creations of these native blacks, whether or not they were entitled to be called American and whether or not they were worthy of consideration as foundational elements for a school of American composition."[39] If slave songs were composed by "native blacks"—a child-like people who only could act imitatively and without agency—then slave songs did not have to be taken seriously as poetry, definitely not as American poetry. Many white American cultural arbiters were reluctant to acknowledge that an aesthetic expression produced by African Americans could have a place in the American literary canon. At the same time, many African Americans were equally unwilling to celebrate slave songs. They preferred to distance themselves from what they perceived as humiliating vestiges of slave culture that they understandably wished to leave in the past.

John Mason Brown recognized in 1868 that the creators of slave songs were working in artists' territory, yet still provided caveats reinforcing the fact of their group production and aesthetic marginalization:

> What if its words were rude and its music ill-constructed? Great poets like Schiller have essayed the same theme, and mighty musicians like Beethoven have striven to give it musical form. What their splendid genius failed adequately to express, the humble slave could scarce accomplish; yet they but wrought in the same direction as the poor negro, whose eyes unwittingly swam in tears, and whose heart, he scarce knew why, dissolved in tenderness, as he sang in a plaintive minor key some such song.[40]

In 1899, Marion Alexander Haskell expressed another reason why African Americans would have been reticent about slave songs: "The negro feels that the white man's religion is very different from his own, and is sensitive about submitting to an uncomprehending critic a sacred thing, which he fears may be ridiculed, or at best regarded as strange and peculiar."[41] During Reconstruction and continuing into the twentieth century, there is ample evidence that many African Americans viewed slave songs as embarrassing and painful products of plantation culture best left behind—an attitude that was intensified by the depictions of minstrelsy. The reluctance of many newly freed African Americans during and after Reconstruction to have anything to do with slave culture and the inability of some American cultural arbiters to take a black vernacular product seriously as art coincided to marginalize slave songs from the canons of either African American or American poetry.

Eileen Southern agrees with Fisher that the roots of slave songs are African, and her sources suggest that the slaves might have continued to sing and dance in an African style until the eighteenth century, though surely a new kind of black music had developed by the time of the Emancipation Proclamation in 1863.[42] There seems to be general scholarly agreement that, by the nineteenth century, songs of work, lament, social comment, and worship had developed with their own synthetic character that retained such African features as Southern refers to as an "overlapping" call-and-response structure, that is, a continuous cacophony of sound where all parts intersect one another.[43]

In 1913, Henry Edward Krehbiel refers to "primitive African music" and "the savage ancestors" of the negro slaves to show that "the essential elements [of the spirituals] came from Africa," thus proving that they were not imitative of white hymns and separating the African Americans from the primitivism from their own forebears. Ironically, Krehbiel uses this explanation of their African origins and survivals in slave songs to prove their Americanness and their originality. Krehbiel's scholarship is excellent, sympathetic, and among the best of its age, but it is also of its age in displaying an underlying ambivalence toward questions of Americanness and primitive authenticity relating to slave songs. These are not wholly different from the issues that Jerome Rothenberg was shown to be grappling with in chapter 1 regarding his own desire to respectfully present "primitive" oral poetry. Krehbiel writes of slave songs, "They are the fruit of the creative capacity of a whole and ingenuous people, not of individual artists, and give voice to the joys, sorrows and aspirations of that people." In offering this statement of "appreciation," Krehbiel particularly reinforces the identity of slave songs as not being the work of "individuals" but rather the work of a mass. Perhaps he wishes to echo the comments of W. E. B. Du Bois and the values of the African oral tradition in stating that this poetry represents an entire community. But Krehbiel's statement, which follows, does seem to pull back very slightly at considering them to be representative of American poetry with a bit of *sotto voce* elitism that might suggest his lingering awareness of those "primitive" African roots. They will do as American songs for the time being, in other words:

> These people all speak the language of America. They are native born. Their songs are sung in the language of America *(albeit in a corrupt dialect)* [my emphasis], and as much entitled to be called American songs as would be the songs, *were there any such* [my emphasis], created here by any other element of our population. They may not give voice to the feelings of the entire population of the country, but for a song which shall do

that we shall have to wait until the amalgamation of the inhabitants of the United States is complete. Will such a time ever come? Perhaps so; but it will be after the people of the world stop swarming as they have swarmed from the birth of history till now.[44]

In an interesting contrast, when Irving Sablosky comments on the music alone, apart from the words, he has no difficulty stating in 1969 that slave songs are "a musical expression that has since affected every kind of music identifiable as American."[45]

Abolitionists and those with abolitionist sympathies used slave songs to show the peace-loving and harmonious nature of a unified population deserving of freedom. But even well into the twentieth century, by demonstrating that slave songs reflected shared values of universal humanity, their uniqueness remained under erasure. "There are points of resemblance and similarity in all the music that has ever been produced by any people, however different in race, or however far separated by ages. In essentials, all men have been and are still the same," wrote Krehbiel, further complicating his point of view.[46]

The esteemed African American scholar and preserver of slave songs, John Wesley Work, echoed a similar perspective to Du Bois, writing, "These songs certainly express the feelings of the Negro 'as a whole.'" But then he boldly expanded that vision to claim them as truly American and African American expressions as "the Americans of Americans," based on the conditions of slavery itself. I read this astonishing quotation as itself loudly "signifyin'" or "gittin' ovuh," with more than a subtle level of irony reinforcing the powerful message that, in building the most heinous institution in its history, America has produced the truest and realest of all Americans. The slaves' capacity to surmount, survive, and create lasting poetry was an emblem of some of the nation's core values: persevering and speaking out for the cause of justice. Slavery was the pressure that produced slave songs and revealed the American character to itself:

[I]t is not difficult to understand why there is no folk song that expresses the soul of America. America was settled by people who came from countries whose civilization was centuries old and who brought their institutions, customs, literature, and music with them. They were stronger than their surroundings. . . . Each brought his own song from his fatherland. . . . There is, however, a real indisputable folk song in

America—an American production. It was born in the hearts of slaves and consequently expresses the life, not of the whole, but of a part, of our country. . . . The African was vastly different from the other men who came to America. . . . he had not the means of conquering this rugged land, he was not stronger but weaker than his surroundings in America. He did not appropriate, but was appropriated; he did not assimilate but was assimilated; more than any other immigrant he became American, and to-day he is the American of Americans. . . . It was slavery that gave color to his music. Slavery was the starting point and heaven was the goal of his life.[47]

In the preceding quotation, John Wesley Work refers to slave songs as folk songs and not as art or poetry. But Work also cites Carl Holliday, an early twentieth-century English instructor at the University of Virginia, who uses the argument of racial exceptionalism (along with Krehbiel) to justify the Americanness of slave songs as "lyric verse": "Of all the builders of the nation the Negro alone has created a species of lyric verse that all the world may recognize as a distinctly American production."[48]

In an example of how quickly slave songs became a body of echo and allusion in African American literature, we see how their imagery of home and its complicated set of inputs and implications resonate throughout the poetry collections of Paul Laurence Dunbar, who is often referred to as the first "Poet Laureate" of African American poetry, although he lived a life of tragedy and destitution.[49] The influence includes Dunbar's appropriation, reconstruction, and adaptation of slave songs' imagery of home, where "'home'" remains a concept charged with ambiguity, desire, self-determination, loss, absence, and myth-making. The Kiquotan Kamera Klub's photographic illustrations of Dunbar's poetry collections worked in fascinating conjunction with this imagery of home—sometimes illuminating a stunning paternalism, and at other times exhibiting a disturbing romanticization of the fragments of plantation culture. The Kamera Klub photographs narrowed the viewer's angle of perspective to a space that looms large in the imaginary of home in slave songs and in Dunbar's poetry to show how the creative blend of image and substance becomes encapsulated in a simple and profoundly resonant objective correlative—that is, the doorway, the vestibule.

When we refer to image and substance, we are referring to all of the issues addressed in this chapter having to do with the identity of the slaves and slave songs as being on the perimeter, hanging in the cultural balance, not categorized, not claimed, and not fully dealt with. Dunbar's poetry—as the bridge from slave songs into the modern and contemporary African American poetry tradition—is the ideal vehicle to move us forward and send us back to figure out what it all adds up to. To summarize, slave songs are American and not American, African and not African American, poetry and not poetry, authentic black songs and stolen objects from white culture, primitive and knowing, valuable and trivial, products locked in plantation culture and objects that have meaning beyond the era of slavery, solely religious and about a variety of topics, sincere in content and tricky messages with double meanings, commentaries about the value of life on earth and about finding meaning only in the afterlife, vernacular products and artistic creations, and so on. Slave songs, in short, reside in several doorways: neither in nor out of secure spaces of identity, nationality, ownership, production, culture, art, poetry, value, originality, meaning, and interpretation.

The dialogue between the Kamera Klub illustrations and Dunbar's view of the past and future, as represented by "home," both extend and challenge slave songs' views of home. Similarly to slave songs, Dunbar's poems and the accompanying illustrations abstract and fragment the concept of home to address various nineteenth-century myths of cabin life in relation to the construction of a new and modern sense of African American place, history, community, and identity. It can hardly be missed that many of the photographs accompanying Dunbar's poems show figures—most often males—in the doorway of a home, neither in the fields nor solidly ensconced "on the inside," in a place of safety and self-determination. This liminal state applies to time as much as politics and the psychological ramifications of Reconstruction.

In the illustration that accompanies "Long Ago," for instance, which appeared in *Joggin' Erlong* (1906), we see three separate images of male figures in the doorway of a cabin. These images accompany the first three stanzas of the poem. Stanzas 1 and 2 focus on the loss of the "old times" and the hymns of the past (slave songs), which are explicitly connected to community through nostalgia for the "meetin'," and their image is a figure who is literally poised in the space between. But the third illustration accompanies stanza 3, which is the transitional moment where the reader realizes that nostalgia for the cultural and chronological past was actually the metaphor and not the literal meaning. The persona's advancing age appears to be the central subject rather than the political juxtaposition of the past contrasted with the present. Yet this too is represented by a figure in a doorway, extending the imagery of home in slave songs—when the slaves figuratively, and sometimes literally, were homeless, as discussed in chapter 2—into Dunbar's world on the verge of the twentieth century.

Similarly to the representations of home in slave songs, we see that home in Dunbar's poetry is often evanescent or a constellation of fragmented references, gesturing toward multiple sites at once that are not all in the same conceptual plane. We see similar images in numerous Kamera Klub illustrations where figures are either hovering on the external perimeter of a cabin or set in a doorway. This combination of literary and visual imagery becomes a virtual icon of deliberate and controlled ambivalence, ambiguity, and cognitive dissonance. We see this frame of mind reflected in the poetry's stylized and strategized mourning for slave songs themselves, which rapidly became seen in Reconstruction by the newly freed people as part of the history of slavery. Dunbar's representations of home, which allude to slave songs, remind us that slave songs themselves and the plantation life that they depicted already were characterized by ambiguities associated with the state of deprivation of a stable and unitary sense of home, homeland, and being at home in the world.

Dunbar's poem "Long Ago" explicitly addresses romantic nostalgia attached to advancing age absent of racial signifiers, but the setup is generated through the evocation of the persona's youth on the plantation, as visually represented by a dual image of a man perched half in and half out. We see a male figure standing on the steps of a home in "At Candle-Lightin' Time," a woman leaning against the door of a house in "The Deserted Plantation," and a man sitting immediately outside a home in the same poem. In "A Banjo Song" a large group of individuals sit and lean against the perimeter of a house, including two men leaning against the front door and one against the front window. In another photo illustrating the same poem, a whole family is grouped outside the home, and in still another, a woman sits alone next to the door. The non-locatability of home in slave songs is strongly consonant with the ambivalence that later appears in Dunbar's poems.

The illustration to "The Banjo Song" shows figures either leaning against the exterior wall of a cabin or huddling in a group immediately outside the cabin's perimeter, with the focal point of the photo being the vertical angle of the corner of the cabin. Home—as in slave songs—might mean being locked out, but it also relates to community. We see the stress on family as representing the true essence of home in poems such as "At Candle-Lightin' Time" and "When de Co'n Pone's Hot." Home in Dunbar's poems and the photographic illustrations—as in slave songs—often refers to family rather than a place, which we also see in "The Banjo Song."

On the verge of the twentieth century, it was unclear in this new world what the role would be of African Americans, but the roots of this uncertainty had already appeared in slave songs in their representations of a home that was, almost by definition, "elsewhere." We have seen a range of meanings of "home" in slave songs, allusions in Dunbar's poems to slave songs' engagements with ideas of home, and the mediation performed by the photographic illustrations between the world of Dunbar's poems and slave songs, as well as the way that Dunbar was mediating between worlds in his poetry, often through imagery of home and by allusions to the world represented—both in image and substance—by slave songs.

In 1874, the first of three editions was published of *Cabin and Plantation Songs* as they were then sung by the first class of Hampton University students and arranged and compiled by the first director of the Hampton Student Singers, Thomas P. Fenner. This early collection contrasts with the second and third edition of this collection and with the 1941 collection of Hampton-based slave songs edited by R. Nathaniel Dett, in large part because of Fenner's expressed lack of interest in the concert tradition. We may take the 1874 edition as being as one of the more "authentic" compilations of slave songs. The stanzaic symmetry, for instance, that often characterizes the poetic structure of slave songs is missing, and instead of extended metaphors, we have discontinuous metaphors from one stanza to the next.

In October 1895, Miss J. E. Davis, a founding member of the Kiquotan Kamera Klub, suggested that each member of the group illustrate a poem; this idea was taken up with enthusiasm, and Kamera

Klub minutes suggest that this activity began with Dunbar's poem "The Deserted Plantation." The homes in the Kamera Klub photos tend to be simple cabins showing signs of deterioration; the intent is to show the ravages of time. But if the goal also is to romanticize the simplicity of black life and culture, it contrasts with one of the most frequent themes of slave songs where the complexity of slave life is foregrounded.

The Kamera Klub minutes of June 1899, printed in *The Southern Workman*, said that the most valuable work the club had ever done was the Dunbar illustrations as "the study of the old-time life of coloured people," because "[t]he poems themselves are wonderfully true in their descriptions of a life which is rapidly passing away."[50] As Nancy McGhee notes, "Although the old way of life was fading from the Hampton community at the turn of the century, the illustrations for Dunbar's lifelike plantation images came from actual scenes" in the locality. We know that Dunbar saw and either approved or rejected the photos from various Kamera Klub notes and minutes—for example, handwritten notes in the dummy of "Chris-mus is a-Comin'" says "Mr. Dunbar says *no* to the first picture."[51] It is reasonable to say that Dunbar's poetry must stand alone from its illustrations, yet we know from the Kamera Klub's meticulously maintained minutes, which are in the archives at Hampton Institute, that Dunbar did have something like veto power over the photos presented to him for inclusion in the six books that they illustrated, and so they might enter the allusive conversation that joins Dunbar's poetry so intimately to slave songs and plantation life. The influence of slave songs on Paul Laurence Dunbar would have come to him directly as part of his biographical inheritance and his own cultural legacy, especially from his mother Matilda who presented him with "positive" images of slave culture and whose nurturing of his literary talents has been carefully documented by Joanne M. Braxton in her introduction to the definitive edition of Paul Laurence Dunbar's *Collected Poetry*, which she edited.

In this vein of struggling between attempting to acknowledge the possibility of something positive—even potentially classic lyric poetry—emerging from slavery, while acknowledging the conditions under which they were produced, we are reminded that even a staunch supporter such as Henry Edward Krehbiel refers to "primitive African music" and "the savage ancestors" of the negro slaves in showing that "the essential elements [of slave songs] came from Africa,"[52] another justification for not considering them as high art in the Western tradition and as not American. Krehbiel does discuss the importance of Antonin Dvořák finding slave songs a source of inspiration in writing "From the New World,"[53] but then of course Dvořák was not an American composer, and his symphony inspired by slave songs was not American music. As observed by Shelley Fisher Fishkin, "[Mark] Twain's awareness of his countrymen's failure to appreciate the value of the spirituals is echoed by Alain Locke, who noted in 1925 in 'The Negro Spirituals,' that 'only recently have they come to be recognized as artistically precious things. It still requires vision and courage to proclaim their ultimate value and possibilities.'"[54]

CHAPTER 4

Border Crossing in Slave Songs

Slave songs *were* the slaves' traveling shoes. This traveling across conceptual and material boundaries was often managed through the direct evocation of biblical narratives, allusions, and typology, through the use of ideas that reflected both African and Western Christian philosophical and theological traditions, and through processes of conceptual integration. By these means, the slave poets were able to cross a variety of borders as a transformative and liberating response to the linguistic, physical, religious, intellectual, and cultural constraints of their lives. Slave songs were a metaphorical freedom train. They became a conceptual space where the slaves were able to build a platform of poetic liberation in response to their radically constrained circumstances by means of the Bible, creative metaphors, and a new combination of African and Western Christian views of mind and spirit.

It is commonly accepted that slave songs are metaphorical, which is an ancient and central literary trope that historically accounts for much of the complexity and resonance of lyric poetry. Slave songs typically convey a literal surface meaning (or meanings that might have been subjected to multiple interpretations), and one or several subtextual readings embedding coded "other" meanings, which were intended to be selectively translated or deciphered by the "right" audience. Metaphor itself, like allusion, is a figure of transference, transformation, or transition, connected to the classical concept of metalepsis or transumption, and it serves as a bridge to join two ideas together or carry a word or idea somewhere else.[1]

In *The Poetics*, Aristotle called metaphor "the application of a strange term either transferred from the genus and applied to the species or from the species and applied to the genus, or from one species to another or else by analogy."[2] We will find Aristotle's further explanation of analogy to be significant in relation to the transference or outright substitution of meaning by way of "hidden" metaphors in slave songs. Aristotle's ideas on metaphor as analogy are relevant to our discussion of two types of situations that predominate in slave songs where the needed term did not exist. First, there are states of partial embodiment, partial humanness, and being midway in the crossing of spaces or borders culturally, physically, and mentally.

Second, we will find Aristotle's metaphor theory useful in addressing the common circumstance in slave songs where certain aspects of the metaphor are meant to be selectively activated but others are intended to be unseen by some audiences. An example is slave songs whose lyrics foregrounded a primary meaning to slaves that would be invisible or unintelligible to slavery advocates, requiring that two sets of meanings needed to be simultaneously functional but differentially decipherable by insiders and outsiders. Aristotle elaborates:

> Metaphor by analogy means this: when B is to A as D is to C, then instead of B the poet will say D and B instead of D. . . . For instance, . . . old age is to life as evening is to day; so he will call the evening "day's old age" . . . and old age he will call "the evening of life" or "life's setting sun." Sometimes there is no word for some of the terms of the analogy but the metaphor can be used all the same. For instance, to scatter seed is to sow, but there is no word for the action of the sun in scattering its fire. Yet this has to the sunshine the same relation as sowing has to the seed, and so you have the phrase "sowing the god-created fire."[3]

Some of the most famous historical examples of the use of lyrics from slave songs to convey metaphorical meanings are associated with Harriet Tubman. According to Dwight N. Hopkins, "Tubman sang these words to her fellow slaves as she prepared to run away from Delaware slavery to freedom up north":

> When dat ar ole chariot comes
> I'm gwine to lebe you

> I'm boun' for de promised land
> Firen's, I'm gwine to lebe you.
> I'll meet you in de mornin'
> When you reach de promised land
> On de oder side of Jordan
> For I'm boun' for de promised land.[4]

Tubman is widely reported to have used the slave songs "Go Down, Moses" and "Swing Low, Sweet Chariot" as a means of communication in operating the Underground Railroad. In "Swing Low," the lines "Swing low, sweet chariot, / comin' for to carry me home" and "A band of angels comin' after me" are interpreted as a metaphorical reference to the Underground Railroad and the "angels" who are prepared to help slaves ride "home" to freedom. "Go Down, Moses" is a reference to the nickname of Tubman herself. She was metaphorically called Moses for her role in delivering so many slaves to their version of the Promised Land, in an analogy to the Exodus in the Old Testament, by helping them escape to freedom through the Underground Railroad.

Nat Turner is often credited as being the author of one of the most famous slave songs, "Steal Away," which is said to have been used as the rallying cry for the secret meetings that led to his divinely inspired 1831 insurrection:

> Steal away, steal away, steal away to Jesus;
> Steal away, steal away home,
> I ain't got long to stay here.
>
> My Lord calls me,
> He calls me by the thunder;
> The trumpet sounds within-a my soul,
> I ain't got long to stay here.
>
> Steal away, steal away, steal away to Jesus;
> Steal away, steal away home,
> I ain't got long to stay here.
>
> Green trees are bending,
> Poor sinner stands a-trembling;
> The trumpet sounds within-a my soul,
> I ain't got long to stay here.

Steal away, steal away, steal away to Jesus;
Steal away, steal away home,
I ain't got long to stay here.

Tombstones are bursting,
Poor sinner stands a-trembling;
The trumpet sounds within-a my soul,
I ain't got long to stay here.

Steal away, steal away, steal away to Jesus;
Steal away, steal away home,
I ain't got long to stay here.

My Lord calls me,
He calls me by the lightning;
The trumpet sounds within-a my soul,
I ain't got long to stay here.

Steal away, steal away, steal away to Jesus;
Steal away, steal away home,
I ain't got long to stay here.

Whether Turner's authorship is real or apocryphal, this poem is certainly intended on the literal and metaphorical levels to be about crossing boundaries, but even within these interpretive planes—which do not form such simple binaries—there are additional levels of implied movements and translations. The literal Christian reading that the slaves would have intended to be heard by their masters would have been meaningful to the slaves themselves—in other words, it was not wholly a mask or ruse. That message would have been that Jesus calls to Christians by natural signs, as the deity often communicates in slave songs through thunder, lightning, clouds, rainbows, and rain, as well as rocks, mountains, rivers, and the sky.

We have a cognitive blend in the crossing of time frames found so frequently in slave songs. The refrain and stanzas 1, 2, and 4 take place in a sphere that could be in the speaker's present but also could be taking place atemporally, in the speaker's past, present, future, or all of these frames. Stanza 3 explicitly is located in the future, in relation to the speaker's present, at Judgment Day.

The uncanny repeated line—one of the most beautiful and famous in the whole body of slave songs—"The trumpet sounds within-a my soul" echoes such lines in slave songs as "My soul is a witness for my Lord," where body and soul seem to have been separated, but the soul is still invested with capabilities associated with the physical body. This operation will be discussed later in this chapter in relation to Pascal Boyer's concept of "ghost physics."

The revolutionary dangers and conceptual difficulties entailed in having lyrics understood by one audience and only partially understood by another produce appreciable cognitive challenges, especially when the process is oral and improvisatory. Often the meaning that was intended to be conveyed on the purely literal level—which was still metaphorical as an expression of Christian faith and doctrine—would operate successfully in its quasi-subterfuge. John Lovell Jr. discusses the explicit encouragement offered in slave songs to run away and to send the message that this desire was not an impossible goal (like reaching heaven). Lovell imagines a plausible scenario of the compositional process of slave songs and the risks entailed in their dual purposes. His always excellent analysis also highlights the value of considering the meaning of the constituent parts of slave songs as units rather than as the aesthetic totality to which we are generally oriented in the textually based lyric poetry tradition:

One of the creative singers wishes to remind the crowd that freedom is not an impossible way out of their troubles. He comes by a suitable rhythm and stretches it into a song,

> Steal away,
> Steal away,
> Steal away.

And then the danger of his position confronts him. He cannot openly advocate escape and insurrection; it would do him no good. He knows that his yearning is already shared by the crowd around him and that they will understand what he is trying to say. He searches for a medium with appeal and force. Knowing the religious bent of his companions, he settles on "To Jesus!"

Now, he is in the clear. From now on, he can say what he pleases. The oppressor, always close by, is satisfied that this is a purely religious enterprise; his suspicion, aroused by the first "Steal away" is fully allayed. But the slave poet goes on,

> Steal away, steal away home,
> I ain't got long to stay here!

The trusting oppressor never knew (or believed) until too late that the slave had probably already made contact with the Underground Railroad or some other slave stealing organization.[5]

The specific metaphorical subtexts of "Steal Away" seem to have varied from region to region according to their most effective practical use. Perhaps it was the call to battle for Nat Turner and his revolutionaries. A missionary from Choctaw Mission in Texas named Alexander Reid claimed to have taught a version of the song to the Jubilee Singers that he learned from a slave named Uncle Wallace, who said it was used by "the slaves on a neighboring plantation 'stealing away' across the Red River in canoes to worship at Reid's mission."[6]

We also know that the surface or literal message alone sometimes failed to be conveyed to the oppressors, and the subversive intent—whether by implication or the specific details—was understood. Following the Nat Turner Rebellion, which was one of the largest rebellions in the history of American slavery,[7] scrutiny and restrictions for the slaves markedly increased, and the following commentary contains yet another metaphorical reference for "Steal Away." A former slave from the Heathsville, Virginia region reported that before 1836,

I commenced holding meetings among the people, and it was not long before my fame began to spread as an exhorter. I was very zealous, so much so that I used to hold meeting all night. . . . The singing was accompanied by a certain ecstacy of motion, clapping of hands, tossing of heads, which would continue without cessation about half an hour; one would lead off in a kind of recitative style, others joining in the chorus. . . . When Nat Turner's insurrection broke out, the colored people were forbidden to hold meetings among themselves. . . . Notwithstanding our difficulties, we used to steal away to some of the quarters to have our meetings.[8]

A former slave named Charity Bowery from North Carolina provided another report that many in the white pro-slavery population did understand that slave songs had double meanings that could directly generate revolt: All the colored folks were afraid to pray in the time of old Prophet Nat. There was no law about it; but the whites reported it round among themselves that, if a note was heard, we should have some dreadful punishment; and after that, the low whites would fall upon any slaves they heard praying, or singing a hymn, and often killed them before their masters or mistresses could get to them.[9]

Nevertheless, the subtextual messages of slave songs and their perpetuation remained a vital presence within the slave community. In R. Nathaniel Dett's *Religious Folk-Songs of the Negro*, the introduction to "Run to Jesus, Shun the Danger" (credited to the Fisk Collection) provides this background: "This song was given to the Jubilee Singers by Hon. Frederick Douglass, at Washington D.C., with the interesting statement that it first suggested to him the thought of escaping from slavery."[10] The lyrics provide an excellent example of the Du Boisian double voicing, or the metaphorical invisibility and surface transparency that characterizes so many of these poems:

> Run to Jesus, shun the danger,
> I don't expect to stay much longer here.
> He will be our dearest friend,
> And will help us to the end,
> I don't expect to stay much longer here.
> Run to Jesus, shun the danger,
> I don't expect to stay much longer here.
>
> Oh, I thought I heard them say,
> There were lions in the way,
> I don't expect to stay much longer here.
> Run to Jesus, shun the danger,
> I don't expect to stay much longer here.
>
> Many mansions there will be,
> One for you and one for me,
> I don't expect to stay much longer here.
> Run to Jesus, shun the danger,
> I don't expect to stay much longer here.[11]

It is not difficult to see how such lyrics could persuade overseers, masters, and other auditors of slave songs that their creators were focused solely on religion. The first line of the refrain would have been interpreted as an exhortation to urgently devote oneself to Jesus and disregard all obstacles. The second line would have been taken as a comment on the brevity of life on earth (the referent of "here") compared to the eternal life promised to Christian believers. Slaves such as Douglass, however, would have understood the lyrics as a message that it was a good time to run for freedom because God and his "angels"—who were helpers of any sort, whether other slaves who had escaped to freedom, those working on the Underground Railroad, abolitionists, or anyone sympathetic and helpful to the cause—would be a "friend" in providing safe passage and escape from the "lions," who were the patrollers and other risk factors. The message of Christian protection is not negated: it is simply accompanied by a second message that, in terms of practical action, is as important as the first.

The target audience for the poems' metaphorical or hidden meanings could have been

- the slaves themselves in the now-past from their synchronic perspective in time;
- the slaves' ancestors;
- their absent relatives;
- their immediate community on their plantation;
- slaves on other American plantations;
- their extended African diasporic community;
- other slaves (past, present and future);
- biblical figures;
- all Christians throughout time;
- listeners or readers in a future period in time.

These future audiences include us, from our diachronic perspective—but deliberately excluding the contemporaneous class of slave holders in the nineteenth-century American South, though this was not a foolproof system.

The history of interpretation of slave songs—and a perspective that frequently extends into the present—offers a widely held view that they are inherently but asymmetrically double-voiced. That is, they contain a coded structure that is universally fixed and decipherable along racial lines. They are often interpreted as being selectively metaphorical to the black slaves but somehow mono-semantic to most of the white southern slaveholding population. In other words, the full complexity of their plural meanings would be illegible to the white pro-slavery population that came in contact with the slaves but would be understood by the slaves themselves.

One of the best known and strongest statements to support the idea that slave-owning culture interpreted the singing of slaves as signs of happiness rather than expressions of sadness, comes from the *Narrative of the Life of Frederick Douglass, An American Slave, Written by Himself*:

> I have often been utterly astonished, since I came to the north, to find persons who could speak of the singing, among slaves, as evidence of their contentment and happiness. It is almost impossible to conceive of a greater mistake. Slaves sing most when they are most unhappy. The songs of the slave represent the sorrows of his heart; and he is relieved by them, only as an aching heart is relieved by its tears.[12]

If anyone could possibly misunderstand the strength of Douglass's point on the importance and function of slave songs—so ardently articulated throughout the *Narrative*—he makes it clear in *My Bondage and My Freedom* that "[e]very tone was a testimony and against slavery, and a prayer to God for deliverance from chains."[13]

Yet we still find accounts such as this one from Rev. Horace James describing the African Americans at the end of the Civil War entering the Eastern sea-board towns, which appears in the *Annual Report of the Superintendent of Negro Affairs in North Carolina, 1864–5*:

> Pitiable was the condition of many of them, when they entered our lines. Footsore and weary, ragged and dusty from travel, mostly without covering for either their feet or heads, some of them emaciated and already marked as victims of death, afflicted with hoarse hollow coughs, with measles, with malarial chills, it seemed like anything but a land of promise into which they had come. But they were happy, and did not complain. With the characteristic cheerfulness of the negro, which is an admirable and beautiful feature of his character, they went singing along, and still, though living in want and destitution, they continue to sing.[14]

James's somewhat reductive, if sympathetic, description underscores Douglass's comments in overlooking the complex functions, meanings, and mixed emotions expressed in the singing of these obviously suffering individuals by calling them "happy" though "already marked

as victims of death" because they are singing, as a sign of the "characteristic cheerfulness of the negro."[15]

There can be no doubt of the validity of Douglass's claim that some
slave owners and overseers misunderstood the meanings of the black
songs during the time of slavery. There are plentiful descriptions of ill,
starving, and terrified kidnapped Africans being ordered to dance on
ships in the Middle Passage for the amusement of sailors. There are
many reports of slaves in America being summoned to the plantation
house to sing, play, and dance as entertainment for the guests and fam-
ilies of their owners, and of boasting about the musical talents of slaves.
There is abundant documentation of overseers who ordered slaves to
sing while working so that they could be kept better track of or because
it made them work faster and in more precise unison. This function
was even seen as being of benefit to the quality of the African
Americans' singing of slave songs after Emancipation. According to J.
B. T. Marsh, Henry Ward Beecher wrote a letter recommending the
Fisk Jubilee Singers to a friend in Boston: "They will charm any audience, sure; they make their mark by giving the 'spirituals' and plantation hymns as only they can sing them who know how to keep time to
a master's whip. Our people have been delighted."[16]

Reinforcing that divide of misunderstanding from the opposing
perspective, part of the intended purpose of slave songs *was* to be misunderstood. John Wesley Work wrote, "These songs were never
intended for the world at large. On the contrary, they were lines of
communication between the slaves and God, and between the slave
and slave."[17] Linguistic communities maintain self-circumscribed
patterns of private communication, which is part of their social function. In part, the slaves wanted their owners to be baffled by their
singing, which was such an important source of cohesion, survival,
and information amongst themselves. As discussed so cogently by
Geneva Smitherman, throughout African American history, oral
communication has served as a means of preservation of black heritage and culture, as well as for enabling the process of adaptation to
new and changing situations over time:

> Both in the old-time black Gospel song and in black street vernacular,
> "gittin' ovuh" had to do with surviving. While the religious use of the
> phrase speaks to spiritual survival in a sinister world of sin, its secular
> usage speaks to material survival in a white world of oppression. . . . In

Black America, the oral tradition has served as a fundamental vehicle for gittin ovuh. That tradition preserves the Afro-American heritage and reflects the collective spirit of the race. Through song, folk sayings, and rich verbal play among everyday people, lessons and precepts about life and survival are handed down from generation to generation. Until contemporary times, Black America relied on word-of-mouth for its rituals of cultural preservation. (For instance, it was not until the late nineteenth century that the Negro spirituals were written down, though they date well back to the beginning of slavery.) . . . Indeed the core strength of this tradition lies in its capacity to accommodate new situations and changing realities.[18]

One of the functions of slave songs was undoubtedly to convey a multiplicity of meanings, some of which were intended to be hidden from anyone but the slaves. But as is now fully evident from interviews and other documentation, there was ample suspicion among many of the slave owners and overseers that not all slave songs (and the slaves' communication in general) expressed acceptable Christian values, and their messages hardly upheld the standards of slave-holding culture. Source materials are filled with examples of slaves being prevented from attending church, talking on the way to and from church, praying in the fields, singing, attending their own prayer meetings, and working alongside other slaves in order to disrupt communication—which, of course, simply took other forms and went underground, often at secret meetings.

In *Slave Songs of the United States*, an editorial note written by Thomas Wentworth Higginson to accompany the lyrics to "Many Thousand Go" states that this song "had been sung in secret to avoid detection."[19] "Many Thousand Go"[20] disproves the stereotypes that, on the literal level, all slave songs were religious in content and the slaves focused all of their attention on their religious life and heaven. It also strongly disproves any possible belief that slave songs' importance was solely as music; it was the words that were threatening, incendiary, filled with agency, and viewed as powerful and challenging—no less than the warnings of Plato about the dangers of poets in the new Republic.

It is illuminating to observe which slave songs seem to have fallen from favor and which seem to have increased in popularity over time, a topic also addressed in chapter 1. There are some slave songs, though surprisingly a smaller quantity than one might think, that have appeared in virtually every collection of slave songs from the earliest collections to the present. These core slave songs would include "Go Down Moses," "Roll, Jordan, Roll," "Didn't My Lord Deliver Daniel," "I'm a-Rollin' Through an Unfriendly World," and "Nobody Knows the Trouble I've Seen." The relatively infrequent appearance of "Many Thousand Gone" in some of the later collections of slave songs seems to support the theory that the image of African Americans underwent a process of sanitization after Emancipation. It is interesting to note that this song does not appear in John W. Work, Johnson and Johnson's *The Books of American Negro Spirituals*, or Hogan's *The Oxford Book of Spirituals*, leading to the speculation that over time, it became increasingly accepted and believed that slave songs were entirely religious and those that did not fit the pattern fell away.

Using slave songs as evidence, the range of these poems was distilled into the separate categories of "spirituals" and "seculars" with particular stress on the spirituals, which promoted the idea that the slaves had separate songs for separate purposes (which is far too facile a generalization) and that religion and the afterlife were all that they cared about. Lyrics such as those to "Many Thousand Gone" would not fit the category of "spirituals" so neatly, and the major collections of slave lyrics do primarily consist of the slaves' "religious folk songs." John W. Work is one exception by including songs falling into diverse categories. Similarly, Barksdale and Kinnamon's brilliant representation of "Songs" listed under "Folk Literature" very appropriately intermixes such lyrics as "Do, Lawd," "The Stoker's Chant" and "Raise a Ruckus Tonight."[21] Ultimately, the ambiguity of slave songs would rest more neatly with the category of lyric poetry than liturgical hymns or historical remnants, which underscores the central argument of this book.

We have seen that many slave songs were not explicitly religious, and even those that were had a simultaneous message of release from bondage on earth as much as deliverance to eternal life in the Christian vision of heaven. Previous discussion in this chapter makes it evident that there were slave insurrections inspired and subversive messages conveyed by slave songs that were complex and multifaceted poetry. They achieved a stunning range of purposes and were designed to function on two and often more levels: aesthetically, emotionally, politically, ideologically, and pragmatically. By delivering the slaves across so many boundaries, it is hard to conceive of any body of poetry that could achieve more than that.

The lyrics to "Many Thousand Gone" cannot be taken as the stereotype of religious hymns containing coded messages. If there is any "religious" message, it might be that you should treat others as you would have them treat you, but that is about as far as a "Christian" meaning goes. Their literal meaning has no pretense of being obfuscatory, pious, or remotely acceptable to slaveholders. If we are searching for a metaphorical meaning, perhaps one could be found in the tremendously poignant last line of each stanza: "Many thousand go," which we could interpret as "I have been preceded in my condition by countless others and I won't stand for it much longer: soon there will be an end to this treatment for me, and for us all." The lyrics that Higginson provided with his editorial comment are as follows:[22]

> No more peck o' corn for me,
>   No more, no more;
> No more peck o' corn for me,
>   Many thousand go.
>
> No more driver's lash for me.
>   No more, no more;
> No more peck o' corn for me,
>   Many thousand go.
>
> No more pint o' salt for me,
>   No more, no more;
> No more peck o' corn for me,
>   Many thousand go.
>
> No more hundred lash for me,
>   No more, no more;
> No more peck o' corn for me,
>   Many thousand go.
>
> No more mistress' call for me,
>   No more, no more;
> No more peck o' corn for me,
>   Many thousand go.[23]

For all of the accounts of overseers being entertained by the slaves' singing and dancing, and even ordering them to do so for their amusement, there are many examples of church attendance where singing and socializing was forbidden. This prohibition resulted from the masters' justified suspicion that this contact and slave songs that were developed and were shared contained subversive contents, served undermining purposes, encouraged rebellious cross-plantation activities, and presented plantation figures as the butt of jokes.

In "Acculturation Amongs the Gullahs," William R. Bascom reports of some plantations where cooperative work patterns existed and labor took place in unison to music. But this pattern, which Bascom attributes to African roots, was not necessarily the norm. Such practices were determined by individual slaveholders and varied from one plantation to the next: "There was no singing while farming on St. Helena, where they said they had to 'sing with the hoe.' . . . About Darien and on Harris Neck, on the Georgia mainland, . . . the work was not done in unison to music."[24] In Frances Anne Kemble's *Journal of a Residence on a Georgian Plantation in 1838–1839*, she writes, "I mounted my horse, and resumed my ride and my conversation with Israel. He told me that Mr. K——'s great objection to the people going to church was their meeting slaves from other plantations."[25] In her diary between 1860 and 1861, Keziah Goodwyn Hopkins Brevard becomes enraged at the impudence of one of her slaves for singing in the kitchen[26] and decides that they are a duplicitous race: "Negroes are strange creatures—I cannot tell whether they have any good feelings for their owners or not—sometimes I think they have—then I think their [sic] is nothing but deception in them."[27]

This image is consistent with the self-fashioned characterizations of the slaves as tricksters—or as those who are "gittin ovuh," as termed by Geneva Smitherman. It also reflects the external perception of the slaves by some members of white Southern culture as being two-faced and untrustworthy.[28] Those images of the slaves' characters as being essentially conniving held that the slaves enjoyed trying (usually unsuccessfully) to outwit a white person, who would be able to catch and reveal their tricks, ridiculousness, and errors (hence the popularity of burlesquing black speech, blackface minstrel shows, producing verbally exaggerated imitation slave songs, and so forth). These images of the slaves and how they are connected to the lyrics of their songs relate to topics addressed in chapter 3, including: the concepts of semblance and reality, naturalness and deviation, material substance and figments, imitation and the thing itself, model and copy, the normative and the deviant, appearance and deception, and Americanness and the alien.

In addition to their awareness of the coded messages being transmitted, some early collectors also realized that not all slave songs were religious. They recognized that slave songs to which they were not given access—that is, those that did not necessarily have an overtly religious surface veneer—were the most privately guarded of all, though these collectors had differing explanations as to why. William Francis Allen, in the introduction to *Slave Songs in the United States*, mentions that

> 'fiddle-sings,' 'devil-songs,' 'corn-songs,' 'jig-tunes,' and what not, are common. . . . We have succeeded in obtaining only a few songs of this character. . . . It is often, indeed, no easy matter to persuade them to sing their old songs, even as a curiosity, such is the sense that dignity has come with freedom.[29]

In "The Negro Spiritual," Robert W. Gordon discusses his familiarity with non-religious slave songs and the African Americans' reluctance to share them: "Again and again I have talked with older negroes about songs other than those of the church. They admitted freely they had heard them, had once sung them. But that was before they became church members. Sometimes they claimed that they had forgotten, but more often they admitted they still knew the songs in question though they would not sing them."[30]

As I discuss in chapter 2, in slave songs it cannot always be determined if the slave poets were imagining themselves in the biblical past, if biblical figures and stories were being projected forward to the slaves' present, or if a future meeting were being imagined in heaven. As mentioned, these time shifts were observed as early as 1867 by Thomas Wentworth Higginson, who wrote: "Sometimes the present predominates, sometimes the future; but the combination is always implied."[31] Higginson saw the past and present as interconnected for the slaves but distinctly demarcated when they shifted from one chronological frame to another. I view the separation of time and place as far less determinable in slave songs and as reflective of some of their most crucial work in crossing boundaries. Part of the confusion of some commentators and auditors relates to their understanding of the equivocal weights of "reality" attributed by the slaves to alternative states of metaphysical, spiritual and biological presence.

Higginson was able to distinguish between the slaves' references to the present and the future because, from his perspective, these realms were neatly mapped out for the slaves themselves. Higginson expressed an interpretive stance commonly held among past and some present critics that the slaves' profuse references to the future demonstrated their patient faith as Christians. Anticipating their reward in heaven enabled them to tolerate an otherwise intolerable present: "The attitude is always the same, and, as a commentary on the life of the race, is infinitely pathetic. Nothing but patience for this life,—nothing but triumph in the next."[32] Similarly, John Wesley Work wrote:

> In all his song there is neither trace nor hint of hatred or revenge. It is most assuredly divine in human nature, that such a stupendous burden as human bondage, with all of its inherent sorrows and heartbreakings could fail to arouse in the heart of the slave sentiments of hatred and revenge against his master.[33]

Sterling A. Brown expressed his reservations on this perspective, pointing out that the idea of a future reward was important for slaves who were Christians, but was not the whole story:

> Too many rash critics have stated that the spirituals showed the slave turning his back on this world for the joys of the next. The truth is that he took a good look at this world and told what he saw. Sometimes he was forthright in denouncing slavery, as in "No Mo' Driver's Lash for Me" or in that trumpet call:
>
> > Go down, Moses
> > Way down in Egypt land
> > Tell ole Pharoah
> > To let my people go![34]
>
> It is not surprising that this class of songs is no larger: these songs were dangerous in a South on the fringe of hysteria.[35]

As Brown, Arthur Davis, and Ulysses Lee elaborated, the present mattered too: "It is only a half-truth to see the spirituals as other worldly."[36]

John Lovell Jr. also complains about this sentimental vision of the slaves as entirely consumed by the rewards of the afterlife, and he holds W. E. B. Du Bois, James Weldon Johnson, Alain Locke, and Maud Cuney Hare responsible for this attitude by writing such comments as, "These were hymns that glowed with religious fervor and constant belief in ultimate victory through the gateway of death."[37] Lovell discredits this sentimentalism for reflecting and promulgating the premise "that the spiritual was exclusively a method of escape from a troublesome world to a land of dreams, before or after death; and that its chief motivation is pure religion." According to Lovell, the slaves were interested in what he calls "the possibilities of various escapes"— that is, religion, but also "underground railroads, swamps, abolition, colonization—anything that might provide a way out of the dark."[38]

Dwight N. Hopkins supports the idea that the slaves had varied and full lives and identities, as expressed in their songs, but that part of that wholeness necessitated a level of doubleness based on their circumstances: "The songs they sang denoted duplicitous theological, spiritual, and earthly meanings."[39] Such dualities and paradoxes resonate in slave songs, showing us how the "other world" and "this world" were inextricably bound in the slave poets' literary expressions and philosophical and religious beliefs. But Hopkins's further explanation suggests that this vision of multiple and simultaneous planes, which he views as an African survival, was less a matter of deception and splitting and more an expression of the absence of boundaries and categories that define Western ontological and spiritual experiences:

These Africans had not been broken by colonial European or Euro-American philosophies and divested of their indigenous West African religious sensibilities and beliefs. They harbored conscious memories of what it meant to be a human being created by the Supreme Being, to remain in proximity to the presence of the ancestors. Their faiths and cosmologies had not been totally shattered or damaged by the warped Christian catechism and preaching from hired plantation preachers. . . . For them, there existed no separation of sacred and secular; everything, including walking, breathing, laboring, and lovemaking, was deemed a religious activity putting the person in constant contact with God. Religion appeared in the practice of their political economy, linguistics, culture, and microdimensions of being in the world. They took care of themselves as Africans—quite aware of the knowledge of who they were as stolen strangers in a foreign land.[40]

Even in my own teaching, I find that students are surprised to learn that slave songs are on the syllabus in classes in American and African American poetry. Their impression is that they are "nothing more" than slave artifacts—that we now know them to be transparently decipherable instructions that sounded piously Christian on the surface, but that they were "really" secret verbal maps to escape routes. While it does not take long to persuade the students of the literary complexity and beauty of slave songs and of how much similarity they bear to other poems that they have studied that are considered part of the lyric tradition, they cannot initially fathom why we would read them as poems. Ironically, it is precisely this neat and tidy vision of slave songs' dual function that has masked the far greater ingenuity and lasting importance of their literary value and operations.

I will now demonstrate how the issues coalesce into a central figure of bifurcation by connecting these related issues of metaphorical and literal meanings: slave songs as being powerfully meaningful but also harmless entertainment, slave songs' lyrics as meaning one thing to the slaves and something else to white pro-slavery culture, and characterizations of slaves as both wholly consumed by religious morality and fundamentally deceptive. In showing the actual eliding of these apparently conflicting visions of twoness, I will utilize Kwasi Wiredu's ideas on African and Western Christian concepts of quasi-material spirits, Mark Turner's ideas on creative blends, Len Talmy's work on fictive motion, and Pascal Boyer's ideas on ghost physics. I will look especially at how these related concepts from philosophy, linguistics, cognitive science, religious studies, and literary studies manifest themselves in slave songs in breaking physical, social, and imaginative barriers, navigating between images of stasis and movement, wholeness and fragmentation in relation to identity, and being alive versus being in spirit. These metaphorical domains include traveling in time and space, passing over or through geographical and other material barriers, and breaking free of various laws of physics. Slave songs provide a wealth of examples in these categories to show how they served as a means for their creators of crossing borders to attain a sense of personhood and hope.

We see examples in slave songs of a type of blend that Len Talmy refers to as "fictive motion." These are "expressions that depict motion when there is no physical occurrence of motion."[41] These poems are replete

with such constructions. The following are common constituent elements
of slave songs that would be classified as examples of fictive motion:

> A wheel in a wheel, Oh, my Lord,
> It runs by love, Oh, my Lord,
> It runs by faith, Oh, my Lord,[42]

~

> Roll, Jordan, roll,
> My home is over Jordan.

~

> Steal away to Jesus.

~

> I'm a-trav'ling to the grave,
> I'm gwine to sing along the way.

~

> Hear dat mournful thunder
> roll from door to door.

~

> Do Lord remember me,
> until the year roll round.

~

> Grief from out my soul shall fly,
> I am bound for Sweet Canaan's happy land.[43]

~

> Oh, stand the storm, it won't be long,
> We'll anchor by and by;

> We're crossing over Jordan,
> We'll anchor by and by,[44]

~

> I'm a poor wayfarin' stranger,
> While journeyin' thro' this world of woe,
>
> . . .
>
> I'm just goin' over Jordan,
> I'm just goin' over home,[45]

~

> One ob dese days about twelve o'clock,
> Dis ol wor'l's goin' to reel and rock,[46]

~

> I'm a-rolling through an unfriendly world.

These examples of fictive motion—versus the potential for actual mobility—was brilliantly compensatory and another means by which biblical imagery and the slave poets' religious faith enabled them to use slave songs to represent the metaphorical crossing of boundaries, to travel, and create a sense of self-determination and action in a state of enforced stasis and absence of freedom.

With limitations to their ability to move through space, motion in slave songs took a variety of dynamic forms, which resulted in their authors becoming easy time travelers. Travel could take place in disembodied form, as we have already seen, and was also sometimes presented as imminent or on the verge, something like stored energy. Speakers in these poems seem to be at an earthly starting block, ready to spring up in the air, down into the earth, across water, to heaven, back in history, ahead to freedom, crossing over physical limitations of what it means to be "here" and "now," even what it means to be human in their present situation. We find examples in such images as "All God's chillun got wings," "I spread out my wings and fly," "I'll take my wings and cleave de air" and "Sometimes I feel like a feather in the air."

They were often seen as embarking for someplace else or in a state of transit:

Git yo' bundle reddy I know it's time[47]

~

Say, don't you want to go to hebben?
How I long to see dat day![48]

~

My ship is on de ocean,
I'm goin' away

De ship begin to sail,
It landed me over on Canaan's shore
an' I'll never come back no mo'

You go, I'll go wid you
One ob dese mornin' bright and fair,
Goin' to take muh flight in de middle ob de air, [49]

~

I'm going there to see my mother (father, sister, brother, Lord)
Oh wither shall I flee?
My ship is on de ocean,
Po' sinner, fare you well.
I'm goin' away to see good ol' Daniel,
I'm goin' away to see my Lord.[50]

~

One o' dese mornin's and it won't be long,
yo look fo' me an' I'll be gone.[51]

Talmy links fictive motion to the linguistic and conceptual phenomena resulting from what Pascal Boyer calls "ghost physics." That is, "ghosts obey all the usual causal expectations for physical entities, except for a few strange exceptions,"[52] such as having the ability to pass through walls, to appear and disappear at will, and to only partially interact with the world of the living. We see numerous examples of ghost physics in operation in slave songs. Instantiations that fit Boyer's definition of "ghost physics" are especially poignant and powerful when we realize how many of these examples refer to the living, not to the deceased: "I've heard of a city called heaven / And I've started to make it my home," "I've got a home in-a dat Rock, don't you see, / Between de earth an' sky,"[53] and "Sometimes I'm up, Sometimes I'm down, / Sometimes I'm almos' to de groun'."[54] The concepts of ghost physics and fictive motion apply very usefully to the frequent references in slave songs to "home," which is a concept discussed in detail in chapter 2.

Slave songs generally provide locative information in terms of what is missing, absent, has just appeared or disappeared, is "away," "over yonder," just out of reach, half-glimpsed, or maybe just imagined: "I thought I saw" is a phrase that we frequently encounter. Sometimes the sense of incomplete physicality is conveyed in a way that is clearly metaphorical—for instance, "sometimes I feel like I'm almost gone, / a long way from home." At other times, we could be encountering either the literal or metaphorical plane or dealing with either the spiritual or physical world, as in these examples: "My soul wants something that's new,"[55] "Sometimes I feel like a motherless child," "I lie in de grave an' stretch out my arms, / I lay dis body down," "Dark midnight was my cry." Human materiality is described as profoundly partial or qualified, almost like the poetic inverse of ghost physics, where aspects of ordinary physics feel as if they do not apply to human beings: "Sometimes I feel like I'm almost gone," "Now I must go across, an' I want to go across,"[56] and "I'm tossed in dis wide worl' alone."[57] The speaker's status seemed transitional, as if in the process of dissolving into an ancestral spirit and embarking for a future that might have seemed more imaginably real (and closer) than an unimaginable present.

The power to cross barriers in slave songs derives from particular conceptions of the relationships among body, mind, and spirit, with the biblical texts as one pivot on which temporal and spatial boundaries are made to dissolve. The slave poets might have been located at any given moment in one temporal space but then, in a state of metaphysical impossibility, abruptly head off for the past or future: "I'm goin' away to see good ol' Daniel," "Steal away to Jesus," or "I'm goin' away to see de weepin' Mary." Sometimes the spirit truly appears to propel or even override the body as a force of equal or greater agency and determinism. Cartesian dualism does not apply to the worldview in operation here. If, for the slaves, more than the material universe was needed in order to have a satisfactory experience of the material universe, then what was the something more? If the "more than" enabled a fuller understanding of the material universe, what was the nature of that "universal joint"? Assuming that there had to be a metaphysical seam, how did the material and immaterial worlds interact, and how was the divide between the two negotiated? The "spirit" in slave songs should be understood as an essential part of the hinge between these worlds for the slave poets.

The examples we have focused on in slave songs bring us directly for an explanation to a non-substance conception of mind, which views "mind" as processes of the brain—that is, "a capacity" rather than an object. This implies that physical matter also becomes, at points, what Kwasi Wiredu calls "quasi-physical" or "quasi-material." According to Wiredu, the African afterlife is imagined as populated by beings that are largely material, but not wholly so because of their exemptions from properties of physics, which echoes Pascal Boyer's concept of ghost physics. In terms of African culture, Wiredu calls these beings "spirits." He defines a spirit as "a being or entity existing in space and possessing a basic material imagery but enjoying exemptions from the laws of motion and optics that govern the entities of the ordinary world."[58] In considering spirits as quasi-material or quasi-physical beings for whom laws of "motion, vision and impenetrability" are suspended, Wiredu believes that the African conception of spirits "fits English semantics to perfection" in binding Western Christian and African concepts of mind and spirit: "When we talk of spirits in English-speaking discourse, common, theological or philosophical, we are standardly thinking of such things as ghosts and ethereally embodied beings such as angels, or, to anticipate an alleged eschatological destiny, the finely reconstituted bodily persons of the Christian 'resurrection of the dead.'"[59] Wiredu sees the term that he uses to describe these entities, "quasi-material," as corresponding to "spirits" in the Western Christian and African senses as beings with a quasi-physical dimension.

Wiredu's specific focus is the Akan people of Ghana on the West Coast, but he believes that these views are widely applicable to other African peoples. To start with the African conception, spirits belong to those who have departed from Earth, maintain a close connection with the life of the living, and inhabit a basically anthropocentric world and existence in terms of values, geography, and abilities. For the Akans, this other world is not a metaphorical construction but an actual place on the other side of a river, which is consistent with the geography of slave songs and their imagery of crossing rivers, especially the Jordan River. Spirits can inhabit places, such as mountains and rivers, and can be entities or phenomena, such as witches, thunder, winds, and ghosts.

This concept of spirits is closely linked to Akan ideas of the living character of humans as already possessing features that are immaterial as part of their existence and identity, which would also apply to aspects of the slaves' self-identity. In their ontology of human personality, the Akans refer to some elements that are conceptually quasi-material. Wiredu explains: "A person is understood to consist, apart from the body, of something called *okra*" (a speck of the divine substance, for example, of the same ontological character as God), which provides animation.[60] At the time of death, the *okra* leaves the body to travel by land and water to the world of the dead, where it eventually turns into an ancestor. This spirit remains actively involved in the lives of its descendants and relatives, looking over them, staying responsible for them, holding them accountable for their actions, staying in dialogue, being able to move through ceilings and doors, and appearing and disappearing at will.

Sunsum is another quasi-material element of human personality (literally meaning "shadow"), which is thought of—not in embodied terms—as accounting for one's "degree of personal presence."[61] Wiredu considers the idea of *sunsum* to be foundational to Akan thought (and by extension to other African peoples) in that it allows for the acceptance of quasi-physical aspects of human existence. This underlying assumption appears throughout slave songs, for instance, in such lines as "Better mind, sister, / how you walk on de cross / Yo' foot might slip an' yo' soul get lost," "My soul is a witness for my Lord," or "The trumpet sounds within-a my soul." Here we see examples of part-whole relations in operation reflecting a frame of mind that accepts that there are aspects of being that are separable from the body or immaterial. This model then maps over conceptions of spirits that are like people in many ways—including having the same personality traits as on earth and performing the same work after death—but able to move in ways that embodied beings cannot, with greater powers, and unable to fully interact with the living. These are demonstrations of ways that people are like spirits and spirits are like people in slave songs.

Linking Turner's cognitive science to Wiredu's philosophy, because humans are conceived of as having souls, it is possible to create a conceptual blend in which "escape from mortality" can be imagined. "It seems to be routine for human beings to create blends in which the intentional agent that causes the body to move is something inside us that is separate from the body: the soul."[62] When the soul leaves the body, as it is capable of doing, what is left behind in the blend is an absence: the result is a space in which a body devoid of its soul ceases to be that person. Similarly, in the case of ghosts or spirits, the imagery of ghosts or spirits can only apply because that entity used to be a person. Because the soul has departed from the body, the ghost has to give up that living status and become what Wiredu would consider to be quasi-physical or quasi-material. In this blend, according to Turner, "when the soul is absent from the body, it is because it is present somewhere else; that death is the departure of the soul from the body as it journeys to another place." Similarly, when dreaming, we are in a state where "we have perceptions that do not fit our surroundings . . . we are someplace other than the place in which our body is located."[63]

The soul can do all of this "exactly because it is immaterial."[64] It can defy certain laws of physics, which we have already seen take place in Wiredu's account of spirits in African philosophy and in instantiations from slave songs that support this view of body and mind. The slave poets needed to be able to create such human scale blends in order to account for what was unfathomable. Such concepts would have made it possible for them to touch something that seemed more permanent and real than physical and psychological chains, and more real than the deprivations of their present existence if envisioned and experienced without these added dimensions. In the blended space, the slave poets could be anywhere. They could interact with ghosts, angels, spirits, biblical figures, ancestors, or God. They could be free.

Vestigial concepts such as those described by Wiredu were present in the thinking and belief of the slaves in the development of their Christian cosmology and in all of their cultural products, which resulted from their experiences of American oppression coupled with African philosophy and theology. Samuel A. Floyd Jr. writes that

> Praying had been part of the Africans' religious behavior in the homeland, and the call-and-response and ejaculatory interjections . . . were part of the African narrative and musical expressive technique. It was new[65] only to Europeans and Americans who were uninformed about the slaves' past. This preaching, praying, and singing event was a syncretized product, born of the synthesis of African religion and Christianity, and it was to pervade all aspects of African-American culture. [66]

The idea of quasi-materiality would also closely correspond to the slaves' actual state and self-image in terms of whole personhood, where in some respects their condition could be considered closer to that of spirits or entities than people. Floyd elaborates specifically that "Protestantism, with its more direct access to the High God through song and praise [versus the African-Catholic syncretism that took hold in Latin America and some parts of America, notably New Orleans], made possible the emergence of a new song for African Americans in which they could express themselves as freely as they had in their homeland. This new song was the African American spiritual."[67] Floyd also cites Sterling Stuckey's stress on the importance of the composite influences and contextual considerations when appreciating slave songs, though Stuckey emphasizes their ritual and ceremonial dimensions as opposed to their integration in all aspects of the slaves' daily life.[68] James Cone described the slaves' basic sense of humanness as profoundly qualified and compromised in psychological, practical, social, and legal terms, with particular implications for freedom and self-determination:

> Slavery meant being regarded as property, like horses, cows and household goods. . . . It has been observed that American law was not consistent in viewing slaves as property. In some measure their personhood was acknowledged, as in laws requiring owners to feed them, clothe them, take care of them in sickness and old age. . . . Under the law, then, slaves were property *and* persons. But the two definitions together were absurd. The concept of property negated the idea of personhood. To be a person is to be in control of one's destiny, to set certain concrete limitations on the movement of self and of other selves in relation to self. It is to be free.[69]

Some features of individuated self-identity were applied selectively to the slaves while others were denied or effaced. As a result, we can imagine the slaves using their songs to both depict and reconstitute this contingent or partial sense of human wholeness or quasi-materiality. We might also view their use of biblical figures as necessary inventions and as successfully compensatory in their present circumstances in this regard, as talismans or sources of inspiration that were anthropomorphic but who had also been chosen by God and had special abilities or features. This quasi-materiality, in having a soul and personality that could be viewed as separate from the body, was likely to have functioned in a powerful and productive way for the slaves, which was reflected in slave songs. This ontological system, philosophically and theologically modeled on African and Christian views, could have enabled these poets to connect with parts of themselves that could not be touched or destroyed by the system of slavery. African philosophy and theology provides a link to join with Christianity in establishing key characteristics of slave songs relating to the expression of power and identity. The sacred and secular both demarcated a communal and shared social fabric. The living and dead remained attached with lives that mirrored one another's. This condition allowed the ability to exist both "elsewhere" and "here"—in mind for the living and in a state imagined to be quasi-physical for the dead, so they could remain an inspiring presence for the enslaved who were alive.

The similarities between African and Western Christian views (including the fact that a stronghold of Christianity was established in Africa) call into question the idea that the slaves accepted Christianity in submission to the missionary will of the oppressors, and rather enable us to understand how it could become a religion of their own making because of these shared features. One of the distinctive characteristics of slave songs was their ability to create a map that had direct historical and conceptual contiguity between theological and ontological systems. Jesus had a body and also existed in resurrected form. Like an Akan spirit, he could appear and disappear in a way that living people could not. As Wiredu has written, to exist is to exist in space and time. But if an entity is quasi-material, as with spirits or ghosts or the Supreme Being, the laws of space and time can be suspended.

Akan thought, then, is similar to Western Christian belief in relation to the acceptance of quasi-material beings, the properties they possess, and the result of those beliefs and assumptions: that it is possible to suspend certain laws of physics in order to create a complete account of the nature of experience. The okra resonates with Christian concepts of the soul. For the slaves, the idea of the ancestors as being reachable would easily map over the belief that they could directly communicate with biblical figures. It would explain how slave songs could reflect a belief in active interventions, if we imagine Jesus, Mary, Daniel, and Joshua as ancestors and elders. The revived individual contained a material aspect that would be revived in the future. This is the Christian idea that the dead will live again, and that the already dead remain present in spirit.

By examining the idea of creative blends in relation to the highly imaginative use of the Bible and the conceptions of mind and spirit that join African and Christian ontology, we can see how the slave poets used slave songs to forge some almighty bridges and cross otherwise insurmountable earthly barriers. This achievement of impressive cognitive mobility could have mediated against an array of physical and other constraints. Slave songs reflect Western Christian and African philosophical and theological traditions, as well as the use of higher order human conceptual operations that help us understand how these belief systems were made to correspond. Some inventive cognitive work took place in slave songs through the operation of creative blends. We see how closely "ghost physics" corresponds to Wiredu's discussion of quasi-materiality in relation to African concepts of mind and spirit. Conceptual integration allowed the slave poets to create a new framework for reality, which permitted them freedom and escape through the imagination and in concepts of Christian eternity in spite of physical and experiential restrictions and controls. This ontological framework, which expressed a state of being able to interact partially with the world of the human, closely reflected the mental and physical state of the slaves in their lives on earth.

What kind of borders were the slaves able to cross with slave songs? Borders of physical materiality when the mind needed separation from the pains and travails of the body. Borders of servitude that defined the life of chattel when it became necessary to fully assert their personhood. Borders of earthly existence when life became intolerable in order to enter into the promise of a better life in Christ. Borders that kept loved ones away when they were separated from living family, connections with ancestors, or culture. In short, borders that separated the living from the dead.

Bibliography

Abarry, Abu. "The African-American Legacy in American Literature." *Journal of Black Studies* 20, no. 4 (1990): 379–98.

Abbington, James. "Biblical Themes in the R. Nathaniel Dett Collection *Religious Folk-Songs of the Negro* (1927)." In *African Americans and the Bible: Sacred Texts and Social Textures*, edited by Vincent L. Wimbush, 281–96. New York: Continuum, 2001.

Abrams, M. H. "Middle English Lyrics." In *The Norton Anthology of English Literature*, 6th ed., vol. 1., 286–87. New York: W. W. Norton, 1993.

———. *Natural Supernaturalism: Tradition and Revolution in Romantic Literature*. New York: W. W. Norton, 1973.

Addison, Joseph. "An Essay on Virgil's Georgics." 1697. In *Criticism and Aesthetics 1660–1800*, edited by Oliver F. Sigworth, 119–29. San Francisco: Rinehart, 1971.

Allen, William Francis, Charles Pickard Ware, and Lucy McKim Garrison, eds. *Slave Songs of the United States*. 1867. Reprint, Bedford, MA: Applewood, 1995.

Alter, Robert. *The Art of Biblical Narrative*. New York: Basic, 1981.

———. *The Pleasures of Reading in an Ideological Age*. New York: Touchstone/Simon and Schuster, 1989.

Anderson, Bernhard. *Understanding the Old Testament*. 4th ed. Englewood Cliffs, NJ: Prentice Hall, 1986.

Andrews, William L. *To Tell a Free Story: The First Century of Afro-American Autobiography, 1760–1865*. Urbana: University of Illinois Press, 1988.

Andrews, William L., Frances Smith Foster, and Trudier Harris, eds. *The Oxford Companion to African American Literature*. New York: Oxford University Press, 1997.

Aristotle, *The Poetics*. 384–322 BCE. In *The Poetics, "Longinus" on the Sublime, Demetrius on Style*, edited by E. Capps, T. E. Rouse, and W. H. D. Rouse, translated by W. Hamilton Fyfe. London: William Heinemann, 1927.

Assmann, Jan. *Moses the Egyptian: The Memory of Egypt in Western Monotheism*. Cambridge, MA: Harvard University Press, 1997.

Auerbach, Erich. "Figura." 1959. In *Scenes from the Drama of European Literature*, 11–76. Minneapolis: University of Minnesota Press, 1984.

Awoonor, Kofi. "Some Ewe Poets." In *Symposium of the Whole: A Range of Discourse Toward an Ethnopoetics*, edited by Jerome Rothenberg and Diane Rothenberg, 162–68. Berkeley: University of California Press, 1983.

Bailey, Wilma Ann. "The Sorrow Songs: Laments from Ancient Israel and the African American Diaspora." In *Yet with a Steady Beat: Contemporary U.S. Afrocentric Biblical Interpretation*, edited by Randall C. Bailey, 61–83. Atlanta: Society of Biblical Literature, 2003.

Baker, Barbara A. "Jamming with Julius: Charles Chesnutt and the Post-Bellum–Pre-Harlem Blues." In *Post-Bellum, Pre-Harlem: African American Literature and Culture, 1877–1919*, edited by Barbara McCaskill and Caroline Gebhard, 133–145. New York: New York University Press, 2006.

Baker, Houston A., Jr., and Patricia Redmond, eds. *Afro-American Literary Study in the 1990s*. Chicago: University of Chicago Press, 1989.

Baldwin, James. *Notes of a Native Son*. Boston: Beacon Press, 1955.

Ballanta-(Taylor), Nicholas George Julius. "Saint Helena Island Spirituals: Recorded and Transcribed at Penn Normal Industrial and Agricultural School, St. Helena Island, Beaufort County, South Carolina." MA thesis, Institute of Musical Arts, New York, 1924.

Barksdale, Richard, and Keneth Kinnamon, eds. "Folk Literature." In *Black Writers of America: A Comprehensive Anthology*, 230–41. Upper Saddle River, NJ: Prentice-Hall, 1972.

Bartlett, Andrew. "Airshafts, Loudspeakers, and the Hip Hop Sample: Contexts and African American Musical Aesthetics." *African American Review* 28, no. 4 (Winter 1994): 639–52.

Barton, William E. *Old Plantation Hymns; a collection of hitherto unpublished melodies of the slave and the freeman, with historical and descriptive notes*. 1899. Reprint, New York: AMS, 1972.

Bascom, William R. "Acculturation Among the Gullah Negroes." In *Shaping Southern Society: The Colonial Experience*, edited by T. H. Breen, 59–66. New York: Oxford University Press, 1976. Originally published in *American Anthropologist* 43, no. I (1941).

Bell, Bernard W. "The Debt to Black Music: Contemporary Afro-American Poetry as Folk Art." *Black World* (March 1973): 17–26, 74–87.

Benston, Kimberly W. *Performing Blackness: Enactments of African-American Modernism*. London: Routledge, 2000.

Beringer, Richard E., et al. "Religion and the Chosen People." In *Why the South Lost the Civil War*, 82–102. Athens: University of Georgia Press, 1986.

Bhabha, Homi. Introduction to *Locations of Culture. The Critical Tradition: Classic Texts and Contemporary Trends*, edited by David H. Richter, 1331–44. Boston: Bedford, 1998.

Blassingame, John W. *The Slave Community: Plantation Life in the Antebellum South*. New York: Oxford University Press, 1979.

———, ed. *Slave Testimony: Two Centuries of Letters, Speeches, Interviews, and Autobiographies*. Baton Rouge: Louisiana State University Press, 2003.

Bontemps, Arna. "Spirituals." In *Princeton Encyclopedia of Poetry and Poetics*, edited by Alex Preminger, 807. Princeton, NJ: Princeton University Press, 1974.

Boyer, Pascal. *The Naturalness of Religious Ideas: A Cognitive Theory of Religion*. Berkeley: University of California Press, 1994.

———. *Religion Explained: The Human Instincts that Fashion Gods, Spirits and Ancestors*. London: Vintage, 2002.

Braxton, Joanne M. *Black Women Writing Autobiography: A Tradition Within a Tradition*. Philadelphia: Temple University Press, 1989.

Bremer, Fredrika. *The Homes of the New World: Impressions of America*. Translated by Mary Howitt. Vols. 1 and 2. New York: Harper & Brothers, 1853.

Brevard, Keziah Goodwyn Hopkins. *A Plantation Mistress on the Eve of the Civil War: The Diary of Keziah Goodwyn Hopkins Brevard, 1860–1861*, edited by John Hammond Moore. Columbia: University of South Carolina Press, 1996.

Brown, John Mason. Letter to *Lippincott's Magazine*. 1868. *The Social Implications of Early Negro Music in the United States*, edited and with an introduction by Bernard Katz, 617–23. New York: Arno Press and the *New York Times*, 1969.

Brown, Sterling. "Negro Folk Poetry." In *Negro Poetry and Drama and The Negro in American Fiction*, 15–31. New York: Atheneum, 1972.

Brown, Sterling A., Arthur P. Davis, and Ulysses Lee, eds. Section 4, "Folk Literature." In *The Negro Caravan*, eds. Brown, Davis, and Lee, 412–91. New York: Arno Press and the *New York Times*, 1970.

Burnim, Mellonee V. "Religious Music." In *African American Music: An Introduction*, edited by Mellonee V. Burnim and Portia K. Maultsby, 51–77. New York: Routledge, 2006.

Burnim, Mellonee V., and Portia K. Maultsby. "Intellectual History." With contributions from Susan Oehler. In *African American Music: An Introduction*, edited by Burnim and Maultsby, 7–32. New York: Routledge, 2006.

Christy, E. P. *Christy's Plantation Melodies: Originator of Ethiopian Minstrelsy and the First to Harmonize Negro Melodies*. Philadelphia: Fisher & Brother, 1851.

Ciment, James. *Atlas of African-American History*. New York: Checkmark, 2001.

Coleman, Will. *Tribal Talk: Black Theology, Hermeneutics, and African/American Ways of "Telling the Story."* University Park, PA: The Pennsylvania State University Press, 2000.

Collins, John J. *Introduction to the Hebrew Bible*. Minneapolis, MN: Fortress, 2004.

Cone, James H. *A Black Theology of Liberation*. 1986. Twentieth Anniversary Edition. Maryknoll, NY: Orbis, 2003.

———. *The Spirituals and the Blues*. 1972. 6th printing. Maryknoll, NY: Orbis, 1999.

Congleton, J. E. "Georgic." In *Princeton Encyclopedia of Poetry and Poetics*, edited by Alex Preminger, 311. Princeton, NJ: Princeton University Press, 1974.

Connor, Kimberly Rae. "Spirituals." In *The Oxford Companion to African American Literature*, edited by William L. Andrews, Francis Smith Foster, and Trudier Harris, 693–96. New York: Oxford University Press, 1997.

Cope, Trevor. "Izibongo: Zulu Praise-Poems." In *Symposium of the Whole: A Range of Discourse Toward an Ethnopoetics*, edited by Jerome Rothenberg and Diane Rothenberg, 125–28. Berkeley: University of California Press, 1983.

Coquet, Cécile. "My God is a Time-God: How African American Folk Oratory Speaks (of) Time." In *African Americans and the Bible: Sacred Texts and Social Textures*, edited by Vincent L. Wimbush, 514–36. New York: Continuum, 2001.

Crite, Allan Rohan. *Were You There When They Crucified My Lord: A Negro Spiritual in Illustrations*. Cambridge, MA: Harvard University Press, 1944.

Cruz, Jon. *Culture on the Margins: The Black Spiritual and the Rise of American Cultural Interpretation*. Princeton, NJ: Princeton University Press, 1999.

Darden, Robert. *People Get Ready!: A New History of Black Gospel Music*. New York: Continuum, 2004.

Davies, Samuel. *The Duty of Masters to their Servants: In a Sermon*. Lynchburg, VA: William W. Gray, 1809.

Davis, Arthur P., J. Saunders Redding, and Joyce Ann Joyce, eds. *Selected African American Writing from 1760 to 1910*. New York: Bantam, 1991.

Dett, R. Nathaniel, ed. *Religious Folk-Songs of the Negro As Sung at Hampton Institute*. New York: AMS, 1972. First published 1927 by Hampton University Press.

Douglass, Frederick. *Narrative of the Life of Frederick Douglass, An American Slave, Written by Himself*. 1845. Norton Critical Edition, edited by William L. Andrews and William S. Feely. New York: W. W. Norton, 1997.

Dozeman, Thomas B. *God at War: Power in the Exodus Tradition*. New York: Oxford University Press, 1996.

Du Bois, W. E. B. *The Souls of Black Folk*. 1903. Reprint, Boston: Bedford, 1997.

Dunbar, Paul Laurence. *The Collected Poetry of Paul Laurence Dunbar*, edited with an introduction by Joanne M. Braxton. Charlottesville: University of Virginia Press, 1993.

Ellison, Ralph. *Shadow & Act*. New York: Signet Books Edition, 1966. First published in 1953 by Random House.

Empson, William. *7 Types of Ambiguity: A Study of its Effects in English Verse*. 1955. Reprint, New York: Meridian, 1957.

Epstein, Dena J. *Sinful Tunes and Spirituals: Black Folk Music to the Civil War*. Urbana: University of Illinois Press, 1977.

Epstein, Dena J. "Secular Folk Music." With contributions from Rosita M. Sands. In *African American Music: An Introduction*, edited by Mellonee V. Burnim and Portia K. Maultsby, 35–50. New York: Routledge, 2006.

Fenner, Thomas P., Frederic G. Rathbun, and Miss Bessie Cleaveland, arrangers. *Cabin and Plantation Songs as Sung by the Hampton Students*. 3rd ed. New York: AMS, 1977. First published 1901 by G. P. Putnam's Sons.

Finnegan, Ruth. "Drum Language and Literature." In *Symposium of the Whole: A Range of Discourse Toward an Ethnopoetics*, edited by Jerome Rothenberg and Diane Rothenberg, 129–39. Berkeley: University of California Press, 1983.

Fishbane, Michael. *Biblical Text and Texture*. Oxford: Oneworld, 1998.

Fisher, Miles Mark. *Negro Slave Songs in the United States*. 1953. Reprint, New York: Citadel, 1990.

Fishkin, Shelley Fisher. *Was Huck Black? Mark Twain and African-American Voices*. New York: Oxford University Press, 1993.

Floyd, Samuel A., Jr. *The Power of Black Music: Interpreting its History from Africa to the United States*. New York: Oxford University Press, 1995.

Forché, Carolyn. "El Salvador: An Aide Memoire." *American Poetry Review* 10 (July/August 1981): 6. Cited in "Responsibilities of the Poet," Robert Pinsky. *Politics and Poetic Value*, edited by Robert von Hallberg, 11. Chicago: University of Chicago Press, 1987.

Fox-Genovese, Elizabeth. *Within the Plantation Household: Black and White Women of the Old South*. Chapel Hill: University of North Carolina Press, 1988.

Fraser, Robert. *West African Poetry: A Critical History*. Cambridge: Cambridge University Press, 1986.

Frye, Northrop. "Introduction: Lexis and Melos." In *Sound and Poetry: English Institute Essays 1956*, edited by Northrop Frye, ix–xxvii. New York: Columbia University Press, 1957. 3rd printing, 1967.

Gates, Henry Louis, Jr. "The Master's Pieces: On Canon Formation and the African-American Tradition." *The South Atlantic Quarterly* 89, no. 1, (Winter 1990): 89–111.

Gates, Henry Louis, Jr., and Nellie Y. McKay, eds. "The Vernacular Tradition: Spirituals." In *The Norton Anthology of African American Literature*. 2nd ed., 8–19. New York: W. W. Norton, 2004.

Genovese, Eugene. *Roll, Jordan, Roll: The World the Slaves Made*. New York: Vintage, 1976.

Gilroy, Paul. *The Black Atlantic: Modernity and Double Consciousness*. Cambridge, MA: Harvard University Press, 1993.

Gilyard, Keith. "The Bible and African American Poetry." In *African Americans and the Bible: Sacred Texts and Social Textures*, edited by Vincent L. Wimbush, 205–20. New York: Continuum, 2001.

Glaude, Eddie S., Jr. *Exodus!: Religion, Race, and Nation in Early Nineteenth-Century Black America*. Chicago: University of Chicago Press, 2000.

Gomez, Michael A. *Reversing Sail: A History of the African Diaspora*. Cambridge: Cambridge University Press, 2005.

Goodheart, Lawrence B., Richard D. Brown, and Stephen G. Rabe, eds. *Slavery in American Society*. 3rd ed. Lexington, MA: D. C. Heath, 1993.

Gordon, Robert. "The Negro Spiritual." In *The Carolina Low-Country*, edited by Augustine T. Smythe, Herbert Ravenel Sass, Alfred Huger, Beatrice Ravenel, Thomas Waring, Archibald Rutledge, Joseph Pinckney, Caroline Pinckney Rutledge, DuBose Heyward, Katharine C. Hutson, and Robert W. Gordon, 191–222. New York: Macmillan, 1931.

Goss, Linda and Marian E. Barnes, eds. *Talk That Talk: An Anthology of African-American Storytelling*. New York: Simon and Schuster/Touchstone, 1989.

Hampton Negro Conference Number II, July, 1989. Hampton: Hampton Institute Press.

Harris-Lopez, Trudier. "Genre." In *Eight Words for the Study of Expressive Culture*, edited by Burt Feintuch, 99–120. Champaign: University of Illinois Press, 2003.

Haskell, Marion Alexander. "Negro 'Spirituals.'" In *The Social Implications of Early Negro Music in the United States*, edited and with an introduction by Bernard Katz. New York: Arno Press and the *New York Times*, 1969. Previously published in *The Century Magazine* XXXVI (1899): 577–81.

Hatfield, Edwin F. *Freedom's Lyre: or, Psalms, Hymns and Sacred Songs, for the Slave and His Friends*. New York: S. W. Benedict, 1840.

Hayes, Roland. *My Songs: Aframerican Religious Folk Songs Arranged and Interpreted by Roland Hayes.* Boston: Atlantic Monthly, Little Brown, 1948.

Higginson, Thomas Wentworth. *Army Life in a Black Regiment and Other Writings.* 1870. New York: Penguin, 1997.

———. *Atlantic Essays.* Boston: James R. Osgood, 1871.

Hendel, Ronald. "The Exodus in Biblical Memory." *Journal of Biblical Literature* 120, no. 4 (2001): 601–22.

Hill, Patricia Liggins, ed. "Go Down, Moses, Way Down in Egypt's Land." In *Call & Response: The Riverside Anthology of the African American Literary Tradition*, 35–58. Boston: Houghton Mifflin.

Hogan, Moses, ed. *The Oxford Book of Spirituals.* New York: Oxford University Press, 2002.

Hollander, John. *The Figure of Echo.* Berkeley: University of California Press, 1988.

Hopkins, Dwight N., and George Cummings, eds. *Cut Loose Your Stammering Tongue: Black Theology in the Slave Narratives.* Maryknoll, NY: Orbis, 1991.

Hopkins, Dwight N. *Down, Up, and Over: Slave Religion and Black Theology.* Minneapolis, MN: Fortress, 2000.

Horton, James Oliver, and Lois E. Horton. *Slavery and the Making of America.* New York: Oxford University Press, 2005.

Hungerford, James. *The Old Plantation and What I Gathered There in an Autumn Month.* New York: Harper & Brothers, 1859.

Hutner, Gordon, ed. *American Literature, American Culture.* New York and Oxford: Oxford University Press, 1999.

Hutson, Katharine C., Josephine Pinckney, and Caroline Pinckney Rutledge, arrangers. *Spirituals of the Carolina Low Country.* Charleston, SC: Society for the Preservation of Spirituals, 2004.

Irele, F. Abiola. *The African Imagination: Literature in Africa and the Black Diaspora.* New York: Oxford University Press, 2001.

Jackson, J. W. "Lyric." In *Princeton Encyclopedia of Poetry and Poetics*, edited by Alex Preminger, 460–70. Princeton, NJ: Princeton University Press, 1974.

James, Rev. Horace. *Annual Report of the Superintendent of Negro Affairs in North Carolina, 1864–5.* Boston: W. F. Brown.

Johnson, James Weldon. Preface from *The Book of American Negro Poetry.* 1921. In *The Norton Anthology of African American Literature*, edited by Henry Louis Gates Jr. and Nellie Y. McKay, 2nd ed., 883–905. New York: W. W. Norton, 2004.

Johnson, James Weldon, and J. Rosamond Johnson. 1926. *The Books of American Negro Spirituals.* New York: Da Capo Press, 1977.

Johnson, W. R. *The Idea of Lyric: Lyric Modes in Ancient and Modern Poetry.* Berkeley: University of California Press, 1982.

Jones, Arthur C. *Wade in the Water: The Wisdom of the Spirituals.* Maryknoll, NY: Orbis, 1993.

Jones, Bessie. *For the Ancestors: Autobiographical Memories,* collected and edited by John Stewart. Urbana: University of Illinois Press, 1983.

Jones, LeRoi. *Blues People: The Negro Experience in White America and the Music that Developed from It.* New York: William Morrow, 1963.

Joyce, Joyce A. "Bantu, Nkodi, Ndugu, and Nganga: Language, Politics, Music, and Religion in African American Poetry." In *The Furious Flowering of African American Poetry,* edited by Joanne V. Gabbin, 99–117. Charlottesville: University Press of Virginia, 1999.

Katz, Bernard. *The Social Implications of Early Negro Music in the United States.* New York: Arno Press and the *New York Times,* 1969.

Krehbiel, Henry Edward. *Afro-American Folksongs: A Study in Racial and National Music.* 1913. Reprint, New York: Frederick Ungar, 1962.

Kemble, Frances Anne. *Journal of a Residence on a Georgian Plantation in 1838–1839.* London: Longman, Green, Longman, Roberts & Green, 1863.

Lakoff, George, and Mark Johnson. *Metaphors We Live By.* Chicago: University of Chicago Press, 1980.

Lakoff, George, and Mark Turner. *More Than Cool Reason: A Field Guide to Poetic Metaphor.* Chicago: University of Chicago Press, 1989.

Leonard, Keith D. *The African American Bardic Poet From Slavery to Civil Rights.* Charlottesville: University of Virginia Press, 2006.

Levine, Lawrence W. "African American Music as Resistance." In *African American Music: An Introduction,* edited by Mellonee V. Burnim and Portia K. Maultsby, 587–98. New York: Routledge, 2006.

———. *Black Culture and Black Consciousness: Afro-American Folk Thought From Slavery to Freedom.* New York: Oxford University Press, 1977.

Lincoln, C. Eric, and Lawrence H. Mamiya. *The Black Church in the African American Experience.* Durham, NC: Duke University Press, 1990.

Lindley, David. *Lyric.* London: Methuen, 1985.

Locke, Alain, ed. *The New Negro.* 1925. Reprint, New York: Atheneum, 1968.

Long, Charles H. "Perspectives for a Study of African American Religion." In *Down by the Riverside: Readings in African American Religion,* edited by Larry G. Murphy, 9–19. New York: New York University Press, 2000.

Lovell, John, Jr. *Black Song: The Forge and the Flame: The Story of How the Afro-American Spiritual was Hammered Out.* New York: Macmillan, 1972.

————. "The Social Implications of the Negro Spiritual." In *The Social Implications of Early Negro Music in the United States*, edited and with an introduction by Bernard Katz. New York: Arno Press and the *New York Times*, 1969. Previously published in *Journal of Negro Education* (October 1939): 634–43.

Magesa, Laurenti. *African Religion: The Moral Traditions of Abundant Life.* Maryknoll, NY: Orbis, 1997.

Marini, Stephen A. *Religion, Music and Public Culture.* Urbana: University of Illinois Press, 2003.

Marsh, J. B. T. *The Story of the Jubilee Singers; with their Songs.* 4th ed. London: Hodder and Stoughton, 1875.

Maultsby, Portia K. "Black Spirituals: An Analysis of Textual Forms and Structures." *Black Perspectives in Music* 4 (Spring 1976): 54–69.

————. "The Use and Performance of Hymnody, Spirituals, and Gospels in the Black Church." *The Western Journal of Black Studies* 7, no. 3 (1983): 161–71.

Mbiti, John S. *African Religions and Philosophy.* 2nd ed. Oxford: Heinemann, 1990.

McClintock, Anne. "'Azikwelwa' (We Will Not Ride): Politics and Value in Black South African Poetry." In *Politics and Poetic Value*, edited by Robert von Hallberg, 225–51. Chicago: University of Chicago Press, 1987.

McDowell, Deborah E. "In the First Place: Making Frederick Douglass and the Afro-American Tradition." In *African American Autobiography: A Collection of Critical Essays*, edited by William L. Andrews, 36–58. Englewood Cliffs, NJ: Prentice-Hall, 1993.

McGeachy, M. G. *Lonesome Words: The Vocal Poetics of the Old English Lament and the African-American Blues Song.* New York: Palgrave Macmillan, 2006.

McGhee, Nancy. "Portraits in Black: Illustrated Poems of Paul Laurence Dunbar." In *Stony the Road: Chapters in the History of Hampton Institute*, edited by Keith L. Schall, 63–104. Charlottesville: University Press of Virginia, 1977.

McKim, Mr. J. "Negro Songs." In *The Social Implications of Early Negro Music in the United States*, edited and with an introduction by Bernard Katz. New York: Arno Press and the *New York Times*, 1969. Previously published in *Dwight's Journal of Music* (August 9, 1862).

Meffert, John, Sherman Pyatt, and the Avery Research Center. *Black America Series: Charleston, South Carolina: America is Woven of Many Strands.* Charleston, SC: Arcadia Publishing, 2000.

Miller, Keith D. "City Called Freedom: Biblical Metaphor in Spirituals, Gospel Lyrics, and the Civil Rights Movement." In *African Americans and the Bible: Sacred Texts and Social Textures*, edited by Vincent L. Wimbush, 546–57. New York: Continuum, 2001.

Miller, Ruth. "Folk Poetry." In *Blackamerican Literature*, edited by Ruth Miller, 216–24. Beverly Hills, CA: Glencoe Press, 1971.

Morgan, Sarah. *The Civil War Diary of a Southern Woman*, edited by Charles East. New York: Simon & Schuster, 1991.

Morrison, Toni. "Unspeakable Things Unspoken: The Afro-American Presence in American Literature." In *American Literature, American Culture*, edited by Gordon Hutner, 538–58. New York: Oxford University Press, 1999.

Nelson, Cary, ed. *Anthology of Modern American Poetry*. New York: Oxford University Press, 2000.

Odum, Howard W., and Guy B. Johnson. *The Negro and His Songs: A Study of Typical Negro Songs in the South*. Chapel Hill: University of North Carolina Press, 1925.

———. *Negro Workaday Songs*. Chapel Hill: University of North Carolina Press, 1926.

Packer, Barbara. "Origin and Authority: Emerson and the Higher Criticism." In *Reconstructing American Literary History*, edited by Sacvan Bercovitch. Cambridge, MA: Harvard University Press, 1986.

Palmer, Michael. *Code of Signals: Recent Writings in Poetics*. Berkeley, CA: North Atlantic, 1983.

Patterson, Orlando. *Slavery and Social Death: A Comparative Study*. Cambridge, MA: Harvard University Press, 1982.

Peterkin, Julia. *Roll, Jordan, Roll*. With photographic studies by Doris Ulmann. New York: Robert O. Ballou, 1933.

Peters, Erskine. "The Poetics of the Afro-American Spiritual." *Black American Literature Forum* 23, no. 3 (Autumn 1989): 559–78.

Piersen, William D. *Black Legacy: America's Hidden Heritage*. Amherst: University of Massachusetts Press, 1993.

Pike, Rev. Gustavus D. *The Singing Campaign for Ten Thousand Pounds: Jubilee Singers in Great Britain*. Rev. ed. New York: American Missionary Association, 1875.

Pinsky, Robert. "Responsibilities of the Poet." In *Politics and Poetic Value*, edited by Robert von Hallberg, 7–19. Chicago: University of Chicago Press, 1987.

Poe, Edgar Allan. "The Poetic Principle." 1850. In *Criticism: Major Statements*, edited by Charles Kaplan and William Anderson, 3rd ed., 337–56. New York: St. Martin's Press, 1991.

Preminger, Alex, ed. *Princeton Encyclopedia of Poetry and Poetics*. Princeton, NJ: Princeton University Press, 1974.

Raboteau, Albert J. "African Americans, Exodus, and the American Israel." In *Down by the Riverside: Readings in African American Religion*, edited by Larry G. Murphy, 20–25. New York: New York University Press, 2000.

———. *Slave Religion: The "Invisible Institution" in the Antebellum South*. New York: Oxford University Press, 1978.

Ramey, Lauri. "The African American Slave Songs." In *Encyclopedia of American Poetry*, edited by Jeffrey Gray, vol. 1, 17–19. Westport, CT: Greenwood, 2005.

———. "The Theology of the Lyric Tradition in African American Poetry." *Journal of the American Academy of Religion* 70, no. 2 (June 2002): 347–63.

Ramey, Martin. "'Dragging in its Rear the Bible': The 'Lost Cause' and the Status of African Americans Before and After the American Civil War." *Humanitas: The Journal of the George Bell Institute* 5, no. 1 (October 2003): 43–73.

Randall, Dudley. "Folk Poetry." In *The Black Poets*. 5–32. New York: Bantam, 1971.

Redding, J. Saunders. *To Make a Poet Black*. 1939. Ithaca and London: Cornell University Press, 1988.

Redmond, Eugene B. *Drumvoices: The Mission of Afro-American Poetry: A Critical History*. Garden City, NY: Anchor, 1976.

Ricks, Christopher, and William L. Vance, eds. *The Faber Book of America*. London: Faber and Faber, 1992.

Rothenberg, Jerome, ed. *Technicians of the Sacred: A Range of Poetries from Africa, America, Asia & Oceania*. Garden City, NY: Anchor, 1969.

Rothenberg, Jerome, and George Quasha, eds. *America a Prophecy: A New Reading of American Poetry from Pre-Columbian Times to the Present*. New York: Vintage, 1974.

Rothenberg, Jerome, and Diane Rothenberg, eds. *Symposium of the Whole: A Range of Discourse Toward an Ethnopoetics*. Berkeley: University of California Press, 1983.

Sablosky, Irving. *American Music*. Chicago: University of Chicago Press, 1969.

———. *What They Heard: Music in America, 1852–1881, from the Pages of Dwight's Journal of Music*. Baton Rouge: Louisiana State University Press, 1986.

Schmidt, Michael. *Lives of the Poets*. London: Phoenix, 1998.

Scott, J. S., and P. Simpson-Housley, eds. *Mapping the Sacred: Religion, Geography and Postcolonial Literatures*. Amsterdam: Rodopi, 2001.

Seward, Theo. F. Preface. *Jubilee Songs: As Sung by the Jubilee Singers of Fisk University (Nashville, Tenn.), under the auspices of the American Missionary Association.* New York: Biglow & Main, 1872.

Shepperd, Eli (Martha Young). *Plantation Songs for My Lady's Banjo, and Other Negro Lyrics and Monologues.* New York: R. H. Russell, 1901.

Sherman, Joan R., ed. *African-American Poetry: An Anthology, 1773–1927.* Mineola, NY: Dover, 1997.

Singh, Amritjit, and Peter Schmidt, eds. *Postcolonial Theory and the United States: Race, Ethnicity and Literature.* Jackson: University Press of Mississippi, 2000.

Smith, Jonathan Z. *Relating Religion: Essays in the Study of Religion.* Chicago: University of Chicago Press, 2004.

Smith, Rochelle, and Sharon L. Jones, eds. *The Prentice Hall Anthology of African American Literature.* Upper Saddle River, NJ: Prentice-Hall, 2000.

Smith, William. *Smith's Bible Dictionary.* Reprint, Old Tappan, NJ: Spire Books, 1975.

Smitherman, Geneva. *Talkin and Testifyin: The Language of Black America.* Detroit, MI: Wayne State University Press, 1977.

Smythe, Augustine T., Herbert Ravenel Sass, Alfred Huger, Beatrice Ravenel, Thomas Waring, Archibald Rutledge, Joseph Pinckney, Caroline Pinckney Rutledge, DuBose Heyward, Katharine C. Hutson, and Robert W. Gordon, eds. *The Carolina Low-Country.* New York: Macmillan, 1931.

Snyder, Graydon F. *Ante Pacem: Archaeological Evidence of Church Life Before Constantine,* Reprint, Mercer University Press, 1991.

Southern, Eileen, and Josephine Wright. *Iconography of Music in African-American Culture (1770s–1920s).* New York and London: Garland, 2000.

Southern, Eileen. *The Music of Black Americans: A History.* 3rd ed. New York: W. W. Norton and Sons, 1997.

Southern, Eileen, ed. *Readings in Black American Music.* 2nd ed. New York: W. W. Norton, 1983.

Spencer, Jon Michael. *Protest and Praise: Sacred Music of Black Religion.* Minneapolis, MN: Augsburg Fortress, 1990.

———. *Sacred Symphony.* Westport, CT: Greenwood, 1988.

Stepto, Robert B. "Narration, Authentication, and Authorial Control in Frederick Douglass's *Narrative* of 1845." In *African American Autobiography: A Collection of Critical Essays,* edited by William L. Andrews, 26–35. Englewood Cliffs, NJ: Prentice-Hall, 1993.

Stuckey, Sterling. "'My Burden Lightened:' Frederick Douglass, the Bible, and Slave Culture." *African Americans and the Bible: Sacred Texts and Social Textures,* edited by Vincent L. Wimbush, 251–65. New York: Continuum, 2001.

——. *Slave Culture: Nationalist Theory and the Foundations of Black America*. New York: Oxford University Press, 1987.

Talmy, Leonard. *Toward a Cognitive Semantics. Volume 1: Conceptual Structuring Systems. Volume 2: Typology and Process in Concept Structuring*. Cambridge, MA: MIT Press, 2000.

Takaki, Ronald. *A Different Mirror: A History of Multicultural America*. Boston: Little, Brown, 1993.

Taylor, Rev. Marshall W. *Plantation Melodies*. Cincinnati: Marshall W. Taylor and W. C. Echols, 1882.

Thomas, W. H. *Some Current Folk-Songs of the Negro and their Economic Interpretation*. College Station: The Folk-Lore Society of Texas, 1912.

Thurman, Howard. *Deep River and The Negro Spiritual Speaks of Life and Death*. 1945, 1947. Richmond: Friends United, 1975.

Turner, Mark. "The Ghost of Anyone's Father." Unpublished draft version of essay quoted by kind permission of the author, copyright 2003.

——. *The Literary Mind*. Oxford: Oxford University Press, 1996.

Turner, Nat. *The Confessions of Nat Turner and Related Documents*, edited with an introduction by Kenneth S. Greenberg. Boston: Bedford/St. Martin's, 1996. *The Confessions of Nat Turner* was originally published in 1831.

Untermeyer, Louis. "Four Spirituals." *The Britannica Library of Great American Writing*, edited by Louis Untermeyer, vol. 1, 637–41. Chicago: Britannica Press, 1960.

von Hallberg, Robert. *Charles Olson: The Scholar's Art*. Cambridge, MA: Harvard University Press, 1978.

Ward, Andrew. *Dark Midnight When I Rise: The Story of the Fisk Jubilee Singers: How Black Music Changed America and the World*. New York: Amistad, HarperCollins, 2000.

Ward, Jerry W., Jr., ed. *Trouble the Water: 250 Years of African American Poetry*. New York: Penguin Books, 1997.

Washington, Booker T. *Up From Slavery with Related Documents*, edited and with an introduction by W. Fitzhugh Brundage. Boston: Bedford/St. Martin's, 2003. *Up From Slavery* was originally published in 1901.

Washington, Margaret. "The Meaning of Scripture in Gullah Concepts of Liberation and Group Identity." In *African Americans and the Bible: Sacred Texts and Social Textures*, edited by Vincent L. Wimbush, 321–41. New York: Continuum, 2001.

Watson, John F. *Methodist Error Or, Friendly, Christian Advice, to those Methodists, who indulge in extravagant emotions and bodily exercises, by A Wesleyan Methodist*. Trenton, NJ: D. & E. Fenton, 1819.

Weheliye, Alexander G. "'I Am I Be': The Subject of Sonic Afro-Modernity." *boundary 2* 30, no. 2 (2003): 97–114.

Welsh, Andrew. *Roots of Lyric: Primitive Poetry and Modern Poetics*. Princeton, NJ: Princeton University Press, 1978.

Whalley, George. "Metaphor." In *Princeton Encyclopedia of Poetry and Poetics*, edited by Alex Preminger, 490–95. Princeton, NJ: Princeton University Press, 1974.

Whalum, Wendell Phillips. "The Spiritual As Mature Choral Composition." *Black World*. July 1974, 34–39.

Whitman, Walt. *Complete Poetry and Selected Prose*, edited and with an introduction by James E. Miller Jr. Boston: Houghton Mifflin Co., 1959.

Winter, Margaret Crumpton, and Rhonda Reymond. "Henry Ossawa Tanner and W. E. B. Du Bois: African American Art and 'High Culture' at the Turn into the Twentieth Century." *Post-Bellum, Pre-Harlem: African American Literature and Culture, 1877–1919*, edited by Barbara McCaskill and Caroline Gebhard, 231–49. New York: New York University Press, 2006.

Wiredu, Kwasi. "The Concepts of Mind and Spirit: Some African Reflections." Unpublished draft version of essay dated 20 June 2003 and quoted by kind permission of the author.

Women in Jazz Swansea Archive Web site, part of Channel 4's Black and Asian History Map (UK). Fisk Jubilee Singers. Available at http://www.womeninjazzswansea.org.uk.fisk.asp.

Wood, Henry Cleveland. "Negro Camp Meeting Melodies." In *The Social Implications of Early Negro Music in the United States*, edited and with an introduction by Bernard Katz, New York: Arno Press and the *New York Times*, 1969. Previously published in *New England Magazine* (March 1892): 61–64.

Wordsworth, William. "The 1800 Preface to *Lyrical Ballads*." *The Prelude: Selected Poems and Sonnets*. 1850 (*The Prelude*). Reprint. New York: Rinehart, 1948.

Work, John W. *American Negro Songs: 230 Folk Songs and Spirituals, Religious and Secular*. 1940. Reprint, New York: Dover, 1998.

Work, John Wesley. *Folk Song of the American Negro*. 1915. Reprint, New York: Negro Universities Press, 1969. Originally published by Fisk University Press.

Wright, Richard. "Blueprint for Negro Writing." 1937. In *The Norton Anthology of African American Literature*, edited by Henry Louis Gates Jr. and Nellie Y. McKay, 2nd ed. 1403–10. New York: W. W. Norton, 2004.

Yetman, Norman R., ed. *When I Was a Slave: Memoirs from the Slave Narrative Collection*. Material transcribed 1936–38. Reprint, Mineola, NY: Dover, 2002. Originally published as *Voices From Slavery*, 1970.

Zamir, Shamoon. *Dark Voices: W. E. B. Du Bois and American Thought, 1888–1903*. Chicago: University of Chicago Press, 1995.

Zbikowski, Lawrence M. "The Cognitive Tango." In *The Artful Mind: Cognitive Science and the Riddle of Human Creativity*, edited by Mark Turner, 115–31. New York: Oxford University Press, 2006.

Notes

Preface

1. Miles Mark Fisher, *Negro Slave Songs in the United States* (New York: Carol Publishing Group, Citadel, 1990), 183.
2. *Methodist Error Or, Friendly, Christian Advice, to Those Methodists, who indulge in extravagant religious emotions and bodily exercises*, authored anonymously by "A Methodist" (1819) and later attributed to John F. Watson, describes the "growing evil" of hymns that are "often miserable as poetry, and senseless as matter, and most frequently composed and sung by the illiterate blacks of the society." Excerpt appears in *Readings in Black American Music*, ed. Eileen Southern (New York: W. W. Norton, 1983), 62–63.
3. Thomas Wentworth Higginson, "Negro Spirituals," in *Army Life in a Black Regiment and Other Writings* (New York: Penguin), 160.
4. William E. Barton, *Old Plantation Hymns; a collection of hitherto unpublished melodies of the slave and the freeman, with historical and descriptive notes* (New York: AMS, 1972), 10.
5. W. E. B. Du Bois, *The Souls of Black Folk* (Boston: Bedford, 1997), 189.
6. William Francis Allen, Charles Pickard Ware, and Lucy McKim Garrison, eds., *Slave Songs of the United States* (Bedford, MA: Applewood, 1995), iv.
7. Shelley Fisher Fishkin, *Was Huck Black? Mark Twain and African American Voices* (Oxford: Oxford University Press, 1993), 5.
8. John Lovell Jr., "The Social Implications of the Negro Spiritual," in *The Social Implications of Early Negro Music in the United States*, ed. Bernard Katz (New York: Arno Press and the New York Times, 1969), 130. Lovell himself exemplified the commitment of the "patient scholars" that he implicitly called on to undertake serious critical study of slave

songs by doing it himself (and others also produced major scholarly studies after Lovell's essay appeared, notably Dena J. Epstein with her monumental work *Sinful Tunes and Spirituals: Black Folk Music to the Civil War* [Chicago: University of Illinois Press, 1977]). The cited essay by Lovell was written in 1939; he continued to research slave songs until completing his 686-page masterpiece, *Black Song: The Forge and the Flame: How the African-American Spiritual Was Hammered Out*, in 1972. In 1939, Lovell estimated that there were between 800 and 1,000 slave songs. By the time *Black Song* was published, his meticulous research had accounted for more than 6,000 songs.

9. Du Bois, 186.

Introduction

1. Irving Sablosky, *American Music* (Chicago: University of Chicago Press, 1969), 112.
2. William E. Barton, *Old Plantation Hymns; a collection of hitherto unpublished melodies of the slave and the freeman, with historical and descriptive notes* (New York: AMS, 1972), 3.
3. Thomas Wentworth Higginson, *Army Life in a Black Regiment and Other Writings* (New York: Penguin, 1997), 149–50.
4. Ibid.
5. Ibid., 157.
6. Gustavus D. Pike, *The Singing Campaign for Ten Thousand Pounds: Jubilee Singers in Great Britain* (New York: American Missionary Association, 1875), 71.
7. Ibid., 205.
8. I do not wish to suggest that there are not massive historical complexities relating to this issue and era and strongly suggest that readers consult the historical literature on Emancipation, Reconstruction, Jim Crow Laws, and the sociological and political background that provides essential context. I also highly recommend an excellent and extremely relevant essay collection focused on this period in literary studies that provides strong historical contextualization called *Post-Bellum, Pre-Harlem: African American Literature and Culture, 1877–1919*, eds. Barbara McCaskill and Caroline Gebhard (New York: New York University Press, 2006).
9. Andrew Ward, *Dark Midnight When I Rise: The Story of the Fisk Jubilee Singers: How Black Music Changed America and the World* (New York: Amistad, HarperCollins, 2000), 160.
10. Ibid., 134–35.

11. Irving Sablosky, *What They Heard: Music in America, 1852–1881, From the Pages of Dwight's Journal of Music* (Baton Rouge: Louisiana State University Press, 1986), 278.

12. John Wesley Work, *Folk Song of the American Negro: 230 Folk Songs and Spirituals, Religious and Secular* (New York: Dover, 1998), 30–31.

13. Alain Locke, ed., *The New Negro* (New York: Atheneum, 1968), 199.

14. I would consider Lovell's study to be the most exhaustive and focused literary treatment of slave songs, but I believe there would be general agreement that literary studies has become more theoretical than it was in the early 1970s. When this major opus appeared, Lovell had already been researching slave songs for more than thirty years. Though the focus of the discipline and its interpretive strategies, and of Professor Lovell, may have been somewhat different when *Black Song* was published, the exegesis, knowledge, research, and analysis in this work are staggering.

15. Henry Edward Krehbiel, *Afro-American Folksongs: A Study in Racial and National Music* (New York: Frederick Ungar, 1962), 48.

16. Roland Hayes, *My Songs: Aframerican Religious Folk Songs Arranged and Interpreted by Roland Hayes* (Boston: Atlantic Monthly, Little Brown, 1948), 55.

17. Lawrence W. Levine, *Black Culture and Black Consciousness: Afro-American Folk Thought From Slavery to Freedom* (New York: Oxford University Press, 1977), 18.

18. An impeccably researched and detailed treatment of the intersecting political, economic, and religious themes motivating the various movements involved in slavery, Christianity, and abolitionism—and their ultimate impact on African Americans after Emancipation—is found in Martin Ramey's essay "'Dragging in its Rear the Bible': The 'Lost Cause' and the Status of African Americans Before and After the American Civil War" in *Humanitas: The Journal of the George Bell Institute* 5, no. 1 (Oct. 2003): 43–73.

19. James Weldon Johnson and J. Rosamond Johnson, *The Books of American Negro Spirituals*, bk. 1 (Jackson, TN: Da Capo, 1925), 13.

20. Bernard Katz, *The Social Implications of Early Negro Music in the United States* (New York: Arno Press and the New York Times, 1969), 70.

21. Work, 22.

22. Hayes, 113.

Chapter 1

1. Wordsworth, "1800 Preface to *Lyrical Ballads*," in *The Prelude: Selected Poems and Sonnets*, ed. Carlos Baker (New York: Rinehart, 1948), 1.

2. F. Abiola Irele, *The African Imagination: Literature in Africa and the Black Diaspora* (Oxford: Oxford University Press, 2001). I will be building my interpretation of slave songs primarily using Irele's ideas in chapter 2, "Orality, Literacy, and African Literature," 23–38, but the book as a whole is a classic critical text that I cannot recommend more enthusiastically.

3. See Andrew Welsh, *Roots of Lyric: Primitive Poetry and Modern Poetics* (Princeton, NJ: Princeton University Press, 1978) for an early and beautifully developed study of how ancient and international "non-poetic" forms account for much of what we consider to be "poetic" in the modern lyric. This book has become something of the scholarly equivalent of a cult classic. Will Coleman's *Tribal Talk: Black Theology, Hermeneutics, and African/American Ways of "Telling the Story"* (University Park, PA: The Pennsylvania State University Press, 2000) serves as a fascinating parallel text to Welsh's book. Coleman's interdisciplinary study is an excellent overview and analysis of tale-telling patterns in the African diaspora addressed from the perspective of black theology.

4. Edgar Allan Poe, "The Poetic Principle," in *Criticism: Major Statements*, eds. Charles Kaplan and William Anderson, 3rd ed. (New York: St. Martin's, 1991), 337.

5. Jerome Rothenberg and Diane Rothenberg, eds. *Symposium of the Whole: A Range of Discourse Toward an Ethnopoetics* (Berkeley: University of California Press, 1983), xi.

6. Michael Palmer, *Code of Signals: Recent Writings in Poetics* (Berkeley, CA: North Atlantic, 1983), copyright page.

7. Jerome Rothenberg, ed. *Technicians of the Sacred: A Range of Poetries from Africa, America, Asia & Oceania* (Garden City, NY: Anchor/Doubleday, 1969), xx.

8. Ibid., xxvi.

9. Ibid., xxii.

10. Ibid., xxvi.

11. John Lovell Jr., "The Social Implications of the Negro Spiritual" in *The Social Implications of Early Negro Music in the United States*, ed. Bernard Katz (New York: Arno Press and the *New York Times*, 1969), 129. Originally published in *Journal of Negro Education*, October 1939.

12. Cary Nelson, ed., *Anthology of Modern American Poetry* (New York: Oxford University Press, 2000), 491.

13. Ibid., 717–18. The topic of anonymity versus identifiable authorship is one of the major issues of chapter 3 in this book. I focus on the high value placed within the lyric tradition on poetry which is the expression of an individual, as a condition that is in tension with the competing higher

value placed on group identity for African Americans during and after slavery.

14. Ibid., xxx.

15. Joan R. Sherman, ed., *African-American Poetry: An Anthology, 1773–1927* (Mineola, NY: Dover, 1997), iii.

16. Although the anthology itself does not contain slave songs, it comes with an outstanding CD called *Living Words* by Kevin Everod Quashie and Stuart L. Twite, which includes several slave songs, among them Paul Robeson singing "Swing Low, Sweet Chariot"; "Come By Hyar" by Bernice Reagon; and "I Couldn't Hear Nobody Pray" by the Fisk Jubilee Singers, as well as two remarkable recordings of testimonies by former slaves.

17. Henry Louis Gates Jr., "The Master's Pieces: On Canon Formation and the African-American Tradition," *The South Atlantic Quarterly* 89, no. 1 (1990): 97–98.

18. M. H. Abrams, ed., *The Norton Anthology of English Literature*, 6th ed., vol. 1. (New York: W. W. Norton, 1993), 286–87.

19. M. H. Abrams, *Natural Supernaturalism: Tradition and Revolution in Romantic Literature* (New York: W. W. Norton, 1973), 32.

20. Ibid., 32. The citation comes from the "Preface to *Poems* of 1815," *Literary Criticism of William Wordsworth*, ed. Paul M. Zall (Lincoln, Nebraska, 1966), 143.

21. W. H. Thomas, *Some Current Folk-Songs of the Negro and their Economic Interpretation* (College Station: The Folk-Lore Society of Texas, 1912), 5.

22. Roland Hayes, *My Songs: Aframerican Religious Folk Songs Arranged and Interpreted by Roland Hayes* (Boston: Atlantic Monthly Press; Little, Brown, and Co., 1948), 93.

23. Ibid., 94–95.

24. Howard W. Odum and Guy B. Johnson, *The Negro and His Songs: A Study of Typical Negro Songs in the South* (Chapel Hill: University of North Carolina Press, 1925), 17. The citation is taken from Booker T. Washington's introduction to *Twenty-Four Negro Melodies* by Samuel Coleridge-Taylor in *The Musician's Library*.

25. Abrams, *The Norton Anthology of English Literature*, vol. 1, 18–19.

26. Michael Calabrese read and commented on the relevant portions of this chapter and generously shared his expertise by discussing illuminating parallels in the development, construction, and history of reception of medieval poetry and slave songs. I wish to express my gratitude for many of his suggestions that are reflected in this section.

27. Alex Preminger, ed., *Princeton Encyclopedia of Poetry and Poetics* (Princeton, NJ: Princeton University Press), 807.

28. At the same time that I emphasize the importance of music and the African oral tradition for slave songs, I equally wish to stress the point that I am not an expert in music or African literature and make no pretense of being so. Fortunately, there are brilliant scholars and wonderful resources that I have made efforts to cite often, and upon whose works I have relied over and over. Their lifetimes of research and analysis cannot be stressed enough as crucial to a sophisticated understanding of slave songs in these two fields. Religious studies is another field of central importance to slave songs that is outside of my area of academic training where I have similarly attempted to point readers in the direction of true experts. I recommend highly the works of Albert Raboteau, Dwight N. Hopkins, Jon Michael Spencer, James Cone, and Pascal Boyer. For musical insight on slave songs and African American music, some of the experts (with apologies to anyone who has been overlooked) are Eileen Southern, Dena J. Epstein, Portia Maultsby, Samuel A. Floyd Jr., and Mellonee V. Burnim. For African literature, I consistently turn to the work of F. Abiola Irele, of whom Henry Louis Gates Jr. writes, "No one has a subtler appreciation of Africa's present-day cultural complexities." I have also found the work of Robert Fraser, Kofi Awoonor, Ruth Finnegan, and Trevor Cope to be extremely helpful.

29. Preminger, 460–62.

30. Present-day connotations of drama and its presentation as "spectacle" are more akin to the genre that Aristotle described than current views of the lyric. *Poetics*' illuminations of literary language and effect have come to be applied to critical discussions of all literary genres, including historical and modern understandings of lyric poetry and the canon. Aristotle's insights—foundational to general critical analyses of literariness—are especially germane in addressing poetry which may be experienced as performance, as in the case of slave songs.

31. Northrop Frye, "Introduction: Lexis and Melos," in *Sound and Poetry: English Institute Essays 1956*, ed. Northrop Frye (New York: Columbia University Press, 1967), x–xi.

32. David Lindley, *Lyric* (London: Methuen, 1985), 2.

33. Ibid., 41.

34. Ibid., 25. Lindley quotes from Paul Laumonier, ed., *Art Poétique François, Oeuvres Complètes*, XIV (Paris, 1949), 9.

35. W. R. Johnson, *The Idea of Lyric: Lyric Modes in Ancient and Modern Poetry* (Berkeley: University of California Press, 1982), 176–77.

36. Lindley, 4.

37. Ibid., 5.

38. Ibid., 5.

39. Ibid., 2.
40. Preminger, 468.
41. W. R. Johnson, *The Idea of Lyric*, 33.
42. Ibid., 31.
43. Ibid., 30–31.
44. William Francis Allen, Charles Pickard Ware, and Lucy McKim Garrison, eds., *Slave Songs of the United States* (Bedford, MA: Applewood, 1995), 70.
45. John Lovell Jr., *Black Song: The Forge and the Flame: The Story of How the Afro-American Spiritual was Hammered Out* (New York: Macmillan, 1972), 296.
46. R. Nathaniel Dett, ed., *Religious Folk-Songs of the Negro As Sung at Hampton Institute* (New York: AMS, 1972), 127.
47. Ibid., 133.
48. Theo F. Seward, *Jubilee Songs: As Sung by the Jubilee Singers of Fisk University (Nashville, Tenn.), under the auspices of the American Missionary Association* (New York: Biglow & Main, 1872), 8.
49. Ibid., 23.
50. Dett, 10.
51. John W. Work, *American Negro Songs: 230 Folk Songs and Spirituals, Religious and Secular* (New York: Dover, 1998), 212.
52. W. R. Johnson, *The Idea of Lyric*, 34.
53. Ibid., 176–77.
54. Preminger, 310.
55. Joseph Addison, "An Essay on Virgil's Georgics," *Criticism and Aesthetics 1660–1800*, ed. Oliver F. Sigworth (San Francisco: Rinehart, 1971), 125.
56. Ibid., 120.
57. Ibid., 121.
58. Ibid., 120–21.
59. Addison, "An Essay on Virgil's Georgics," 122–23.
60. Robert Pinsky, "Responsibilities of the Poet," in *Politics and Poetic Value*, ed. Robert von Hallberg (Chicago: University of Chicago Press, 1987), 10.
61. Forché is cited by Pinsky, 11.
62. Ibid.
63. Walt Whitman, "Preface" (1855), *Walt Whitman, Complete Poetry and Selected Prose*, ed. James E. Miller Jr. (Boston: Houghton Mifflin, 1959), 426.
64. James E. Miller Jr., "Introduction," *ibid.*, xl.

65. Robert von Hallberg, *Charles Olson: The Scholar's Art* (Cambridge, MA: Harvard University Press, 1978), 34.

66. Ibid., 34.

67. This poem is found in most major in-print anthologies of African American poetry so it is easily accessible, including in Henry Louis Gates Jr. and Nellie Y. McKay, eds., *Norton Anthology of African American Literature*, 2nd ed. (New York: W. W. Norton, 2004), 1619–20.

68. Jerry W. Ward Jr., ed., *Trouble the Water: 250 Years of African American Poetry* (New York: Penguin, 1997), 157.

69. I am discussing such composite and complex metaphorical states in this chapter, specifically in relation to the lyric poetry tradition, but it is an extended topic of consideration that weaves throughout this book. In chapter 2, I discuss the use of such metaphors in relation to Mark Turner's idea of blended spaces in the context of the theology of slave songs. In chapter 3, I discuss metaphors of identity primarily from the perspective of critical reception and explain why contradictory cross-mappings of identity might have prevented African Americans from being recognized as Americans and slave songs from being considered either as art or as American art. In chapter 4, I discuss creative metaphorical blends as a means of transcending time, space, and the body to achieve cognitive freedom based on the conditions that prevailed for the slaves on the plantation, on African concepts of body and mind as survivals in slave culture, and in the human capacity to form such metaphors.

70. William Smith, *Smith's Bible Dictionary* (Old Tappan, NJ: Spire Books, Fleming H. Revell, 1975), 34.

71. Katz, 122.

72. Lovell, "The Social Implications of the Negro Spiritual," 136.

73. Thomas Wentworth Higginson, *Army Life in a Black Regiment* (Boston: James R. Osgood, 1871), 160.

74. Hayes, 13.

75. As one example, see ibid., 127.

76. Ibid., 121.

77. Sterling Brown, *Negro Poetry and Drama and The Negro in American Fiction* (New York: Atheneum, 1972), 17.

78. James Weldon Johnson and J. Rosamond Johnson, *The Books of American Negro Spirituals*, bk. 1 (New York: Da Capo, 1925), 11.

79. Ibid., 42.

80. Ibid., 14.

81. Ibid., 38.

82. Allen, Ware, and Garrison, *Slave Songs of the United States*, iv.

83. Andrew Ward, *Dark Midnight When I Rise: The Story of the Fisk Jubilee Singers: How Black Music Changed America and the World* (New York: Amistad, HarperCollins, 2000), 213.

84. Rev. Gustavus D. Pike, *The Singing Campaign for Ten Thousand Pounds: Jubilee Singers in Great Britain*, rev. ed. (New York: American Missionary Association, 1875), 14–15.

85. Ibid., 61.

86. J. B. T. Marsh, *The Story of the Jubilee Singers; with their Songs*, 4th ed. (London: Hodder and Stoughton, 1875), 89.

87. Dett, xix.

88. Katz, 25.

89. Hayes, 55.

90. Preminger, 310.

91. Irele, 9.

92. Ibid., 10.

93. Ibid.

94. Hungerford, *The Old Plantation and What I Gathered There in an Autumn Month* (New York: Harper & Brothers, 1859), 345.

95. Fredrika Bremer, *The Homes of the New World: Impressions of America*, trans. Mary Howitt, vol. 1 (New York: Harper & Brothers, 1853), 393–94.

96. D'Jimo Kouyate provides an excellent firsthand description of the griot's historical role and current relevance: "The griot was the oral historian and educator in any given society." It was the griot's "responsibility to make sure that the people received all the information about their ancestors. . . . What the griot gave to African society in oral history, cultural information, and ancestral wisdom and knowledge is the key with which all people of African descent can progress and maintain a high level of understanding of their true heritage." D'Jimo Kouyate, "The Role of the Griot," in *Talk That Talk: An Anthology of African-American Storytelling*, eds. Linda Goss and Marian E. Barnes (New York: Simon and Schuster/Touchstone, 1989), 179–81.

97. Irele, 11.

98. Ibid., 19.

99. Ibid.

100. Frances Anne Kemble, *Journal of A Residence on a Georgian Plantation in 1838–1839* (London: Longman, Green, Longman, Roberts & Green, 1863), 3.

101. Ibid., 199.

102. Marsh, 225.

Chapter 2

1. Dwight N. Hopkins, *Down, Up, and Over: Slave Religion and Black Theology* (Minneapolis, MN: Fortress, 2000), 267.

2. J. B. T. Marsh, *The Story of the Jubilee Singers; with their Songs*, 4th ed. (London: Hodder and Stoughton, 1875), 202.

3. Ballanta-(Taylor), Nicholas George Julius, "Saint Helena Island Spirituals: Recorded and Transcribed at Penn Normal Industrial and Agricultural School, St. Helena Island, Beaufort County, South Carolina" (master's thesis, Institute of Musical Arts, New York, 1924), 72.

4. A marvelous recorded version of "Scandalize My Name" appears on the CD *Toil and Triumph: African American Spirituals* by Anthony Brown with The Spirituals Project Choir, which is available from http://www .spiritualsproject.org.

5. Ballanta-(Taylor). This manuscript was Ballanta-(Taylor)'s thesis. In spite of its date, these transcriptions were intended to record the original slave songs that had been preserved and were still part of the cultural life of the residents. The thesis is located in the Moorland-Spingarn Research Center at Howard University, and I am extremely grateful to Joellen ElBashir, Curator of Manuscripts, for pointing it out to me and generally offering expert assistance while conducting my research in this outstanding collection.

6. R. Nathaniel Dett, ed., *Religious Folk-Songs of the Negro As Sung at Hampton Institute* (New York: AMS, 1972), 129.

7. Ibid.

8. Ibid., 122.

9. William Francis Allen, Charles Pickard Ware, and Lucy McKim Garrison, eds., *Slave Songs of the United States* (Bedford, MA: Applewood, 1995), 46.

10. Dett, 130.

11. Ibid., 125.

12. Thomas Wentworth Higginson, *Army Life in a Black Regiment and Other Writings* (New York: Penguin, 1997), 159.

13. James Weldon Johnson and J. Rosamond Johnson, *The Books of American Negro Spirituals*, bk. 2 (Jackson, TN: Da Capo Press, 1925), 68–69.

14. Ibid., 134.

15. Moses Hogan, ed., *The Oxford Book of Spirituals* (New York: Oxford University Press, 2002), 145.

16. William E. Barton, *Old Plantation Hymns; a collection of hitherto unpublished melodies of the slave and the freeman, with historical and descriptive notes* (New York: AMS, 1972), 11.

17. Norman R. Yetman, ed., *When I Was a Slave: Memoirs from the Slave Narrative Collection* (Mineola, NY: Dover Thrift Editions, 2002), 107.
18. Eileen Southern and Josephine Wright, *Iconography of Music in African-American Culture (1770s–1920s)* (New York: Garland, 2000), 17.
19. Barton, 20.
20. Andrew Ward, *Dark Midnight When I Rise: The Story of the Fisk Jubilee Singers: How Black Music Changed the World and America* (New York: Amistad, HarperCollins, 2000), 241–42.
21. Ibid., 156.
22. Marsh, 32.
23. John W. Blassingame, ed., *Slave Testimony: Two Centuries of Letters, Speeches, Interviews, and Autobiographies* (Baton Rouge: Louisiana State University Press, 2003) and Yetman, ed., *When I Was a Slave*, which was originally published as *Voices From Slavery*, fully document the disorientation and incomprehension of countless slaves when being told that they were freed. Many of them remained on the plantations where they resided because they were too old or infirm to go elsewhere, or because they had no better alternatives. For a thoroughly chilling firsthand account of the conditions immediately after Emancipation, there are two newly released recordings of interviews with former slaves on the CD *Living Words* by Kevin Everod Quashie and Stuart L. Twite (tracks 9 and 10) that is included in Rochelle Smith and Sharon L. Jones, eds., *The Prentice Hall Anthology of African American Literature* (Upper Saddle River, NJ: Prentice-Hall, 2000).
24. Paul Laurence Dunbar, *The Collected Poetry of Paul Laurence Dunbar*, ed. Joanne M. Braxton (Charlottesville: University Press of Virginia, 1993), 259–60.
25. Jan Assmann, *Moses the Egyptian: The Memory of Egypt in Western Monotheism* cited in Ronald Hendel, "The Exodus in Biblical Memory," *Journal of Biblical Literature* 120, no. 4 (2001), 603.
26. Ibid.
27. Ibid.
28. Ibid.
29. Johnson and Johnson, 159.
30. Ibid., 78.
31. Richard Barksdale and Keneth Kinnamon, eds., "Folk Literature," in *Black Writers of America: A Comprehensive Anthology* (Upper Saddle River, NJ: Prentice-Hall, 1972), 237. This particular song contains the interesting suggestion—supporting Barton—that prayer is focused on the end times, and when eternal life is reached, prayer is no longer necessary.
32. Dett, 110.

33. Ibid., 111.
34. Johnson and Johnson, bk. 1, p. 62.
35. Ibid., 100.
36. Higginson, *Army Life in a Black Regiment*, 158.
37. Dett, 169.
38. Thomas P. Fenner, Frederic G. Rathbun, and Miss Bessie Cleaveland, *Cabin and Plantation Songs as Sung by the Hampton Students* (New York: AMS, 1977), 127.
39. John S. Mbiti, *African Religions and Philosophy*, 2nd ed. (Oxford: Heinemann, 1990), 27.
40. Dett, 70.
41. Johnson and Johnson, 75.
42. Hogan, 194.
43. Dett, 153.
44. Johnson and Johnson, 65. The diachronic development of slave songs poses fascinating issues in relation to authenticity, as discussed in chapter 4, and also reveals how some of them appeared, disappeared, and reappeared in collections over time. Allen, Ware, and Garrison say that they have rejected a song called "Climb Jacob's Ladder" for inclusion in *Slave Songs of the United States* as a spurious slave song since they found the same song in Methodist hymnbooks (vi). "We Am Climbin' Jacob's Ladder" or variants of that song did not appear in Dett or Fenner either, but then it reappeared in the later collections of Johnson and Johnson and John W. Work, (*American Negro Songs: 230 Folk Songs and Spirituals, Religious and Secular* [New York: Dover, 1998]) and is now generally regarded as an authentic slave song.
45. Dett, 54.
46. Ibid., 69.
47. Ibid., 71.
48. Johnson and Johnson, 59.
49. Fenner, Rathbun, and Cleaveland, 55.
50. Johnson and Johnson, 168–69.
51. Ibid., 118–19.
52. Fisher, 56–58, 117–18.
53. Higginson, *Army Life in a Black Regiment*, 161.
54. Henry Cleveland Wood, "Negro Camp Meeting Melodies" in *The Social Implications of Early Negro Music in the United States*, ed. and intro. Bernard Katz (New York: Arno Press and the *New York Times*, 1969), 73.

55. Rev. Gustavus D. Pike, *The Singing Campaign for Ten Thousand Pounds: Jubilee Singers in Great Britain* (New York: American Missionary Association, 1875), 143–44.

56. Theo F. Seward, ed., *Jubilee Songs: As Sung by the Jubilee Singers of Fisk University (Nashville, Tenn.), under the auspices of the American Missionary Association* (New York: Biglow & Main, 1872), 17.

57. Allen, Ware, and Garrison, 43.

58. Blassingame, *Slave Testimony*, 541.

59. Nat Turner, *The Confessions of Nat Turner and Related Documents*, ed. and intro. Kenneth S. Greenberg (Boston: Bedford/St. Martin's, 1996).

60. Lawrence W. Levine, *Black Culture and Black Consciousness: Afro-American Folk Thought From Slavery to Freedom* (Oxford: Oxford University Press, 1977), 77.

61. Barton, 20.

62. Ibid., 19.

63. Mark Turner, *The Literary Mind* (Oxford: Oxford University Press, 1996), 57–84. The richest reference guide to books, journals, handouts, conferences, symposia, and essays focused on this burgeoning subject may be found on the "Blending Website": http://markturner.org/blending.html.

64. Mark Turner, "The Ghost of Anyone's Father" (unpublished draft version of essay, 2003), 4.

65. Ibid., 8.

66. Ibid., 9.

67. Alice Ogden Bellis suggested that the startlingly underexplored area of Kush and the development of African religions would be a fruitful way to consider the existing frame of mind of the slaves that enabled them to adapt their own brand of Christianity during slavery.

68. Johnson and Johnson, 136–37.

69. Dett, 204.

70. Allen, Ware, and Garrison, 10.

71. Ibid., 39.

72. Johnson and Johnson, 166–67.

73. Work, 124.

74. This version of the lyrics is the same one that appears in Fenner, Rathbun and Cleaveland, 139.

75. Dett, 102.

76. Ibid., 146.

77. Ibid., 188.

78. Ibid., 27.

79. Ibid., 42–43.

80. Johnson and Johnson, 104.

81. Some slave songs are more unusual and appear in a limited number of collections. Or in some cases, I wish to refer to a particular variant among several that exists. In both sets of cases, I have provided complete bibliographic citations. Some other slave songs appear in the most commonly accessible collections of the "spirituals," and at times I am making a point that applies to the generic traits of all common versions of particular slave songs. In both of those situations (for example, "We Are Climbing Jacob's Ladder") I have not thought it necessary to include particular citations.

82. Dett, 196–97.

83. Johnson and Johnson, 30–31.

84. Ibid., 96.

85. Marsh, 225.

86. Allen, Ware, and Garrison, 19.

87. Johnson and Johnson, 25.

88. Frederick Douglass, *Narrative of the Life of Frederick Douglass, An American Slave, Written by Himself*, eds. William L. Andrews and William S. Feely, Norton Critical Edition (New York: W. W. Norton, 1997), 41. The contrast between the slaveholding culture's interpretation of Christianity and its application to support the institution of slavery is brilliantly contrasted by several major scholars through the Christianity of both the slaves themselves and the abolitionists. See especially these indispensable works offering varied perspectives on the topic: Albert Raboteau, *Slave Religion: The "Invisible Institution" in the Antebellum South* (New York: Oxford University Press, 1978); Dwight N. Hopkins, *Down, Up, and Over: Slave Religion and Black Theology* (Minneapolis, MN: Fortress Press, 2000); Eddie S. Glaude Jr., *Exodus!: Religion, Race, and Nation in Early Nineteenth-Century Black America* (Chicago: University of Chicago Press, 2000); and James H. Cone, *A Black Theology of Liberation* (Maryknoll, NY: Orbis Books, Twentieth Anniversary Edition, 2003).

89. Roland Hayes, *My Songs: Aframerican Religious Folk Songs Arranged and Interpreted by Roland Hayes* (Boston: Atlantic Monthly, Little, Brown and Co., 1948), 41.

90. Ibid., 43–44.

91. Dett, 225.

92. Portia K. Maultsby's article "Black Spirituals: An Analysis of Textual Forms and Structures," *Black Perspectives in Music* 4 (Spring 1976): 54–69 is one of the most thorough and cogent explanations that I have read of the major patterns and variations in slave songs.

93. George Lakoff and Mark Turner, *More Than Cool Reason: A Field Guide to Poetic Metaphor* (Chicago: University of Chicago Press, 1989), 40.

Chapter 3

1. John Lovell Jr., *Black Song: The Forge and the Flame: The Story of How the Afro-American Spiritual was Hammered Out* (New York: Macmillan, 1972), 92–94.
2. James H. Cone, *The Spirituals and the Blues* (Maryknoll, NY: Orbis, 1999), 10.
3. Lovell, *Black Song*, 91.
4. Lawrence W. Levine, *Black Culture and Black Consciousness: Afro-American Folk Thought From Slavery to Freedom* (New York: Oxford University Press, 1977), 22.
5. Lovell, *Black Song*, 94.
6. Miles Mark Fisher, *Negro Slave Songs in the United States* (New York: Citadel, 1990), 182.
7. Shelley Fisher Fishkin, *Was Huck Black? Mark Twain and African-American Voices* (New York: Oxford University Press, 1993), 44.
8. James Weldon Johnson and J. Rosamond Johnson, *The Books of American Negro Spirituals*, bk. 1 (New York: Da Capo Press, 1925), 14–15.
9. Charles H. Long, "Perspectives for a Study of African American Religion," *Down by the Riverside: Readings in African American Religion*, ed. Larry G. Murphy (New York: New York University Press, 2000), 15.
10. For detailed treatments of the Exodus myth and its meaning in African American culture, see Albert Raboteau, "African Americans, Exodus, and the American Israel," in *Down by the Riverside: Readings in African American Religion*, ed. Larry G. Murphy (New York: New York University Press, 2000), 20–25; Eddie S. Glaude Jr., *Exodus!: Religion, Race, and Nation in Early Nineteenth-Century Black America* (Chicago: University of Chicago Press, 2000); Martin Ramey, "'Dragging in its Rear the Bible': The 'Lost Cause' and the Status of African Americans Before and After the American Civil War," *Humanitas: The Journal of the George Bell Institute* 5, no. 1 (October 2003): 43–73; and Jon Michael Spencer, "Promises and Passages: The Exodus Story Told Through the Spirituals," in *Protest & Praise: Sacred Music of Black Religion* (Minneapolis, MN: Augsburg Fortress, 1990), 3–34. Extremely helpful background on the Exodus motif itself is provided in Michael Fishbane, "The 'Exodus' Motif/The Paradigm of Historical Renewal," in *Biblical Text and Texture* (Oxford: Oneworld, 1998), 121–40.
11. Raboteau, "African Americans, Exodus, and the American Israel," 20–25.
12. Richard E. Beringer, et al., *Why the South Lost the Civil War* (Athens: The University of Georgia Press, 1986), 82–102.
13. Ibid., 63.

14. Henry Edward Krehbiel, *Afro-American Folksongs: A Study in Racial and National Music* (New York: Frederick Ungar, 1962), 26.

15. William E. Barton, *Old Plantation Hymns; a collection of hitherto unpublished melodies of the slave and the freeman, with historical and descriptive notes* (New York: AMS, 1972), 17.

16. The concept of "wandering" choruses is closely aligned with the literary principles associated with the oral text as identified by F. Abiola Irele, discussed in chapter 1. Some of these features are improvisation, performativity, and the deliberate evasion of a fixed literary object as a candidate for canonicity in the "oral" lyric tradition, all of which have been issues that have resulted in slave songs' history of marginalization. Southern also addresses the concept of "wandering" choruses in further detail in *The Music of Black Americans* (New York: W. W. Norton, 1983), 199–201.

17. For examples from Allen's hymnal, see Eileen Southern, ed., *Readings in Black American Music*, 2nd ed. (New York: W. W. Norton, 1983), 52–61.

18. Southern, *The Music of Black Americans*, 198.

19. Ibid.

20. Satan's religious and cultural role offers another parallel between slave songs and medieval texts, which is discussed in chapter 1. According to William E. Barton, Satan is "at once a terror and source of joy to the negro" who can blame the devil for his earthly hardships: "The place he holds in negro theology is not unlike that which he occupied in the miracle plays of the middle ages" (11).

21. Ibid., 198–200.

22. Ibid., 202.

23. Barton, 12.

24. Thomas P. Fenner, Frederic G. Rathbun, and Miss Bessie Cleaveland, *Cabin and Plantation Songs as Sung by the Hampton Students* (New York: AMS, 1977), 126–27.

25. R. Nathaniel Dett, ed., *Religious Folk-Songs of the Negro As Sung at Hampton Institute* (New York: AMS, 1972), 19.

26. Lovell, *Black Song*, 526.

27. Moses Hogan, ed., *The Oxford Book of Spirituals* (New York: Oxford University Press, 2002), 123–29.

28. Bernard Katz, *The Social Implications of Early Negro Music in the United States* (New York: Arno Press and the *New York Times*, 1969), 71.

29. Howard W. Odum and Guy B. Johnson, *The Negro and His Songs: A Study of Typical Negro Songs in the South* (Chapel Hill: University of North Carolina Press, 1925), 36.

30. Thomas Wentworth Higginson, *Army Life in a Black Regiment and Other Writings* (New York: Penguin, 1997), 168–69.
31. Ibid., 169.
32. Rev. Gustavus D. Pike, *The Singing Campaign for Ten Thousand Pounds: Jubilee Singers in Great Britain*, rev. ed. (New York: American Missionary Association, 1875), 18.
33. Ibid., 143–44.
34. Ibid., 170.
35. Ibid., 205.
36. Katz, 70.
37. Rev. Marshal W. Taylor, *Plantation Melodies* (Cincinnati: Marshall W. Taylor and W. C. Echols, 1882), 3.
38. Irving Sablosky, *American Music* (Chicago: University of Chicago Press, 1969), 277.
39. Krehbiel, vi.
40. Katz, 28.
41. Ibid., 121.
42. Southern, *The Music of Black Americans*, 204.
43. Ibid., 197.
44. Krehbiel, 27.
45. Sablosky, *American Music*, 41.
46. Krehbiel, 279.
47. John Wesley Work, *Folk Song of the American Negro* (New York: Negro Universities Press, 1969), 27.
48. Ibid., 33.ß
49. See, first and foremost, the introduction to the collected poems by Joanne M. Braxton, but also recent work by Shelley Fisher Fishkin and David Bradley, Gene Jarrett and others, as well as a special issue of *African American Review* on Dunbar, Vol. 41, No. 2 (Summer 2007). Much of this fine work results from the marvelous centennial conference held in 2006 at Stanford University.
50. Nancy McGhee, "Portraits in Black: Illustrated Poems of Paul Laurence Dunbar," *Stony the Road: Chapters in the History of Hampton Institute*, ed. Keith L. Schall (Charlottesville: University Press of Virginia, 1977), 81.
51. Ibid., 84.
52. Ibid., ix.
53. Ibid., vi.
54. Allen, Ware, and Garrison, iv.

Chapter 4

1. In Alex Preminger, ed., *Princeton Encyclopedia of Poetry and Poetics* (Princeton, NJ: Princeton University Press, 1974), 490–95; the section on metaphor by George Whalley provides a thorough history of the trope. For additional background on image and substance—or forma and figura—topics relevant both to chapters 3 and 4 of this book, please see Erich Auerbach's chapter "Figura" from *Scenes from the Drama of European Literature* (11–76), which is essential and inspired reading on this subject. In *The Figure of Echo*, John Hollander makes the very useful connection between these tropes that call out to other references (the entire body of operations considered to be under the umbrella of metaphor, as well as the specific operation of allusion as an indirect reference, which might or might not contain an implied metaphorical relationship but often does) and classical tropes. Hollander's summary of the ideas of Quintilian, Sophocles, Susenbrotus, and Isidore of Seville, among others, is pertinent to our discussion here, as well as brilliant and a delight to read. There is an excellent chapter on allusion—like Hollander's approach, it is both historical and analytical—in Robert Alter, *The Pleasures of Reading in an Ideological Age* (New York: Touchstone/Simon and Schuster, 1989), 111–40, that discusses the way tropes that link operate in the literature of all ages, including biblical and classical literature.
2. Aristotle, *The Poetics*, ed. E. Capps, T. E. Rouse, and W. H. D. Rouse, trans. W. Hamilton Fyfe (London: William Heinemann, 1927), 81–83.
3. Ibid.
4. Dwight N. Hopkins, *Down, Up, and Over: Slave Religion and Black Theology* (Minneapolis, MN: Fortress, 2000), 129–30.
5. John Lovell Jr., *Black Song: The Forge and the Flame: The Story of How the Afro-American Spiritual was Hammered Out* (New York: Macmillan, 1972), 228.
6. Andrew Ward, *Dark Midnight When I Rise: The Story of the Fisk Jubilee Singers: How Black Music Changed America and the World* (New York: Amistad, HarperCollins, 2000), 160–61.
7. See Nat Turner, *The Confessions of Nat Turner and Related Documents*, ed. and intro. Kenneth S. Greenberg (Boston: Bedford/St. Martin's, 1996), 14–18, for helpful background information on the context, relative magnitude and significance of the 1831 Nat Turner Rebellion in relation to other acts of organized slave resistance, including the conspiracies led by Denmark Vesey and Gabriel Prosser.
8. Dena J. Epstein, *Sinful Tunes and Spirituals: Black Folk Music to the Civil War* (Urbana: University of Illinois Press, 1977), 202–3.

9. Ibid., 229.

10. R. Nathaniel Dett, ed., *Religious Folk-Songs of the Negro As Sung at Hampton Institute* (New York: AMS, 1972), 15.

11. This poem follows the structural pattern of "Oh Mary, Don't You Weep, Don't You Moan" discussed in chapter 2: the opening stanza, which appears to be the verse and serves as the call, transforms in the second stanza and those that follow into the response to the call.

12. Frederick Douglass, *Narrative of the Life of Frederick Douglass, An American Slave, Written by Himself* (New York: W. W. Norton, 1997), 19.

13. Cited in Lovell, *Black Song*, 493.

14. Rev. Horace James, *Annual Report of the Superintendent of Negro Affairs in North Carolina, 1864–5* (Boston: W. F. Brown), 57–58.

15. Ibid.

16. J. B. T. Marsh, *The Story of the Jubilee Singers; with their Songs*, 4th ed. (London: Hodder and Stoughton, 1875), 32.

17. John Wesley Work, *Folk Song of the American Negro* (New York: Negro Universities Press, 1969), 101.

18. Geneva Smitherman, *Talkin and Testifyin: The Language of Black America* (Detroit: Wayne State University Press, 1977), 73.

19. William Francis Allen, Charles Pickard Ware, and Lucy McKim Garrison, eds., *Slave Songs of the United States* (Bedford, MA: Applewood Books, 1995), 48.

20. Variants of this slave song sometimes appear titled "No More Auction Block"—chiefly, the version sung by the Jubilee Singers—and may be found in Rev. Gustavus D. Pike, *The Singing Campaign for Ten Thousand Pounds: Jubilee Singers in Great Britain*, rev. ed. (New York: American Missionary Association, 1875); and Dett's *Religious Folk-Songs of the Negro*, but the verse "No more auction block for me" does not appear in the version provided by Higginson to Allen, Ware and Garrison (*Slave Songs of the United States*). It is also interesting to note that this slave song does not appear in James Weldon Johnson and J. Rosamond Johnson, *The Books of American Negro Spirituals* (New York: Da Capo Press, 1925); John W. Work, *American Negro Songs: 230 Folk Songs and Spirituals, Religious and Secular* (New York: Dover, 1998); or Moses Hogan, ed., *The Oxford Book of Spirituals* (New York: Oxford University Press, 2002), leading to the speculation that over time, it became increasingly accepted and believed that slave songs were entirely religious and those that did not fit the pattern fell away. In intriguing contrast, "No More Auction Block" appears in virtually every teaching anthology of African American literature that does contain slave songs,

including Richard Barksdale and Keneth Kinnamon, eds., *Black Writers of America: A Comprehensive Anthology* (Upper Saddle River, NJ: Prentice Hall, 1972), Henry Louis Gates Jr. and Nellie Y. McKay, eds., *Norton Anthology of African American Literature*, 2nd ed. (New York: W. W. Norton, 2004), 8–19; Ruth Miller, ed., *Blackamerican Literature* (Beverly Hills, CA: Glencoe /Macmillan, 1971); Sterling A. Brown, Arthur P. Davis, and Ulysses Lee, eds., *The Negro Caravan* (New York: Arno Press and the *New York Times*, 1970); and Patricia Liggins Hill, ed., *Call & Response: The Riverside Anthology of the African American Literary Tradition* (Boston: Houghton Mifflin, 1998).

21. Barksdale and Kinnamon, 234–41.

22. Allen, Ware, and Garrison, 48. Higginson's introductory note in this volume also explains that "The peck of corn and pint of salt were slavery's rations."

23. The same lyrics appear in Thomas P. Fenner, Frederic G. Rathbun, and Miss Bessie Cleaveland, *Cabin and Plantation Songs as Sung by the Hampton Students* (New York: AMS, 1977), with the addition of "No More Auction Block" as the title and repeated first and third lines of the first stanza. This version is designated as the one in the Fisk Jubilee Singers collection. The same version appears in Dett, *Religious Folk-Songs of the Negro*, which would be expected, as that is an enlarged and revised edition of Fenner, Rathbun and Cleaveland, but he has categorized this slave song rather oxymoronically with the "Hymns of Tribulation," a somewhat peculiar designation since it contains no references to Christianity or worship.

24. William R. Bascom, "Acculturation Among the Gullah Negroes," *Shaping Southern Society: The Colonial Experience*, ed. T. H. Breen (New York: Oxford University Press, 1976), 63.

25. Frances Anne Kemble, *Journal of a Residence on a Georgian Plantation in 1838–1839* (London: Longman, Green, Longman, Roberts & Green, 1863), 346.

26. Keziah Goodwyn Hopkins Brevard, *A Plantation Mistress on the Eve of the Civil War: The Diary of Keziah Goodwyn Hopkins Brevard, 1860–1861*, ed. John Hammond Moore (Columbia: University of South Carolina Press, 1996), 13.

27. Ibid., 81.

28. Here we have an echo of one aspect of the scholarly contention that slave songs were nothing more than hymns "stolen" from white sources. The other version of that "theory" was that the slaves unwittingly copied the white hymns through no malevolence but rather through lack of originality.

29. Allen, Ware, and Garrison, x.

30. Robert Gordon, "The Negro Spiritual," *The Carolina Low-Country*, eds. Augustine T. Smythe et al. (New York: Macmillan, 1931), 195.

31. Thomas Wentworth Higginson, *Army Life in a Black Regiment and Other Writings* (New York: Penguin, 1997), 154.

32. Ibid.

33. Work, *Folk Song of the American Negro*, 22.

34. Contrast Brown's example with the statement made by Higginson—one echoed by many others—that "[a]lmost all their songs were thoroughly religious in their tone" (154). Also, to avoid any potential confusion, Brown refers here to the slave song discussed earlier in this chapter as "No More Driver's Lash For Me," but in his co-edited anthology, *The Negro Caravan*, the lyrics appear under the title "No More Auction Block For Me." It is, of course, the same song, and he uses the same lyrics as the two Hampton collections which were taken from the Fisk collection.

35. Sterling Brown, *Negro Poetry and Drama and The Negro in American Fiction* (New York: Atheneum, 1972), 18. A thorough examination of sources, including slave songs that appeared in early collections and seem to have fallen from favor in popular later collections; knowledge of African customs of oral communication and socialization; and rethinking the category of "spirituals," "seculars," "work songs," "ballads," "protest songs," and so forth, in favor of "slave songs" suggest that social commentary and slave songs with high levels of satire, protest, and irony were not as rare as Brown's statement might suggest. There is every indication that the slaves would have been extremely clever (as is abundantly clear from the coding, signifyin', and double voicing of these poems) in staying out of harm's way when singing provocative, retaliatory, or insurrectionist songs. But substantial materials indicate that slave songs with themes of hypocrisy, anger, retribution, sexuality, and other non-religious themes were not rare. See, as some examples, the Charles P. Ware Collection in the Moorland-Spingarn Research Center; Kemble, *Journal of a Residence* (for instance, page 201: "they . . . performed a spirited chaunt in honour of Psyche and our bouncing black housemaid, Mary."); some of the St. Helena Island Spirituals transcribed by Nicholas George Julius Ballanta-(Taylor); Lovell and Levine, among others, also comment on the caution that the slaves would naturally have shown in deciding which songs to share; even Allen mentions in the introduction to *Slave Songs of the United States* his realization that some songs are being held back. See for further readily available examples of slave songs that "cross the border" of genres and do not fit the "spirituals" mold the

following: "Screw this Cotton" (238), "Lay Ten Dollars Down" (240), "I Got a House in Baltimo" (241), and "Got No Money" (246) in Work's *American Negro Songs*, and "De Ole Nigger Driver" (234), "Raise a Ruckus Tonight" (235), "Who-zen John, Who-za" (235), "Misse Got a Gold Chain" (235), "Zip e Duden Duden" (236), "Uncle Gabriel" (236–37), and "The Stoker's Chant" (236) in Barksdale and Kinnamon's *Black Writers of America*.

36. Brown, Davis, and Lee, *The Negro Caravan*, 419.
37. John Lovell Jr., "The Social Implications of the Negro Spiritual," in *The Social Implications of Early Negro Music in the United States*, ed. Bernard Katz (New York: Arno Press and the *New York Times*, 1969), 133.
38. Ibid.
39. Hopkins, *Down, Up, and Over*, 130.
40. Ibid., 131.
41. Mark Turner, "The ghost of anyone's father" (unpublished draft version of essay, 2003), 26.
42. Dett, 184.
43. Ibid., 188.
44. Ibid., 189.
45. Ibid., 191.
46. Ballanta-(Taylor), Nicholas George Julius, "Saint Helena Island Spirituals: Recorded and Transcribed at Penn Normal Industrial and Agricultural School, St. Helena Island, Beaufort County, South Carolina" (master's thesis, Institute of Musical Arts, New York, 1924), 16.
47. Ibid., 3.
48. Fenner, Rathbun, and Cleaveland, *Cabin and Plantation Songs as Sung by the Hampton Students*, 71.
49. Ballanta-(Taylor), 16.
50. Johnson and Johnson, bk. 2, 150–51.
51. Ibid., 88.
52. Boyer as cited in Turner, "The ghost of anyone's father," 28.
53. Johnson and Johnson, bk. 1, 96.
54. Ibid., bk. 2, 35.
55. Fenner, Rathbun, and Cleaveland, 147.
56. Ibid., 23.
57. Hogan, *The Oxford Book of Spirituals*, 123.
58. Kwasi Wiredu, "The Concepts of Mind and Spirit: Some African Reflections" (unpublished draft version of essay, 2003), 3.
59. Ibid., 4.
60. Ibid., 9.
61. Ibid.

62. Turner, "Ghost of Anyone's Father," 19.
63. Ibid., 21.
64. Ibid.
65. Samuel A. Floyd Jr., *The Power of Black Music Music: Interpreting its History from Africa to the United States* (New York: Oxford University Press, 1995), 62.
66. Once again we come across this designation of "new," which continues to be such an equivocal term in relation to slave songs throughout the entire span of their critical history continuing to the present and which I believe is a major part of why they have not been considered part of the lyric poetry canon. They are considered both new (and strange) or not new (and humdrum). These are contradictory evaluative positions that cannot be historical or analytical reflections on slave songs themselves but rather on a series of critical developments that has continued to misread them in various ways. See chapter 3 for focused treatment of this topic.
67. Floyd, 39.
68. Sterling Stuckey, *Slave Culture: Nationalist Theory and the Foundations of Black America* (New York: Oxford University Press, 1987), 27.
69. James H. Cone, *The Spirituals and the Blues* (Maryknoll, NY: Orbis, 1999), 21.

Index

Please note that page numbers in *italics* indicate endnotes.

Abbington, James, 9
abolitionism, 10–12, 24, 48, 64,
    109, 115, 130, 139, *169, 180*
Abrams, M. H., 27
Addison, Joseph, 38–39
*African American Poetry: An
    Anthology* (Sherman), 25
African Americans and the Bible
    (Wimbush), 9
African Imagination, The (Irele), 102
African oral tradition, 18, 35, 40,
    51, 54, 111, 114, *171*
Afro-American Folksongs (Krehbiel),
    9
Allen, Richard, 102
Allen, Samuel, 42
Allen, William Francis
    "Climb Jacob's Ladder" and, *178*
    "No More Auction Block" and,
        185
    publication of slave songs, 2, 7,
        12, 46
    on religion and slave songs, 137
    on sharing of slave songs, *187*
America a Prophecy (Rothenberg and
    Quasha), 19, 21
American Missionary Association,
    5, 12, 111, *185*
American Negro Songs (Work),
    83–84

"An Essay on Virgil's Georgics"
    (Addison), 38–41
*Anthology of American Negro
    Literature, An* (Calverton),
    25–26
Aristotle, 32, 35, 124, *172*
Assmann, Jan, 66
"At Candle-Lightin' Time," 118,
    120
Auden, W. H., 41

Bailey, Randall C., 10
Bailey, Wilma Ann, 9
Baldwin, James, 14
"Banjo Song" (Dunbar), 6,
    118–120
Barksdale, Richard, 24, 134
Barton, William E.
    fixed slave songs and, 63, 108
    "mosaics" and, 84, 102–103, 107
    "Poor Pilgrim" and, 106
    prayer and, *177*
    publication of slave songs, 2
    on Satan, *182*
Bascom, William R., 136
Beecher, Henry Ward, 64, 132
"Bein' Back Home" (Dunbar), 65
Berry, Wendell, 20
Beyond Genre (Hernadi), 33
Bhabha, Homi, 69

Black Culture and Black Consciousness (Levine), 8, 94
Black Poets, The (Randall), 24
Black Song: The Forge and the Flame (Lovell), 8, *168, 169*
Black Writers of America (Barksdale and Kinnamon), 24, 134
Blackamerican Literature (Miller), 25
Blake, William, 57
Blassingame, John W., 8, 98
blues, 1, 8, 25, 42
Blues People (Jones), 14
Bontemps, Arna, 25
Books of American Negro Spirituals, The (Johnson and Johnson), 8, 134
Boyer, Pascal, 127, 140, 143, 145
Braxton, Joanne M., 120, *183*
Bremer, Fredrika, 2, 52
Brown, Anthony, 105
Brown, Colin, 63, 65, 76, 110–111
Brown, John Mason, 50, 52, 113
Brown, Sterling A., 14, 24, 46, 138, *187*
Bryant, William Cullen, 22
Burnim, Mellonee, 9, *172*

Cabin and Plantation Songs, 3, 47, 119
"Caedmon's Hymn," 29–30
Call and Response (Hill), 25
call-and-response structure, 31, 53–55, 98, 108, 114, 147
Calverton, V. F., 25–26
Cleaveland, Bessie, 3, 47, *179, 186*
"Climb Jacob's Ladder," *178*
clothing, 62–63
Cone, James, 8, 97, 148, *172*
Confessions of Nat Turner, The (Styron), 14
Connelly, Marc, 105

Cruz, Jon, 10, 57
Culture on the Margins (Cruz), 10
Cuyler, Theodore Ledyard, 64–65

Dark Midnight When I Rise (Ward), 10
Davis, Arthur P., 24, 25, 138
Davis, J. E., 119
"De Angel Roll De Stone Away," 72–73, 82, 87
de Paur, Leonard, 105
Deep River and The Negro Spiritual Speaks of Life and Death (Thurman), 8–9
Dett, R. Nathaniel, 9, 47, 83, 85, 119, 129
    categorization of slave songs, 49
    "No More Auction Block" and, *186*
    "Poor Pilgrim" and, 104–106
    "We Am Climbin' Jacob's Ladder" and, *178*
Dickinson, Emily, 13, 22–23
"Didn't My Lord Deliver Daniel," 76–77, 134
Donne, John, 57
"Don't Yo' Hab Eberybody Fo' Yo' Fr'en," 59–60
double voicing, 69, 99, 106, 129, 130, *187*
Douglass, Frederick, 14, 24, 90, 129–132
Dove, Rita, 41–42
Du Bois, W. E. B., 10, 22, 129
    Krehbiel and, 114
    Lovell and, 139
    "Sorrow Songs" and, 24–25, 112
    Work and, 115
Dunbar, Paul Laurence, 6, 110, *183*
    influence of slave songs on, 65–66, 116
    Kamera Klub and, 116–120

Ellison, Ralph, 14
Emancipation, 3, 6, 64, 98, 108, 114, 132, 134, *168*, *169*, *177*
Emerson, Ralph Waldo, 22
Epstein, Dena J., 8–9, 98, 100, *168*, *172*
ethnopoetics, 18–19, 30, 50
evangelism, 10, 12, 98, 111

Faulkner, William, 14
Fenner, Thomas P., 3, 47, 119, *178*, *179*, *186*
Fisher, Miles Mark, 75, 98, 113
Fishkin, Shelley Fisher, 121, *183*
Fisk Jubilee Singers, 5–6, 12, 46–48, 63–64, 110, 129, 132, *171*, *186*, *187*
Floyd, Samuel A., 147–148, *172*
Folk Songs of the American Negro (Work), 7, 9
Forché, Carolyn, 40
Foster, Stephen, 6
freedom, 11–12, 44, 67–70, 79, 85, 89–91, 93, 97, 106, 111, 115, 123–125, 127, 130–131, 137, 142, 148, 150
Frost, Robert, 41
Frye, Northrop, 32

Garrison, Lucy McKim, 2, 6–7, 12, 112, *178*, *185*
Gates, Henry Louis, Jr., 25, *172*, *174*
Genovese, Eugene D., 9
ghost physics, 127, 140, 143–145, 150
Ginsberg, Allen, 20
"Give Me Jesus," 95
Glaude, Eddie S., Jr., 57
"Go Down, Moses," 42, 46, 108, 125, 134
Green Pastures: A Fable, 105

Hammon, Jupiter, 25
Hare, Maud Cuney, 139
Harper, Frances Ellen Watkins, 25
Harper, Michael S., 25
Haskell, Marion Alexander, 45, 113
Hatfield, Edwin F., 111
Hayden, Robert, 41
Hayes, Roland, 7, 11, 13, 27, 29, 45–46, 50, 91
HBCUs. *See* Historically Black Colleges and Universities
"He Never Said a Mumberlin' Word," 46, 72, 95
Heath Anthology of American Literature, 23
heaven, 70, 74–75, 88–89, 91
Hendel, Ronald, 66
Herbert, George, 57
Hernadi, Paul, 33
Hesiod, 38, 40–41, 50
Higginson, Thomas Wentworth
    discovery of slave songs, 4–5, 45, 108
    "Many Thousand Gone" and, 133, 135
    "No More Auction Block" and, *185*
    on political power of slave songs, 109–110
    Promised Land and, 90
    publication of slave songs, 3, 7, 46
    on religion and slave songs, *187*
    on time shifts, 137–138
    "Wrestling Jacob" and, 75
Hill, Patricia Liggins, 25
Historically Black Colleges and Universities (HBCUs), 5, 12, 46
Hogan, Moses, 105, 134
Hopkins, Dwight N., 57–58, 124, 139, *172*

Hopkins, Gerard Manley, 57
Hopkins, Keziah Goodwyn, 136
Horton, George Moses, 25
Hungerford, James, 51
Hurston, Zora Neale, 98
Hymes, Dell, 18

"I Got a Home in Dat Rock," 95
"I Know Moonrise," 95
"I Thank God I'm Free at Las'," 67,
     95
*Iconography of Music in African-
     American Culture* (Southern
     and Wright), 63
"I'm a-Rollin' Through an
     Unfriendly World," 134
Irele, F. Abiola, *170*, *172*, *182*
   fixed slave songs and, 108
   oral tradition and, 18, 35, 51–54,
     102, 111

Jackson, George Pullen, 97
James, Horace, 131
"Jis Want Tell What a Liar Will
     Do," 60–61
Joggin' Erlong, 117
Johnson, Guy B., 97, 109
Johnson, J. Rosamond, 8, 84, 134,
     178, *185*
Johnson, James Weldon
   on biblical references in slave
     songs, 84
   on creators of slave songs, 46, 109
   Lovell and, 139
   Lovell on, 22
   "Many Thousand Gone" and, 134
   "No More Auction Block" and,
     185
   publication of slave songs, 7, 8
   on spirituals, 12, 99
   "We Am Climbin' Jacob's Ladder"
     and, *178*

Johnson, James William, 34
Johnson, W. R., 33, 34–38
Jones, Arthur C., 10
Jones, LeRoi, 14
Jones, Sharon L., 25, *177*
Joyce, Joyce Ann, 25

Kamera Klub, 116–120
Katz, Bernard, 9
Kemble, Frances Anne, 2, 54, 136,
     187
Kinnamon, Keneth, 24, 134
Krehbiel, Henry Edward
   on creators of slave songs, 112,
     114–116, 121
   Pound and, 97
   on slave songs, 9, 101–102
   on spirituals, 11

Lakoff, George, 94
Langland, William, 57
Lauter, Paul, 23
Lee, Ulysses, 24, 138
Levine, Lawrence W., 8, 12, 77, 98,
     187
Liberia, 75, 90
Lindley, David, 32–34
"Little David," 83, 84–85
Locke, Alain, 7–8, 14, 22, 121, 139
Long, Charles H., 100
"Long Ago" (Dunbar), 117–118
Longfellow, Henry Wadsworth, 47
Lovell, John, Jr.
   on creators of slave songs, 45
   on freedom, 127, 139
   on history of slave songs, 22
   on sharing of slave songs, *187*
   spirituals and, 8, 9, *167–168*, *169*
   on white spiritual theory, 97, 112

MacDonald, George, 5
"Many Thousand Go," 14

"Many Thousand Gone," 133–134, 135–136
Marsh, J. B. T., 2, 47–48, 55, 64, 132
Mary Magdalene, 74–75
Mbiti, John, 61
McGhee, Nancy, 120
McKay, Nellie Y., 25
McKim, Lucy. *See* Garrison, Lucy McKim
Methodist Error (Watson), 100, *167*
Methodist hymns, 97, *178*
"Mighty Day," 77–78
Miller, Ruth, 25
Milton, John, 27–28, 57
Modernism, 17, 35
Morrison, Toni, 14
"Motherless Child," 3, 91, 95, 144
Music of Black Americans, The (Southern), 9, 102, *182*
musicality, 25, 31, 33–35, 42
My Songs: Aframerican Religious Folk Songs Arranged and Interpreted by Roland Hayes, 45

Negro Caravan, The (Brown), 14, 24, *187*
Negro Slave Songs of the United States (Allen, Ware, and Garrison), 2
Nelson, Cary, 23
New Negro Movement, 7
New Negro, The (Locke), 7, 14
"No More Auction Block," *185*, *186*, *187*
"Nobody Knows the Trouble I See," 48, 95, 134
Norton Anthology of African American Literature, 25
Norton Anthology of English Literature, 27
Notes of a Native Son (Ellison), 14

Oberlin College, 6
Odum, Howard W., 109
"Oh Mary, Don't You Weep, Don't You Moan," 88–90, 93, 94, *184*
"Old Black Joe," 6, *187*
Old Plantation Hymns (Barton), 2
Old Testament, 43, 50, 78, 84–85, 89–90, 92, 94, 98, 100, 106, 125
Olson, Charles, 41
Oxford Anthology of Modern American Poetry, 23–24
Oxford Book of Spirituals (Hogan), 105, 134

Pike, Gustavus D., 3, 46–47, 110, *185*
"Pilgrim's Song," 103–105
Pinsky, Robert, 40
Plantation Melodies (Taylor), 3
Poe, Edgar Allan, 22, 34
Poetics, The (Aristotle), 124, *172*
"Poor Pilgrim," 104–105, 106
Pound, Ezra, 18, 41
Pound, Louise, 97
Prentice Hall Anthology of African American Literature, 25
Princeton Encyclopedia of Poetry and Poetics, 30–34, 37, 50
Promised Land, 65, 86, 90, 93, 97, 100, 125

Quasha, George, 19, 21

Raboteau, Albert J., 8, 57, 98, 100, *172*
Randall, Dudley, 24
Rathbun, Frederic G., 3, 47, *179*, *186*
Readings in Black American Music (Southern), 9

Redding, J. Saunders, 25
Reid, Alexander, 128
Religious Folk Songs of the Negro
    (Dett), 9, 47, 83, 85, 104, 129
Reynolds, Mary, 63
Reznikoff, Charles, 41
"Roll, Jordan, Roll," 6, 9, 44, 134,
    141–142
Roll, Jordan, Roll (Genovese), 9
Ronsard, Pierre, 33
Rothenberg, Diane, 19
Rothenberg, Jerome, 18–19, 20–21,
    33, 114
"Run to Jesus, Shun the Danger,"
    129–130

Said, Edward, 3
Sands, Rosita M., 9
"Secular Folk Music" (Epstein), 9
Seward, Theodore F., 2–3, 5, 46,
    111
Shadow & Act (Ellison), 14
Sherman, Joan R., 25
Sinful Tunes and Spirituals (Epstein),
    8–9, 98, *168*
*Singing Campaign for Ten Thousand
    Pounds, The* (Pike), 3, 47, 110
Slave Community, The
    (Blassingame), 8, 98
Slave Religion (Raboteau), 8, 98
Slave Songs of the United States
    (Allen, Ware, and Garrison), 2,
    7, 12, 46, 133, *178*, *187*
Smart, Christopher, 57
Smith, Rochelle, 25
Smitherman, Geneva, 132, 136
Snyder, Gary, 20
*Social Implications of Early Negro
    Music in the United States*
    (Katz), 9
Souls of Black Folk, The (Du Bois),
    10, 24, 110

Southern, Eileen, *172*, *182*
    on creators of slave songs,
        113–114
    fixed slave songs and, 108
    "Poor Pilgrim" and, 106
    publication of slave songs, 9
    on references to Old Testament,
        100
    on slaves' clothing, 63
    "wandering choruses," 84,
        102–103, 107
Spirituals and the Blues (Cone), 8,
    97
Spirituals Project Choir, The, 105,
    176
"Steal Away," 6, 42, 68, 108,
    125–128
Stuckey, Sterling, 148
Styron, William, 14

Talmy, Len, 140, 143
Taylor, Marshall W., 3
Technicians of the Sacred
    (Rothenberg), 19, 20, 21
Tedlock, Dennis, 18–19
Thomas, W. H., 27
Thomas and Beulah (Dove), 42
Thurman, Howard, 9
time shifts, 137
Tolson, Melvin B., 41–42
Trouble the Water (Ward), 24
Tubman, Harriet, 108, 109,
    124–125
Turner, Mark, 78, 82, 94, 140,
    146–147, *174*
Turner, Nat, 77, 108, 109,
    125–126, 128
Twain, Mark, 14, 47, 121
"Two Wings," 91–92

Underground Railroad, 30, 70, 91, 109, 125, 128, 130

"View the Land," 58–59
Virgil, 38–41, 43
von Hallberg, Robert, 41

Wade in the Water (Jones), 10
Walker, Margaret, 42–44
Wallaschek, Richard, 97, 112
Walton, Anthony, 25
wandering choruses, 84, 102–103, 106–107, *182*
Ward, Andrew, 10
Ward, Jerry W., Jr., 24, 67
Ware, Charles P., 2, 7, 12, *178*, *185*, *187*
Washington, Booker T., 24, 28–29, *171*
Watson, John F., 100–101, *167*
Watts, Isaac, 102
"We Am Climbin' Jacob's Ladder," *178*
"Weeping Mary," 97
"Were You There When They Crucified My Lord?," 80–81, 95
Wheatley, Phillis, 22–23, 25
"When de Co'n Pone's Hot," 120
"When Malindy Sings," 6

White, George Leonard, 6, 46
White, Newman I., 97
Whitman, Walt, 13, 22–23, 40, 42, 50
Williams, William Carlos, 18
Wimbush, Vincent J., 9
Wiredu, Kwasi, 140, 145–147, 149, 150
"Witness," 95
Wood, Henry Cleveland, 13, 76–77, 109, 111
Wordsworth, William, 17, 27, 35, 39, 41
Work, John Wesley
  on African American identity, 7
  call-and-response structure and, 98
  categorization of slave songs, 48–49, 115–116
  "Many Thousand Gone" and, 134
  on slave songs, 9, 13, 83–85, 132, 138
  "We Am Climbin' Jacob's Ladder" and, *178*
Works Progress Administration, 63
"Wrestling Jacob," 75
Wright, Josephine, 63

Yeats, William Butler, 41

CPSIA information can be obtained
at www.ICGtesting.com
Printed in the USA
LVHW091919181220
674543LV00004B/120